CHARM OFFENSIVE

*Commodifying Femininity
in Postwar France*

KELLY RICCIARDI COLVIN

UNIVERSITY OF TORONTO PRESS
Toronto Buffalo London

© University of Toronto Press 2023
Toronto Buffalo London
utorontopress.com

ISBN 978-1-4875-0836-4 (cloth)   ISBN 978-1-4875-3809-5 (EPUB)
ISBN 978-1-4875-2582-8 (paper)   ISBN 978-1-4875-3808-8 (PDF)

Library and Archives Canada Cataloguing in Publication

Title: Charm offensive : commodifying femininity in postwar France / Kelly Ricciardi Colvin.
Names: Colvin, Kelly Ricciardi, author.
Description: Includes bibliographical references and index.
Identifiers: Canadiana (print) 20220485631 | Canadiana (ebook) 20220485712 | ISBN 9781487525828 (paper) | ISBN 9781487508364 (cloth) | ISBN 9781487538088 (PDF) | ISBN 9781487538095 (EPUB)
Subjects: LCSH: Femininity – Economic aspects – France – History – 20th century. | LCSH: Feminine beauty (Aesthetics) – Economic aspects – France – History – 20th century. | LCSH: Women – France – History – 20th century. | LCSH: Commodification – France – History – 20th century. | LCSH: Tourism – France – History – 20th century. | LCSH: National characteristics, French – History – 20th century.
Classification: LCC HQ1613.C65 2023 | DDC 305.4094409/045 – dc23

We wish to acknowledge the land on which the University of Toronto Press operates. This land is the traditional territory of the Wendat, the Anishnaabeg, the Haudenosaunee, the Métis, and the Mississaugas of the Credit First Nation.

University of Toronto Press acknowledges the financial support of the Government of Canada, the Canada Council for the Arts, and the Ontario Arts Council, an agency of the Government of Ontario, for its publishing activities.

   Canada Council   Conseil des Arts
for the Arts   du Canada

Funded by the   Financé par le
Government   gouvernement
of Canada   du Canada

To my family

Contents

List of Illustrations   ix
Acknowledgments   xi

Introduction   3
1 Creating the Model Hostess   21
2 Hostessing beyond the Airplane   57
3 Hostessing Global Events   84
4 Selling Postwar French Femininity   103
5 The Gendering and Selling of France   137
Conclusion   165

Notes   171
Bibliography   211
Index   223

Illustrations

1.1 Legendary Air France hostess Solange Catry (1966)   23
1.2 The second group of accepted hostesses in a publicity shot for the airline (1946)   23
1.3 One of the earliest Air France uniforms, designed by Georgette de Trèze (1954)   30
1.4 The Christian Dior uniform (1963)   32
1.5 A company poster from the 1950s reminds hostesses to "always say it with a smile!" (1950s)   36
1.6 Hostesses caring for children (1970)   42
1.7 The "At Your Service" campaign (1960s)   51
2.1 A hostess promotes French Camembert cheese (c. 1950)   58
2.2 The unveiling of the Concorde airplane (1967)   62
2.3 A hostess helps a customer at Air France's headquarters at the Invalides in Paris (1950s)   69
3.1 Pierre de Gaulle at the 1958 World Exposition (1958)   87
3.2 "Good luck Sapporo" (1968)   102
4.1 Reims Cathedral (1961)   106
4.2 Booksellers' stalls along the Seine (1968)   107
4.3 The Tarn River (1954)   108
4.4 A sailing poster (1954)   109
4.5 Brigitte Bardot as Marianne, as sculpted by the artist Aslan (late 1960s)   114
4.6 Brigitte Bardot in the poster for *And God Created Woman* (1956)   117
4.7 Brigitte Bardot (1953)   120
5.1 A hostess features prominently in one of Air France's publicity campaigns (1971)   142
5.2 Springtime in Paris (1962)   144

Acknowledgments

The publication of a book provides a special opportunity to reflect and express gratitude. At first glance, writing a book appears to be a solo affair, but in reality it is the worst group project of all time, in that so many people play important roles, and one person takes the lion's share of credit. Let me try to remedy that injustice here, paying thanks to some of the many who contributed.

Carolyn Dean and Maud Mandel continue to be trusted advisers, colleagues, and friends; I have relied on immensely on their support. I was also fortunate enough to have not one, but two, amazing sets of boots on the ground in France when I was unable to travel. Nathan Vanelli and Nicolas Montano provided invaluable research assistance, and I can honestly say I would not have been able to complete this book without them. Relatedly, archivists at the Air France Museum went above and beyond to help, especially when visiting the museum in person was not an option. Sarah Bochicchio has evolved from my student to my trusted friend and colleague, and she graciously read and commented on every word in this manuscript, a task she undertook with far more enthusiasm than its quality warranted at the time. Various research groups including the Boston French History Group, the Brown University Modern Europe Colloquium, the Soft Power Workshop, and the Gender and French History Group all read selections of this book, which is infused with their generous wisdom and counsel. Friends in the field including (but certainly not limited to!) Michèle Plott, Margie Anderson, Elizabeth Everton, and Joel Revill also provided excellent and needed advice. My colleagues in the history department of UMass Boston are a wonderfully supportive group; their counsel has contributed immensely to this publication, and I feel so lucky to be able to work with them all.

The anonymous readers of the manuscript enormously improved the book, and I am very grateful to them for their dedication and help. Stephen Shapiro at the University of Toronto Press believed in the work and shepherded it through the editorial process with skill and alacrity, and I feel so fortunate that he agreed to work with me.

My family reminds me that I am much more than the words on these pages. My mother, Joanne, transmitted her love of books and learning, while my many siblings and their partners (aka "the outlaws") and children take me out of the library and into the realms of the fun and festive.

My husband, Will, and our children, Alex and William, are my whole world. Their presence, whether they like it or not, infuses the pages of this book, and there is no way this book would exist without them. The love I have for them makes me continue to have hope for the future and believe that all things are possible.

The writing and publication of this book coincided with the COVID-19 pandemic, which has taken so much from so many around the world. For me and for my family, it took our beloved father, Patrick Ricciardi, who passed away in February 2021. He was a happy, funny, generous man; he did not share my interest in French history in any way, but he always offered his pride and support, and that proved to be invaluable. To know that he was always in our corner was an immeasurable gift for me and my family, and we miss him terribly. This one's for you, Dad.

CHARM OFFENSIVE

Introduction

I want to open this book with an experiment: if you close your eyes and try to conjure up a French woman in your mind, what words would you use to describe her? Having performed this thought exercise with many people, I would hazard a few guesses: sexy, elegant, chic, alluring, thin, charming. How did these specific qualities come to dominate popular understandings about French femininity? This book addresses that question, locating the origins of these adoptions of ideal French femininity in a state-run air hostess program, and then tracing how the traits mandated by the state for Air France hostesses reverberated, first to its hostesses on the ground, and then to all French women. The government had a vested interest in tapping into notions of ideal femininity and capitalizing on them.[1] Witnessing the erosion of the country's military and imperial stature, especially in the wake of the Second World War, French officials proceeded to turn to women to lure crucial dollars and prestige to the struggling nation. This book will trace how and why the hostess program developed; it will follow its influence on the female population of France and consider how women around the world came to conflate notions of ideal femininity with the "Hexagon," as people in France sometimes refer to their country. In so doing, the book will demystify postwar French femininity as an aspirational marker and rather pinpoint it as a specific project serving official French concerns, a project over which the women themselves had little control.

In 1969, Roger Delagnes, a senator from Marseille, bemoaned his city's secondary tourist status and especially Marseille's lack of government funding to attract tourists. When he delved into specifics, though, it was not Marseille's airport or train station, nor was it the harbour or hotel situation, or the state of the *autoroutes* leading into and out of town that Delagnes decried. Instead, Delagnes wondered how Marseille, "France's second city," could possibly compete on a touristic field with only "two, three or four hostesses to receive tourists … at the level of an Air France hostess" for its entire area.[2]

Just one year earlier, in 1968, the American sports journalist Will Grimsley, writing for the Associated Press at the Grenoble Olympics, celebrated what he termed France's "pride of the games" in a long piece published in the *Washington Post*. He was not alluding to Jean-Claude Killy or Anne-Marie Goitschel, the hugely famous French skiers who dominated the Chamrousse slopes that year. Nor did he refer to the opening ceremonies, a display of French technology and innovation, held in Grenoble's impressive stadium that another renowned journalist, Fred Tupper of the *New York Times*, called a triumphant "extravaganza," in contrast with the "obscure" displays "on some obscure mountain peak" of games past.[3] Rather, Grimsley told American readers of how France was trying to "sell the Winter Olympic Games with the commodities it knows best: charm, beauty, sex, and mademoiselles." The women Grimsley referred to were hostesses, hired and trained by Air France and the French government to ensure the success of the games. And the women, widely known as "bunnies"[4] among the journalists covering the games, were apparently quite successful: Grimsley reported that he could not even "walk down the street" without being "accosted by a pretty maiden in form-fitting blue ski pants and a red parka asking, 'Pardon, monsieur. Can I help you, monsieur?'"[5]

The external and internal identification of one of France's chief commodities as femininity was not accidental, but rather the product of years of concerted efforts to define and market French women as the most superior of their kind the world over. How did this reputation originate? In the three decades following the Second World War, a new category of female occupation, termed "hostessing," blossomed. In France, hostesses acted as state-defined *ambassadrices*, female ambassadors who could embody the prestige inimical to iterations of postwar French identity. Because of the way the French language is set up in its expression of gender, the word *ambassadrice* can be translated in various ways, all of which have implications for its meaning. In its most basic, literal form, *ambassadrice* can mean simply a woman ambassador, the female version of a male *ambassadeur*. This translation, while technically correct, lacks the nuance implied by users contemporary to the period studied in this project. The more precise meaning is *feminine* ambassador, because an *ambassadrice* projected not only her physical body, but also the traits of femininity that were purportedly natural in all French women. Women were not formal state ambassadors, but their appearance and their deportment carried consequential weight for France in the 1950s and the 1960s, as the government desperately tried to reassert itself as a great power. In her landmark work on gender and diplomacy, the scholar Cynthia Enloe famously asked, "where are the women?" In response, this project will demonstrate both women's ubiquity and their centrality to postwar French efforts at diplomacy and national identity.[6]

Hostesses' femininity in postwar France emerged as a tool wielded by institutional entities in the service of French greatness. In this context, Will Grimsley's use of the word commodity to describe French women is entirely appropriate. French actors in multiple realms – government, tourism, culture – packaged and proffered to the world an image of womanhood that was stylish, sexy, and biddable. I do not wish to suggest that unanimity was a constant, either among officials or among the women themselves. However, overwhelmingly, in internal and external dialogues about France and femininity, attracting tourists, especially Americans, via an idealized vision of femininity became the dominant theme for actors in these realms. Histories of diplomacy, Christopher Endy has argued, must be expanded to include nontraditional subjects, like consumerism, film, and popular culture, for these arenas, he asserts, hold an informal power that is just as potent as more expected sites, such as policy meetings.[7] In this vein, my book tracks how French femininity itself became a valued commodity on the international market.

French women and men had long taken to the skies, well before the postwar era. In its early days, aviation was a space of relative gender equality in France, where one's sexual identity mattered far less than nerve and knowledge.[8] Air France acknowledged that early time in its monthly employee bulletin, *Échos de l'air* (*Echoes of the Air*) in 1947, and then quickly put it to bed. "Already Woman has controlled the airplane via her courage and her daring," the magazine reported, "… but it is with her own feminine genius that today we see her put the finishing touches on that conquest." Hostesses, the company argued, essentially ran their own salons in the air, but solely for the benefit of their passengers, not for themselves. "From the very first second," the company bulletin enthused, "the vivacity of this salon is due to the pretty smile and appealing kindness of the hostess, who does the honors with the grace and enthusiasm of a perfect young girl of the world, playing … the delicate role of Mistress of the House, for the greatest pleasure of her hosts."[9] It was a far cry from the days of flying planes and setting speed records, but in the postwar period, this book shows, being an air hostess was both a way of performing a perfect postwar femininity and serving French global interests.

To be sure, there had been other iterations of hostesses before air hostesses, and much like their later counterparts, they served in front-facing positions where the world would see French women's beauty, tapping into long-standing notions of ideal appearances.[10] Women might work as hotel hostesses, for example, offering a friendly face to welcome weary travellers to the Hexagon. Their beauty and charm led the list of assumed qualities they brought to the role; in taking care of travellers' food and lodging needs, they were, in some ways, the original quasi-public *maîtresses de maison* that air hostesses later embodied. In 1913, during a celebratory dinner for the Hoteliers de France, the president of Paris's Municipal Council saluted those "beautiful hostesses with their black eyes and even their blue eyes that I have admired … and, if I may enlarge this toast, to all French women."[11] This part of the toast came at the tail end of a long speech dedicated to male hoteliers and their contributions to the field. A 1928 tourism trade journal commended male hoteliers for their functionality, but argued for the attraction of the hotel hostess, "who welcomes passing clients like long lost friends, who multiplies herself for them, who gives them attention and consideration, who worries about their fatigue, their tastes and their wants, who finds that mysterious way to be maternal and to transform a place that is foreign to them into a home."[12] The qualities discussed in these sources reflect traditional assumptions about femininity and its manifestation as a beautiful, welcoming force, qualities that would later translate into an aviation setting.

More akin to planes and air travel, auto shows also utilized female hostesses; in the earliest days of these shows, women graced the covers of brochures meant to advertise the spectacular technologies French automakers had designed.[13] Posters for the 1898 Exposition internationale d'automobiles depicted a large figurehead of a goddess-like figure, sitting on a throne and welcoming visitors to the show with a sweep of her hand.[14] The next year, a similarly celestial figure surveyed the show landscape with wings on her back, a tricolour ribbon in her hair, and a hammer in her hand.[15] These images are reminiscent of those discussed in Lynn Hunt's work on Marianne and representation; a female figure could represent the French republic in its earliest days precisely because there was no danger of women actually wielding power.[16] In this case, since technology could be confined to a near-total masculine sphere through formal and informal barriers, a woman could represent France's achievements in that manly realm because she had no chance of actually challenging male supremacy there.[17] In the interwar period, when cultural mores about women in public had eased a bit since the earliest days of the automobile, such figureheads might take a more corporeal form. In 1934, the writer, art critic, and Legion of Honour recipient Paul Sentenac lauded one automaker's idea to "place a young, elegant woman posing ... near his car." He argued that the creation of such a combination was like "a poet who knows how to sense connections [*rapports*] between things and harmonize them." Here, according to Sentenac, the automaker had sensed "how feminine and auto elegance go together so perfectly."[18] Yet again, Sentenac's use of "things" to describe both an inanimate car and a woman reveals a consistent sense of woman as decorative object, there to be looked at as part of a tableau celebrating France's achievements.

As the automobile examples demonstrate, the combination of technology and a warm, pretty female face is not new. What this book brings to the fore is the specific context of postwar France. As I assert, government officials, hoping for economic success, leaned heavily on the nation's traditional renown for romance and beautiful women, meaning that the air hostess, as a symbol of both of those concepts, stood as a bulwark against irrelevance. In her postwar time, the air hostess occupied a role as a crucial figurehead for French femininity, rendered all the more important because she arrived at a moment of doubt in French greatness. The combination of technological intensity – air travel was one of a few arenas where French officials thought they could match other nations' successes – and national self-doubt over France's future served to render hostesses' status all the more central to the project of French rehabilitation in the eyes of government officials and the world.

Hostessing, in an official government-sponsored capacity, had its postwar apogee in the airline industry. Before the Second World War, there were no "air hostesses" in France, and very few anywhere in the world.[19] After the war, though, air hostessing quickly became a desirable profession globally. Beginning in Western Europe and the United States, and then moving across the world, cosmopolitan young women sought independence and adventure in the burgeoning civil aviation industry.[20]

Despite other countries' participation in the hostessing profession, France represents a very specific case for several interconnected reasons. First, the French have a particular record of sexualized tourism, one that dates back to the days of the Enlightenment and the Grand Tour. Well-heeled travellers the world over looked to France for its arts, history, and culture, but also for experiences ranging from the romantic to the licentious that were purported to be unique to France. Dabbling in Paris's seedier districts to garner a view of scantily dressed women performing the can-can, or, for the less adventurous, taking a "Paris by Night" tour and viewing street scenes from carriages and trams became de rigueur experiences consumed by travellers to France.[21]

After the Second World War, though, the context shifted, as the French reputation for sexual openness clashed with American occupiers' physical advances on French women. Like their fellow countrymen and countrywomen of centuries past, American GIs viewed France as a site of potential hedonistic pleasures, and Frenchwomen as "easy pickings," in the words of one historian.[22] As Mary Louise Roberts writes in her study of postwar interactions between American servicemen and French women, "the US military knew that the average Joe equated France with brothels and pretty women. Sex was how they were going to sell the Normandy campaign. In this sense, the soldiers were literally *seduced* into fighting the war."[23] Attesting to the potency – and national specificity – of this sexualized campaign, although British and Canadians, among others, also participated in the liberation of France, neither of those nationalities experienced a level of sexual assault complaints that even approached that of the Americans.[24]

In this sense, the French reputation for sexual permissiveness backfired, and French officials and commentators were quick to both decry American behaviour and assert a new image of moral uprightness on behalf of French women. Contemporary writers described the ideal French woman not as a floozy, but rather as a stolid, righteous woman who had supported France through its penurious trials, in effect reclaiming the virginal, almost Marian, figure from the interwar era that historian Whitney Walton has referred to as the *jeune fille*. The *jeune fille* was a protected entity – her family, society, and the state all having a stake in her purity.[25] Of course neither ideal reflected the complicated reality on either side of the debate: women's actual lives rarely conform(ed) to state vision, a fact that remains important despite this book's focus on cultural ideals rather than biography or demography.[26]

Given the intensity with which actors in France and the United States held to their notions of French femininity, animosity rose on both sides of this sexual divide. French authorities were disgusted by the loutish behaviour of Americans, while their American counterparts found the French, according to Walton, to be "swindlers, lazy, and ungrateful."[27] Some GIs began comparing Germany favourably to France, astonishing in the context of the Liberation, solely on the basis of the permissiveness of each nation's women. As an article in *Newsweek* stated: "[The GI] compares the mercenary, unsavoury French streetwalker with the unprofessional, acquiescent German girl and, of course, prefers the fräulein."[28] The international battle to own French women's sexuality waged on; if the French government had its way, the world's image of a French woman would no longer rest on licentious laurels.

Only a few years later, however, the government softened its stance on the availability of its women, placing the most attractive French *femmes* in positions of high visibility and points of contact with outsiders. Much of the reason for French authorities' revived willingness to showcase its women to the world could be located in two arenas: the struggling French economy and the all-consuming quest for global prestige. First, the nation was desperate for money at the end of the war, and many people in the government particularly coveted American dollars.[29] It is no exaggeration to say that the immediate postwar French economy was in shambles. The country's infrastructure had been destroyed in the war, leading to the striking statistic that industrial production in 1945 was just 38 per cent of what it had been in 1938.[30] Tourism boosters in the government and beyond trumpeted their cause, strains that did not fall on deaf ears.[31] As early as 1946, tourism had become France's second-largest industry,[32] and its champions clamoured for American spending.[33] The equation of France with eroticism helped boost tourist numbers, particularly as the Cold War intensified and Americans sought to escape the political tensions at home.[34]

The French wanted to capitalize on as much foreign tourist money as possible, and they embarked on campaigns across Europe, North America, Asia, and Australia. As early as 1946, in a France still reeling from the physical and psychological destruction wrought by war, tourism was already the second-largest industry.[35] Tourism officials within the government zeroed in on the United States, especially at the outset of the marketing program. The United States was, at the end of the Second World War, the financial powerhouse of the world, a fact that (unevenly) translated into a burgeoning middle class.[36] That new American middle class sought to tap into the mores of bourgeois and upper-class tradition and consume previously unaffordable tourism experiences. Happily for tourism officials, France had long held a place of pride in the American imagination, far more than other European nations. As Christopher Endy argues, this unique fascination stemmed from many historical and demographic factors, such as France's role in the American Revolution and the relative scarcity of French immigrants in the United States.[37]

French officials were hyper-aware of both the power of the French mystique and the growing importance of foreign money, especially the US dollar, over the course of this time period. In 1948, just three years after the end of the war, the head of the French Senate's finance committee, Alexandre Roubert, proclaimed, "each American needs to come to France at least once in their lifetime … If each American came just one time, that would be two million Americans coming to France every year. This would not be a negligible amount of money for our country." Roubert went on to crow about France's success in attracting Americans, a huge boon for the French economy, claiming that "we have not only beaten our record since the Liberation, but this year we have hosted more American tourists than in any year in our history."[38] By 1949, Senator Albert Lamarque reported that it was already "a truism to say that tourism is one of our principal industries, that it is one of the essential elements of our prestige and prosperity." "We need," he continued, "to attract foreign tourists to our country and allow them to admire it."[39]

Flying was not a common activity for most North Americans during the period studied here, and international travel was even more rare. It was generally restricted not only to the more comfortable, but also to men, which adds another dimension to the rationale behind propagating air hostesses. Flying became more democratic in terms of class in the 1970s, with the advent of jumbo jets flying at even greater speeds – and with the diminishing importance of service relative to ticket price.[40] However, within that context, nuance exists. It was in the 1950s and 1960s that "tourist class" ticket pricing, a program from Air France and a few other airlines that was specifically designed to appeal to middle-class people, began and flourished. Christopher Endy argues that, prior to this moment, transatlantic travel was "strictly a first-class affair."[41]

Tourism officials within France were quite aware of the fact that there was a massive untapped market of middle-class Americans who had never visited their country. Long after the initiation of major tourism efforts, French politicians sought to capitalize even further on the American market. Minister of Tourism Édouard Bonnefous announced in 1964 that any American home "with an income of 6,000 dollars or more is a potential target to come to Europe." He went on to detail the untapped potential consumers in the United States, asking the French Senate, "did you know that 80 percent of Americans have never even been on an airplane? That gives you an idea of the possibilities we could have available to us in terms of potential clientele."[42] This clientele, Bonnefous warned, did not consist of the fat cats from years past, "those who smoked cigars and rented luxury cars and spent a month or two." Rather today's consumer was budget-minded, and Bonnefous spoke of a new kind of enemy: "numerous are those books from across the Atlantic that teach Americans how to spend frugally on vacation."[43] Another example from 1973 gives a sense of the continued importance of American spending to the French economy. In the midst of the worldwide recession, French politicians fretted mightily about the drop in American tourism spending and its potentially catastrophic impacts on the entirety of the French economy; "the Americans," remarked one senator, "have not provided the forecast tourist numbers."[44] The secretary of state for tourism, Aimé Paquet, sought to assure the troubled politicians by asserting that "over one half of the budget was spent on a major promotion campaign overseas," to the tune of 280 million francs.[45] Still, Paquet continued, his office would "be vigilant" in the face of this pressing problem of attracting Americans to France.[46]

Meanwhile, the context of the Cold War pushed American officials to promote American tourism to the Hexagon as well, hopeful that American leisure and tourism spending would slow or quash the spread of Communism in France. In 1949, American tourist spending in France was equivalent to four-fifths of French exports to the United States, meaning that American tourism was just as important to France's economy as its exports. Indeed, according to Endy, economic statistics show that from 1945 to 1949, American tourists were injecting almost another 10 per cent of the entire Marshall Plan's value through their spending, making them a crucial component of the country's economic health.[47] As such, French officials were desperate to at least maintain, if not grow, the flow of dollars into the French economy; in 1959, France's powerful Economic Council put out a report on how to expand tourist spending in France, and they reported that the whole project of increasing tourism "almost exclusively depends on developing touristic flow from North America," later repeating in the same report, "*It is on [Americans] that, at the end of the day, the success or failure of our tourist policy depends*" (original emphasis).[48] French tourism officials tapped into this constellation of historical and contemporary trends and created marketing campaigns designed to attract this new set of mobile American tourists.

In a project that asserts the airline and government actors acted in concert to shape femininity, it is important to detail the close relationship between Air France and the rest of the French government. Air France was and remains a state-run airline, having been named in 1948 an official "national company," and that means that many directives, while filtered through a company-led administrative apparatus, originated within the highest levels of the French state, including the development of hostessing. Historian Anthony Sampson has described the government as extremely invested in Air France, having "put all the power of the state behind it," a considerable undertaking both in the context of the postwar period and, looking through a longer historical lens, the immense role of the French state in everyday life.[49] In the interwar period, there were four airlines in France. Deeming air travel a matter of state import, the government of Édouard Daladier, later famous for his acquiescence to the policy of appeasement, voted to merge the four companies into one national airline in 1933, later named Air France. "It was a name," Sampson asserts, "imitated by many of the airlines that followed – which left no doubt that [the French government] was carrying the flag."[50] (Most other major European countries had already consolidated their independent airlines, and France did not wish to fall behind in air travel, an arena in which it was a leading force, second only to the United States.) There was a Minister of Aeronautics in the government cabinet, and its first president was Ernest Roume, who had been a long-standing government official. So the links between Air France and the government were clearly quite strong, although the company retained some autonomy.

During the Second World War, Air France was transferred to direct state supervision, but due to the war and its many related restrictions, the company was relatively inactive, suspending all international travel at some points. There was some effort to link all of the free French territories under the auspices of Charles de Gaulle, but this was a scattershot and disorganized situation. Thus, after the war, in the growing chaos that ensued, it was unclear how – and whether – Air France would reform and what its relationship to the French state would be.

In 1944, the government nationalized key industries, including France's aviation sector, which then-leader Charles de Gaulle quickly made part of the cabinet-level Transport Ministry.[51] The airline minister in 1944–5, Charles Tillon, called for Air France to be a "unique company," one which "absolutely has the hallmark of public service."[52] In this moment, the airline was entirely under state control, which gives additional meaning to its directives about the hostesses working for Air France. The importance of aviation to postwar France's global reputation was paramount. Its first postwar managing director, Henri Desbruères, argued in 1946 that "the radiance of a country can be measured through the importance of its civil air transport."[53] In 1948, the government of France owned about 70 per cent of Air France shares; this percentage would actually increase to almost 100 per cent during the decades studied here. Generally, state actors viewed the role of Air France not simply in economic terms, but in social ones as well, meaning both that it would serve the interests of the French in flying to the far-flung outposts of the French empire, but also that it would garner prestige and power for the people of the nation.[54] Although I assert no unanimity among historical actors, when I do attribute any intention to the French government, I think it is crucial to consider just how high up the chain of promoting and funding aviation – and consequently the hostess project – really went. While there was not necessarily total unanimity in the project of creating *ambassadrices*, there was certainly a common set of goals.

Officials in the highest ranks of government viewed Air France airplanes as mini pieces of France itself, and their subsequent determination of how to present the human side of France was consequential in a world in which tourism mattered profoundly to the economy. However, officials were not the only people in the nation to equate hostesses with France itself and to use language that promoted such a view. As the following chapter shows, major newspapers referred to both the airlines and the nation on a grand scale; in 1955 *Le Monde* declared, "thanks to Air France, France will show a 'beautiful face' to its passengers."[55] Therefore the issue of language is a complicated one, for the sources themselves tend to employ terms like "France" and "the French" with impunity. Here I have tried to retain the spirit of grandeur inherent in their language, while attempting to attribute agency as necessary.

Hostessing may have flourished in French airline cabins in the late 1940s and early 1950s, but in no way did it remain confined to Air France airplanes. It was later, in the late 1950s and through the 1960s, that hostessing diversified milieus, moving from civil aviation to tourism booths to railways to state functions and even private industry. The dissemination of hostessing ensured that the public face of the nation be young, pretty, and feminine, a fulsome canvas on which to paint the powerful interests like the French fashion and beauty industries. This book will demonstrate that the campaign for French resurgence, for battling against narratives of decline, depended not only on "men of action," a category I will explain below, but also on *ambassadrices*, carefully selected hostesses who acted as diplomats within France and internationally, to display a pretty face (literally) for France at this critical moment. As the success of hostessing expanded, so, too, did the call for more and more French women to tap into this idealized femininity, as later chapters in this book will show with their investigations into French actresses like Brigitte Bardot and even the gendering of France itself.

The book makes three direct and indirect interventions in existing scholarship. First, my work expands on gender theorists' work on the decentralization of discipline when applied to female bodies, locating disciplinary forces as external to more traditional institutions of power. It also engages with gender historians' work on the French government and universalism, establishing that officials were far from gender-blind in administering government affairs; rather they actively deployed femininity as a tool to gain money and prestige for the nation. Second, while decolonization is not the project's primary evidentiary focus, it expands the historiography on France and the postwar period, demonstrating how, with decolonization and military defeat as a backdrop, actors in the French government not only weaponized technical expertise, as seen in the work of scholars like Kristen Ross and Gabrielle Hecht, but it also actively utilized femininity, beginning with the nucleus of hostessing, as a means of attracting global attention and money back to the Hexagon in a time of waning empire. Third, it combines gender with soft power theory, an International Relations–based concept. I will address each of these components in more depth here.

French women won the right to vote in 1944, after generations of struggle, but that vote did not translate into increased access to political power. As convincingly argued by historians like Fabrice Virgili, Luc Capdevila, and Todd Shepard, women's continued lack of real power, despite their political status, was partly due to the prolonged crisis of masculinity in postwar France, brought on by the experience of war and decolonization.[56] Actors within the French government turned to newly enfranchised women, weaponizing them in an ambassadorial guise to advocate for the nation as a whole. On the surface, it seems like this weaponization had the potential to lead to far greater political power for the women themselves. And yet this ambassadorial role had serious limits. Women could only represent the nation if their entire person, external to internal, head to toe, had achieved this ideal of charm and beauty, with qualifications mandated by Air France and French government actors.

Air France hostesses embodied models of perfection for a nation of women, and those hostesses received, as we shall see, extensive training from state actors in how to dress, how to apply makeup, and how to comport themselves as representatives of the nation. To that end, this book engages with gender theory on the level of the body and beauty norms. Simone de Beauvoir, a contemporary of the period under study, conceptualized the idea of the female body as essentially shaped by the gaze and desires of other people. As early as girlhood, she wrote, "Through compliments and admonishments, through images and words, [a girl] discovers the meaning of the words pretty and ugly; she soon knows that to be pleased is to be pretty as a picture; she tries to resemble an image, she disguises herself, she looks at herself in the mirror, she compares herself to princesses and fairies from tales."[57] Thus, as Beauvoir points out, a woman's body is not entirely her own, but rather is constituted by the words and actions of other people. She learns to please based on the specific exigencies of the society in which she lives. In the 1970s and 1980s, Michel Foucault's work on how institutions like schools, the army, and industry discipline bodies also prompted a number of feminist scholars to contend with how gender might affect his conclusions.[58] Philosopher Sandra Bartky argued that, in order to apply to women, Foucault's work must be relocated from institutions. Instead, Bartky posited, since women have long been excluded from institutions and institutional records, their bodily discipline is in fact not centrally located, but diffuse, and all the more pernicious and constant for that diffuseness. "The disciplinarian who inscribes power on the female body is everywhere and nowhere," she writes, "the disciplinarian is everyone and no one in particular."[59] And yet that does not render the constitutive processes of femininity any less real for the people who experience them.[60] Bartky isolates three forms of non-institutional disciplinary practices to which women are especially subject: "those that aim to produce a body of a certain size and general configuration; those that bring forth from this body a specific repertoire of gestures, postures, and movements; and those directed toward the display of this body as an ornamental surface."[61] Each of these categories applies across this book. In the case of postwar France, where parts of the state actively promoted a vision of femininity that was thin, elegant, and, crucially, on display to the world. This book traces the origins of those disciplinary practices to the Air France program, but it also looks at how that disciplined femininity became less bounded by institutions as time progressed, with later chapters locating pressure points in the media, literature, and other fields.

Within the field of French history, gender historians have very much pushed back against the notion of a gender-blind universal citizen, one of the bases for justice within France itself.[62] For example, in the more contemporary French context, Joan Scott has argued that the French government has required the public display of women's bodies as a condition of citizenship, underscoring the ongoing tension between French abstract individualism and emphasis on sexual difference. The continuing debates about veils and veil laws, which Scott points out are accompanied by an utter lack of attention to gender inequities in broader French society, underscores this crucial point.[63] My work pushes the point even further, noting that sectors of the French government actively helped to mould women's appearances, rendering them a marketable commodity as a condition of national belonging. As such, women's aesthetic power, moulded by the state, was adjacent to political power, not a part of it. My work demonstrates how the French government actively tapped into notions of gender to cultivate and sell a docile, elegant vision of femininity to the world. In a time of decolonization and waning military and economic might, French officials capitalized on French femininity to attract attention and power to France. Women thus became important pieces in the postwar game of international chess in which the French were playing with a weak hand by traditional measures. Rather than being blind to gender and citizenship, the French government deployed gender as a tool. At no point did the French actors advocating for air hostesses intend for them to become economically or politically empowered in the role, as we shall see in examining their motivations and labour practices. We can imagine that this kind of surface-level aesthetic power, heavily entrenched in heteronormativity, has profound consequences when portrayed, as the government did, as women's crucial role for the state.[64]

One component of this postwar femininity worth interrogating here is the idea that women acting as representations of the nation could be considered a manifestation of empowerment. I would contest this notion. France – along with other Western countries – has long utilized a female figure to represent the nation. The history of Marianne, the symbol of France since the time of the French Revolution, is well documented. Lynn Hunt, for one, has argued that the choice of Marianne on the part of the revolutionaries demonstrates the distance between actual women and political power. She argues that precisely because the revolutionaries had effectively excluded women from the political sphere, Marianne was an unthreatening choice.[65] Hunt's analysis informs my own in regard to the postwar era; if Air France airplanes were meant to be, in the words of one historian, "flying Eiffel Towers," air hostesses were flying Mariannes, and their compatriots on the ground performed similar roles.[66] These hostesses' access to ambassadorial power was, therefore, conditional upon their continued inability to harness political power and threaten masculine authority in a time of anxiety. Though these women shaped and moulded their own roles in ways the state had never imagined, as this book will show, they were not able to fully break the barrier between their aesthetically defined power and the masculine state. The leaders of the French state, embroiled in a prolonged crisis of masculinity, did not intend for women's embarkation into aesthetic diplomacy to be a pathway to liberation.

While the position of air hostess afforded French women access to a sort of aesthetic power, in no way did hostessing's associated status cross the barrier between aesthetic and political power. The program's emphasis on women's physical beauty can instead be seen as entirely separate from political or even representational power. As Susan Sontag wrote in her famous essay on women and beauty, "[the power of beauty] is always conceived in relation to men; it is not the power to do but the power to attract. It is a power that negates itself. For this power is not one that can be chosen freely – at least, not by women – or renounced without social censure. To preen, for a woman, can never be just a pleasure. It is also a duty. It is her work."[67] Interestingly, the kind of feminine power that Sontag describes here is reminiscent of the idea of the passive citizen from the era of the French Revolution, when voting rights, and the attendant agency, were restricted to men.[68]

Second, this book demonstrates how French actors utilized women's femininity to wield power in the context of decolonization and military defeat. The aforementioned project of attracting Americans took on an urgency compounded by a particularly acute crisis of postwar confidence.[69] While before the war, sensuality had been one of many pillars of French reputational greatness in the world, now, with the decline of France's vast empire and international economic might, it appeared that sensuality alone remained firm in propping up French identity. France's involvement in Second World War was a source of national embarrassment, despite the best efforts at rehabilitation provided by de Gaulle and the resistance myth;[70] in addition the French empire was in the process of swift and dramatic decolonization. In 1954–5 alone, France suffered a humiliating military loss at Dien Bien Phu, resulting in a retreat from its colony in Indochina; a major rebellion in Cameroon; and, most devastatingly, the outbreak of the Algerian War. Similarly, anxieties about France's role in NATO and the European Community derived in part from its loss of military and colonial power.[71]

One of the ways that the French government responded to a lesser global role was through the modernization of the economy and the development of specific industries. Historians and international relations scholars have described this as a foreign policy dominated by "grandeur," which manifested in specific triumphs like fast trains, sleek airplanes, space research, and, most crucially, nuclear power.[72] The policy of modernization took on, as Gabrielle Hecht has shown, a decidedly masculine character. "The technologist," she writes, "was virile, decisive, and forward-looking." France's modernization would be led by figures Hecht describes as "men of action."[73]

By the early 1950s, the "men of action" associated with Air France had established the largest network of destinations of any airline, thanks to the company's impressive investment in aviation – and to the Hexagon's far-flung empire, which it serviced via airplanes.[74] Publicity literature for Air France claimed to "serve 36 cities in 73 countries ... a worldwide network that totalled 188,000 miles of routes, and ... 8,000,000 passengers ... between 1952–1957."[75] Indeed the government's air investments lend a new meaning to the famous French saying, "Coloniser, c'est transporter" [Colonization is transportation].[76] In a moment when French people's anxieties about losing the empire heightened, the massive investment in "transporter" must also be considered as part of a triage effort to maintain that empire.[77] This effort was paired with Air France's campaign to, as scholar Emily Katherine Gibson demonstrates, "other" the actual indigenous peoples who inhabited Air France's colonial and postcolonial destinations, all while assuring travellers that Air France would provide all the comforts of the metropole.[78] The government's efforts provide an interesting context when considered alongside the importance with which new postwar – and postcolonial – nations around the world treated their own fledgling airlines. As one historian has argued, "national airlines ... helped to hold the regions together, to reinforce the capital, to forge new routes with neighbouring countries which ignored the ex-imperial lifelines, and to represent their country overseas ... [they were seen] as instruments for [countries'] self-determination and their lifeline to the world."[79] Ironically, the French and these countries were speaking a similar language of self-assertion – within very different contexts, of course.

In terms of technology, "man of action" Henri Desbruères, head of French aeronautics, detailed the many advances the French nation could be proud of; in civil aviation, he argued, the Caravelle model, produced in France, now acted as a "source of pride" as well as an "ambassador" for the nation.[80] Similarly, the French government invested in airports as a vision of French superiority to the world, notably renovating Orly, south of Paris, in 1961. Historian Anthony Sampson called Orly airport "a glittering symbol of French air ambitions," and described both Orly and Charles de Gaulle airports as "monuments to French decisiveness and planning which kept foreign airlines and competition firmly in their place."[81] While Sampson's take was largely positive, Vanessa Schwartz has typified Orly's massive remodelling in a darker way, specifically as a direct response to France's anxieties about losing global prestige.[82] These two arguments – that the French government built glittering temples to modernity and that French national anxiety drove the projects – are, to my mind, not at all mutually exclusive.

If technological development in France like that of the Caravelle airplane and the renovations of Orly airport could be seen as masculine, these innovations also coupled with a relatively docile image of femininity, specifically that of a beautiful and welcoming French woman, who represented France's return to the world stage in the postwar years. The project of recasting French greatness needed Hecht's "men of action" and the masculine industries in which they toiled to restore its reputation globally, like aviation, but it also required *ambassadrices* who would sell the world on the idea of a sensual, available, warm France. For the *ambassadrice*, it was her beauty, her body, and her clothing that defined her superiority. Indeed as one aviation trade publication, *Terre et ciel* (*Earth and Sky*), put it, "these hostesses are going to represent French charm, good taste, and gentility to foreigners; these are the qualities that we [French people] hold most dear."[83] In the eyes of postwar travellers the world over in the early Cold War years, that woman was personified first by the Air France hostess, and later by her counterparts outside of the aviation industry, until, as the following chapters will demonstrate, it actually touched all French women.

The specific contours of the ideal French woman excluded many, if not most, of the actual women living within the borders of France, not to mention the French empire. The state and other relevant stakeholders conjured a vision of femininity that was difficult to emulate for many women, but near-impossible for women who were not white and middle-class. While I address the class question more deeply in the first chapter, I do want to look at the race piece here, because I think it deserves foregrounding, for the very reason of its relative archival absence. Indeed, in all of my research in government and media archive materials I found but one piece of evidence of a hostess who was not white during the time period studied in this book.[84] That whiteness played a prominent role in the moulding of an ideal femininity that took place against the backdrop of decolonization is not accidental. The bold assertion of whiteness as a marker of French female national identity, nay global superiority, negated the ability of non-white women to attain that hierarchical status, just as many were arriving on the shores of the Hexagon.[85] That the French government would want to employ that long-standing racial symbolism via their "Mistress of the House" hostesses, both within the metropole and across the francophone world is, I would argue, not at all accidental, but rather a hearkening back to and an aggressive continuity with a language of race that would have been familiar to people on both sides of that equation. The intersectional analysis of hostessing merits far more attention than this book affords it, especially given that the hostess model remains, as I argue in the conclusion, a global standard of femininity, and I hope that future histories continue to take up this call.[86]

And empire itself, as noted earlier, was a major focus of the French state in the postwar context, especially given anxieties both about losing territory – and prestige – and trailing anglophone countries in global power. The French government consciously set out to make a francophone network, ensuring that passengers could crisscross the globe without having to hear English, which one historian calls "a striking achievement,"[87] given France's precarious economic position at the end of the war. In order to maintain this network, the French had to ban their colonies from holding any air rights, and any nationalist leaders, according to historian Jenifer Van Vleck, "found themselves excluded from aviation policy discussions," a snub which surely impeded those nations' economic growth during this time.[88] Indeed Kristin Ross has argued that the simultaneous developments of decolonization on one hand and modernization and Americanization on the other are not unrelated, but rather two components of the same story, and in some ways the history of Air France and hostessing told here links them directly.[89] Airlines, then, complicate narratives of decolonization; French actions to perpetuate colonial subjects' connections to the metropole appear far more akin to a continuation of empire than a rupture.

Third, this project also explains how French actors in government, tourism, and beyond wielded femininity as a marker of soft power, originated by international relations theorist Joseph Nye, who defined soft power as "the ability to get what you want through attraction rather than coercion or payments. It arises from the attractiveness of a country's culture, political ideals, and policies."[90] Nye argues that the elements of culture alone – food, films, or fashion, for example – are not enough to compel people to change their behaviours or, in this case, spend money and other resources. Rather, Nye posits, direct, "personal" exchanges are crucial to maximizing the assets that a country already possesses.[91] France receives special attention in Nye's assessment: "France spends close to $1 billion a year to spread French civilization around the world … France's soft power has been clearly maintained or even increased in the past fifty years [1954–2004], although Paris may no longer be the prime intellectual, cultural, and philosophical capital of the world."[92] The French investment in attracting the world has clearly paid dividends.

Building on Nye's theory of soft power, this book argues that in postwar France the cultural joined with the political in the physical form of hostesses, young women who performed an important service for France. They rendered France desirable – and hence hopefully relevant – on the world stage through contact with the rest of the world. In making that case, the book exposes how gender operates in the service of institutional entities that often have very little interest in bettering the lives of actual men and women.

Some historians, including (but not limited to) Christopher Endy, Richard Kuisel, and Whitney Walton, have persuasively addressed cultural Franco-American relations during the Cold War and the era of decolonization, but they have not focused on the specific combination of tourism and gender as a source of French soft power.[93] If tourism was the second-largest industry in France by 1946, and hostessing was already the firm nucleus of that industry, then it merits a serious look, especially given the long-lasting implications of the model of the hostess on France and femininity across the world. And this book does just that, examining various models of femininity promoted by stakeholders including the French government and civil servants, cultural commentators and critics on both sides of the Atlantic, travel writers, and women themselves. Actual women, as we will see, sometimes resisted conformity; the experience of air hostesses unionizing is one such example of how the state could never have predicted some of the implications of placing women in proximate work positions, and the enforced happiness mandated by the company proved difficult for some hostesses to maintain in the face of problems ranging from mechanical disasters to passenger disgruntlement.[94] However, this book is more concerned with the idealization of a specific version of femininity, one which, as the conclusion shows, has had profound staying power over time.

In much the same way as actors in the postwar French tourism industry located hostessing directly at the centre of France's global fortunes, this book also considers the hostess as the nucleus of its analysis and builds externally from her. The book's structure reflects that of a pebble dropped in a pond, in which the notion of hostessing expands and ripples out exponentially over the course of the time period covered here. The book begins by examining the construction of the model air hostess, whose body, clothing, and overall appearance were crafted by the state in order to present the most perfect vision of French femininity to the world. The second chapter explores how the project of hostessing, which the state considered a resounding success, began to expand, first beginning with other tourism hostesses stationed across the Hexagon, in such sites as trains, train stations, information booths, rest areas on highways, spas, and camping parks, to name just a few. In the third chapter, the book takes an in-depth look at two key moments of the 1950s and the 1960s when the world's eyes turned to France: the Brussels Exposition of 1958 and the Grenoble Winter Olympics of 1968. It examines how, knowing that international attention would be focused on France, and wanting to maximize the potential monetary gains, diverse branches of the French government made absolutely sure to recruit, train, and display a cadre of aesthetically pleasing women for the world to consume. The fourth chapter tracks the jump of the *ambassadrice* out of the realm of hostessing, showing how "pleasing" became a responsibility of all French women, regardless of their role or station. It utilizes what I refer to as translational figures, people like travel writers, authors, and even Brigitte Bardot, who facilitated the separation of France's feminine reputation from strictly the body of the hostess to all French women, as well as its explanation to an American audience. It also demonstrates how readily many influential Americans accepted French women's superiority not only as an aspirational maxim but as a reason to visit France. The chapter also briefly delves into the heteronormativity of this project through an analysis of how translational figures conceptualized tourism, femininity, and homosexuality. Finally, in the fifth chapter, the book illustrates how state actors and travel writers, French and American, promoted the parallel ideas that France was a place where sex and romance comprised an essential part of the tourist experience. The equation of femininity and sexuality with France reached its apogee, as it were, with the ubiquitous travel literature in which France itself was portrayed as an inviting woman and a land where the women were sensually accessible. The journey from air hostess to sensual nation is an astonishing one, and the chapters of this book will attempt to both trace it and analyse its import.

The origins of standards of feminine appearance and behaviour tend to be opaque and difficult to pinpoint. This project shines light on a government which, along with its subsidiaries, spelled out specific requirements for women for the purpose of promoting itself to the world. My work not only identifies these requirements but also shows how they reverberated from the airplane cabin to all women in France and beyond. It is telling that the government felt it had a right to place these standards on women; when the government of France sent male diplomats out into the world, it felt no need to select them based on their height, weight, and general allure. These standards and requirements which government actors placed on women in these roles resounded throughout the culture and beyond. As the book will demonstrate, these idealized women in the public eye were expected to be perfect, to look perfect, to be constantly happy and charming. They were expected to please rather than be heard as individual human beings worthy of respect. If the most important thing a woman can do to serve her nation is to stand to the side and look pretty, then that speaks volumes about women's value within that nation. And in many ways, the relationship between women and power today reveals that this expectation not only persists, but thrives. This book will show how, in the midst of a crisis of masculinity, France turned to its women to market themselves and the nation internationally, creating a veritable charm offensive on the world stage.

Chapter One

Creating the Model Hostess

On 15 April 1946, Air France's first air hostesses took to the skies, launching, according to the major newspaper *Le Figaro*, a new "revolution in the heavens."[1] Before 1946, Air France employed male stewards in airplane cabins, and their job, according to one former hostess, was to sell as much alcohol as possible to passengers, many of whom would turn to drink to take their minds off of the considerable perils of early air travel.[2] At the end of the war, the French government viewed aviation as a realm in which they could imitate American companies' practices as well as challenge them for supremacy. While most French airplanes had either been destroyed or requisitioned during the war, American planes had continued flying, but the French made it a priority to try to keep up with American aviation. The first air hostess was hired in the United States in the 1930s. The French industry, which up to this point had employed only male graduates of hotelier programs as stewards, would now use hostesses, but ones it deemed superior to their American counterparts.[3] This time around, the "revolution" would be led by women, albeit only those who conformed to the company's very specific vision.

A brief note on methodology: this chapter relies on a wide variety of sources, including official archives of Air France, trade newspapers and magazines, novels, and memoirs. Perhaps the most crucial memoir, though, was Solange Catry's *On the Wings of the Seahorse* (the seahorse being the official symbol of Air France). Catry joined Air France as a hostess in the company's earliest years and later rose to become chief hostess of the airline, actively fighting gender-based labour discrimination at several points along the way. Catry can be read as a complicated figure: an independent woman whose career spanned several decades, she worked her way up through company ranks, never married, and ultimately held a position of power, supervising not only air hostesses but, as chapter 3 will show, hostesses far removed from any airplane. Ultimately, Catry was even awarded the Legion of Honour, France's highest commendation, for her service to the company.[4] As such she is a true pioneer alongside the earliest women pilots. Nevertheless, Catry remained extremely dedicated to the vision of the hostess that forms the backbone of this chapter and this book; she demanded that hostesses on and off the airplane conform to thinness and beauty requirements, although she herself was not sure she qualified on the latter front. And even in interviews as late as the 2000s, Catry spoke fondly of her time with the company. It is not possible to know her innermost feelings, but externally, at least, Catry, and many of her hostess compatriots, portrayed herself as a team player. Like most people, and certainly many pioneering women in fields dominated by men, Catry was not a simple figure to understand, and the chapter makes note of some of her inconsistencies. Still, she is a crucial voice for the book, central as she was to many of the developments characterized here, and her complexity serves as a reminder to read carefully and critically. As for Catry, she remained almost universally positive about her experience at Air France in her memoir; the preface was even written by the widow of the longtime director of the company, Max Hymans.

The actual competitive processes for joining Air France as a hostess consisted of intensive trials for candidates, and very few women who entered their names in contention ultimately joined the company. Annual numbers of hostesses can be hard to determine because of high levels of fluidity within the position, and because the archives do not always differentiate between numbers of hostesses and numbers of Air France employees. Still, there are some hard numbers: there were 30 male stewards in 1945, the year before the company launched the air hostess program (after 1950 the company gradually phased out stewards in favour of hostesses, and men rarely worked in cabins again in large numbers until the 1970s). In 1946, the first class of hostesses included 38 women.[5] In 1948, there were 88 women, a marked increase over two years.[6] By 1959, there were 728 air hostesses and stewards, and then 2,757 hostesses and stewards in 1973, nearly the end date for this study.[7] The data clearly document how the air hostess program grew exponentially, along with the size of planes and an expansion in air travel, as well as air hostesses' expanded ambassadorial duties around the world.[8]

The criteria for being an Air France hostess in this initial cohort were quite strict. Just to qualify for the initial consideration, a woman needed to be 21 to 30 years old and single (or divorced or widowed with no dependents). Requirements also demanded a certain size and shape: a hostess's height had to fall between 1.55 and 1.70 metres (approximately five feet one and five feet seven inches), her weight needed to fall within the range of 45 to 65 kilos (100 to 140 pounds), and her waist measurement could be no more than 70 centimetres (27½ inches). In terms of education, she needed at least the first part of her French baccalaureate degree; barring that, she needed the equivalent of a GED. In addition she was required to have a state certificate for nursing, first aid, or

Creating the Model Hostess 23

1.1. Legendary Air France hostess Solange Catry (1966) (Source gallica.bnf.fr/Bibliothèque nationale de France).

1.2. The second group of accepted hostesses in a publicity shot for the airline (1946). Courtesy of the Air France Museum.

emergency services. Air France also had linguistic requirements; every air hostess had to speak French, English, and either German, Italian, or Spanish.[9]

The demands on women to look a certain way were not necessarily unique to the aviation industry, hinting at a broader ideal that the French government and Air France tapped into rather than created from scratch. Other fields of postwar feminine labour encouraged (some might say forced) women to conform to an aesthetic vision of loveliness. Female politicians, pioneers in their own right, learned how to "think like a man but look like a woman."[10] Even in factories, women were encouraged to tend to their appearances; the Confédération Général du Travail (CGT), the most active postwar union for women, distributed "beauty tips for tired eyes or rough skin," according to historian Claire Duchen.[11] However, nowhere were the requirements anywhere near as strict as in hostessing, nor was the influence of the women involved as far-reaching.[12]

If a woman had the desire and waist size to compete for a position, she would express her interest in a letter to the company or attend one of the large gatherings held to recruit potential hostesses. If the candidate was called to the Air France headquarters at Le Bourget, north of Paris, she could expect to be poked and prodded by company and state representatives. Almost immediately upon arrival, she was weighed and measured to make sure she had not fibbed about her size.[13] If she passed the physical scrutiny, she faced another series of tests, which involved her facility with languages: "Do you speak English?" (in English) was one such quick filter.

If linguistic and bodily criteria were not enough, Air France also mandated that its hostesses meet non-quantifiable marks. For example, the company called for hostesses to possess "an appealing face, good personality, [and] distinctiveness."[14] The nebulousness and subjectivity of these qualities would have allowed the evaluator leeway in selecting particular women and establishing an aesthetic for women who would represent France in the skies. If the prospective hostess survived that test, she would then be called in front of what the major newspaper *Le Monde* called a "severe" jury, with as many as 12 people (mostly men), who would observe her "gestures and her walk," and then rate her "general allure,"[15] a concept that allowed for a good deal of interpretational flexibility, on a scale from one to five. Some were rejected right away: "Mademoiselle, we cannot admit you; your legs are too fat."[16] Barring such a physical misfortune, the prospective hostess was sent away for several days while the team evaluated the candidates.

If she had been deemed alluring and intelligent enough, the candidate later returned to face a new round of psychological and aptitude tests, which *Le Monde* described as "torture,"[17] a weighty word in the wake of the Second World War. Indeed, in an interview with an industry magazine, the head of hospitality for Air France agreed that the first group of hostesses had undergone a "harsh ordeal."[18] Solange Catry described the exams as a series of bewildering activities: "assembling and disassembling cubes, untangling knots, cutting bizarre shapes, perforating cards with mysterious emblems."[19] Philippe Roland of *Le Figaro* echoed her assessment, recalling how the candidates toiled over a series of hieroglyphics in a high-stress environment.[20] And another early hostess, Nicole Darde de Bénazé, remembered urgently trying to quiet a fellow candidate, who was trying to figure out the instructions: "Shush, copy me if you will, but shush!"[21]

The process and qualifications changed little over the time period covered in this book. Max Hymans, the president of Air France, wrote in 1954, eight years after the first competition, about how women needed to "have a good dose of enthusiasm for the job" and an "appealing face"; likewise, they were required to be "amiable" and "gracious," and to always possess "tact" and hold "with ease a conversation on a wide range of subjects that would allow [the jury to assess] her naturalness, character, and spirit."[22] He described the medical exam as "a first barrage," and noted that of "250 or 300 candidates, only perhaps 15 will survive," still a shockingly low number several years later. He again reiterated that this rigour was absolutely crucial, for the hostess was first and foremost "an *ambassadrice* of French taste, elegance, and spirit."[23] Hymans did note that passengers of 1954 were more acclimated to flying than their prewar and immediate postwar counterparts, but he remained firm that the role of the hostess was still to be the "mistress of the house," and should she lapse in either that or her physical person (what he called *lassitude physique*, or "physical laziness"), she would be "dropped."[24]

Thirteen years after Hymans detailed the process of becoming a hostess, in 1967 a reporter for the newspaper *Sud-Ouest* described it again as a "strange exam, where the principal qualifications are exactly those that are not named explicitly. Strange test of charm where the voice, the silences, throat clearings, looks, count as much as linguistic virtuosity. '*We are and we must be cold and lucid*,' one 'selector' told me" (original emphasis). The potential hostess would then enter a room with one woman and one man, who was clearly her superior. There, the panel would pose one question to the hostess: "Tell us about yourself, Mademoiselle." The article continued to describe the role-playing required of the successful candidate: "You forget your nerves, your timidity, your gaucheness, your missteps. You are 'dazzling'! You talk about your active life, your friends and acquaintances, of purely feminine matters. You know that you will have to make sacrifices, but you feel a real vocation and you are courageous. You direct all the seductive powers in the world toward this silent, smiling male examiner who listens and looks at you. The 'Monsieur from Paris' scribbles strange signs on his paper, and it's done. You leave, stoically." Upon departing the room, the two panellists consult one another, scrutinizing the potential hostess's performance for the most minute flaws. Perhaps they find that you did not have enough verve for Air France, that you were not "vibrant" enough.

The candidate would continue on to a second jury, this one focused entirely on looks – judges likely would barely utter a word to the candidate. Asked about the rationale for this process, the selector replied, "We have two juries so we cannot be swayed. The task of the first is to judge in depth the character of the young girl. The second must coldly evaluate the 'punch,' the 'impact force' of her silhouette. And the two must then be in agreement." If, for example, the second jury's verdict was "*too bad her thighs are too large*" (original emphasis), the candidate would be sent home, having been "graciously assassinated" by Air France.[25]

Years after her own selection, Solange Catry took part in hostess selection as a jury member (usually the only female on the panel), and she recalled it as a curious experience. Catry wrote that one "needed, in a few minutes, to grade the allure, poise, culture, education, the spirit of repartee and initiative." Such a brief, intense evaluation often tripped up even qualified candidates; forgetting basic rules, like not to wear their glasses, they would be rejected by the jury.[26]

All of these long-standing rigours and regulations beg the question why any woman would subject herself to this level of scrutiny. And yet it is important to remember that the women themselves viewed the opportunity to become a hostess as an exciting, momentous possibility, perhaps unsurprising given the labour and life possibilities open to women in these postwar years. Hostesses tended to fall in the upper echelons of economic strata, but in a complicated way. Labour options for women were limited across class, but for middle- and upper-middle-class women, who had some higher education, as was required of Air France hostesses, it could be extremely difficult to find work. These were young women who, according to Solange Catry, were often (but not always – Catry, who would become the most powerful hostess in the company, referred to herself as a "provincial") well-to-do *parisiennes*. She described them as "brilliant, sure of themselves, remembering their winters spent in the Alps, the plays of Sartre or Thornton Wilder."[27] These women were barred from most of the *grandes écoles*, France's most prestigious bastions of higher education, including the one that trained pilots and aviation engineers. They also faced extreme barriers, formal and informal, to other professions.[28]

Furthermore, the difficulties posed by the immediate postwar context cannot be underestimated. The initial *concours*, in 1946, occurred in the context of extreme postwar deprivation, when basic goods were still rationed by the government. Solange Catry recalled the difficulties of everyday life as motivating her interest. She was residing in a single room in Rouen, eking out a living as an English language tutor: "Heat was almost nonexistent, the décor was austere, and any chance to escape my solitude was good."[29] Additionally, the salary offered by Air France of 90,000 (former) francs per month for 90 hours of flying was relatively generous, given the other available options.

Many of the women sought adventure and excitement, to see the world and have interesting experiences before settling down. Air hostess Alix d'Unienville, who was born into a prominent French family and had won the prestigious Croix de guerre for her activities in the resistance, wrote in her prize-winning memoir that her reason for entering the Air France corps was simple: "I wanted to do aviation to see the world."[30] Similarly, in a letter to an aviation personnel magazine, hostess Madeleine Marillonet wrote of how she had longed to "live a life of excitement, and in this profession I am not disappointed … I can have breakfast in London and dinner in Vienna."[31] Former hostess Aude Malapert remembered some of her time at Air France as spectacular: "Running around the world at 20 years old and finding yourself in four-star hotels with a team of friends with whom to go out and discover a city or to go dancing; it was magnificent. Especially when you lived in Paris in a small studio with a folding shower and a non-flushing toilet."[32] When Solange Catry served on the Air France candidate jury, she believed that the thirst for new experiences, especially for a few years before marriage and family curtailed a woman's possibility for independence, was the most "convincing" answer she received when inquiring about candidates' motivation.[33] For some of the women, Catry recalled, simply coming to Paris was the great adventure of their lives.[34]

The company's promotion of air hostess as a glamorous profession was enormously successful in attracting candidates and whetting the appetites of potential hostesses. One journalistic television show, "Young Girl," designed to attract adolescent girls, broadcast an episode entitled "Marie-Josée: Air Hostess" in 1967. In the episode, the host surveyed random women at Orly Airport, asking them to comment on the profession of air hostess generally. "Do you find this to be a feminine profession?" the host queried the women. "Yes, *very* feminine," answered one female respondent. "Does this career tempt you?" the host continued. "Yes, enormously," she replied.[35]

The cachet associated with being an air hostess extended beyond the individual herself. Entire regions celebrated when one of their own became an air hostess. In 1958, the Bordeaux newspaper *Sud-Ouest* lauded one of its own, Françoise Lagarde, who was chosen to represent Air France internationally in New York, citing how "pretty" Lagarde was, this "little *dacquoise* [woman from Dax, France]."[36] The paper rejoiced again in 1968, a full 12 years after the first competition, when it excitedly announced, "Eight charming *girondines* [women from the Gironde region] will be hostesses for Air France."[37] The article then went on to proclaim that one of the successful women was the "model air hostess" because of her perfect appearance. The successes of these young women from the Gironde were celebrated; that the population there could produce models of French perfection reflected well upon the whole region. Thus the social capital associated with being an air hostess emerged as a collective phenomenon.

Back in Le Bourget, if a candidate persevered through those initial tests, she would be called back again several days later for still further medical testing, and then finally she would have to succeed at all aspects of job training. For Air France hostesses, job training lasted around a month and primarily focused on matters of safety.[38] For the duration of training, the company boarded the women together in an old chateau near Orly airport, just south of Paris. There was little time for leisure; prospective hostesses worked all day, perfecting their brains and their bodies, in preparation for their air hostessing duties. The smallest error could lead to reprisal and even dismissal. As one hostess trainer, Mme. Boursin, said in a television interview, mistakes needed to be loudly and publicly criticized so that "everyone can learn" from other people's errors.[39]

Hostess training comprised an astonishing variety of subjects and activities, but if the goal of the preparation was to create *ambassadrices* who could embody an ideal image of France, then all material that supported that idealization had to be absorbed. In terms of traditional academic subjects, hostesses learned geography, history, and international relations, along with what Solange Catry recalled as "international air law, aerodynamics, geopolitics and other disciplines with strange names that left us terribly perplexed about our future."[40] Catry even remembered a daily press briefing at which the women learned about politics, economics, and society "as though we were going to be called to play, in our cabins, the Scudérys [a celebrated French literary family], Mme de Staël, and the countess of Noailles in one!"[41]

Attention to hostesses' bodies formed another, at least equally important, pillar of job training; the hostess's perfect education also necessitated the perfect packaging. The company demanded that hostesses project a flawless appearance as part of their job. The 1954 Personnel Manual concluded its section on hostess appearance by stating "the hostess must always be clean, impeccable, fresh, simple, and discreet."[42]

Each inch of a hostess's physical person had its own set of regulations; if she was to represent France, perfection was necessary. The few women who had initially conformed to the company's corporal requirements now found themselves facing intense calisthenics sessions at 6:30 every morning, when all of the women would line up and move as one while performing a script of exercises.[43] Hostesses' hair, for example, had an official style, designed for maximum efficiency, diplomacy, and allure. It was not acceptable, the company noted in its manual, to hear passengers "complain that the hostess is poorly coiffed or not even styled at all."[44] When France's General Aviation Regulation board wanted to promote the country's aerospace agency in 1961, it used hostesses' hair for publicity. The company magazine *France-aviation* published a large photograph of two hostesses with the following caption: "The commercial service of [GAR] had the idea to launch a new hairstyle, named 'Space,' specially studied for air hostesses by the French Haute Coiffure [specialists], using two Air France hostesses [as models]. Mlles Meyer ... et Leonard, our new and charming 'Space' pioneers, will, without a doubt, inspire many space missions." The marriage of fashion and technology met on the hostess's body in an assertion of French worthiness, if not superiority, and the hostess's appearance would "inspire" others to covet the women of France.[45]

The beauty education of the Air France hostess involved an extensive amount of work with industry professionals. The company devoted a lot of ink to instructions on proper makeup, down to the level of products and application, in its 1954 Personnel Manual; makeup, the manual insisted, "is of a capital importance."[46] Hostesses underwent a course in makeup application, led by an aesthetic specialist from Lancôme, the French luxury cosmetics company, who would teach the trainees (and often re-teach the hostesses years later) "how an air hostess ought to be made up."[47] As such, Air France itself noted in an article for its on-board magazine, *Air-France Revue*, "Air France has even entrusted its hostesses to Lancôme *techniciennes*. [Our hostesses] learn at Chevilly, between flights, how best to bring out [*mettre en valeur*] their type of beauty, and to correct, in any climate, their imperfections, thanks to the perfect products from these ultra-modern laboratories."[48] This article unites three of postwar France's pillars of national identity: technology (Lancôme labs), hostesses, and beauty standards (a woman ought to look perfect in any setting). If the hostess's face was essentially currency for French diplomacy, it needed to be absolutely flawless – and because of the rigorous aesthetics education, it was. As *Le Monde* declared in 1955, "thanks to Air France, France will show a 'beautiful face' to its passengers."[49]

The hostess had one last task to complete before boarding the plane: donning the Air France uniform. "It is not possible," the Air France Personnel Manual advised in 1954, "to have an elegant comportment without an immaculate uniform and a proper self-presentation."[50] The 1948 hostess manual emphasized the connection between dress and social judgment even more explicitly, arguing that "one is judged on one's personality by words, actions, and dress ... it is through the care one takes in dressing that one forges a strong and active personality."[51] The external aesthetics of a hostess, Air France is arguing here, are indicators to all who observe them of hostesses' internal fitness. Her dress reflected her worthiness to represent France.

A hostess needed to dress the part, a fraught enterprise in a country that was so identified with the fashion industry and that desperately counted on fashion to parlay clothing and design into international grandeur. For Air France *ambassadrices*, then, their sartorial obligations were not simply in sporting company uniforms; their clothing had to communicate the genius of the Gallic mind to the world, on the perfect form of the hostess's body. If uniforms once categorized soldiers' bodies for war, in the case of air hostesses they proclaimed

1.3. One of the earliest Air France uniforms, designed by Georgette de Trèze (1954). Courtesy of the Air France Museum.

corporate allegiance. As one hostess described it, "in uniform I am Marie-Josée Dragon *and* Air France."[52]

Air France hostesses' uniforms were particularly important for two reasons. First, Air France, like other European airlines, historical and contemporary, was owned and operated by the state, and its uniforms thus served as symbols of a major nation. Second, France had a historical association with fashion and the fashion industry, which meant that the uniforms were expected to be a cut above. As one industry publication put it in 1947, wedding two of France's most important postwar commodities, fashion and femininity, "our '*ambassadrices*' of French grace shall have a uniform worthy of our best designers."[53]

It is useful to look at Air France's uniform mandate for hostesses within a historical context. In his landmark work on the development of military uniforms in the *ancien régime*, historian Daniel Roche argues that uniforms are expressly meant to erase individuality and condition uniformity, that they are an important method of soldiers' "training," much like physical or intellectual exercises. Further, he continues, when the individual consents to adopt the uniform, they display "obedience" and contribute to "collective power."[54] Virginia Woolf, who often explored the connections between fashion and power in her works, also laid out the link between institutions and uniforms in her *Three Guineas*, when she argued that the most highly valued arenas in society – war, law, and universities – all required a sort of uniform to designate their import. In each space, she wrote, "we find the same love of dress."[55] Air hostesses, for their part, served the company and the state, and the uniform they wore thus signalled at least tacit acceptance of the company's strictures of behaviour and appearance for them, which were themselves specific to their femininity (unlike pilots, for example, who faced no size or beauty requirements).[56]

The very first Air France hostess uniforms were designed by Georgette Renal, head of a prominent couture house. These garments corresponded in many ways to the exigencies of the time rather than to more creative couture. In 1946, the New Look had not yet appeared, and material deprivations relating to the war abounded. Reflecting the sober conditions, early uniforms took on what Solange Catry described as a military look.[57] In its on-board magazine, the company singled out the importance of one piece of the ensemble: "the national beret that the hostesses of our national company wear with panache, and which symbolizes the warm welcome and the smile of France."[58]

The regulations associated with hostess uniforms betray the company's belief in their importance. The 1948 hostess manual delineated exactly how hostesses should present themselves. Upon acceptance into the hostess program, hostesses received what the company referred to as a "trousseau," a loaded word implying a deep, almost marital, union with Air France, not inappropriately as they were unable to wed and remain in their careers at this time.[59] The company forbade any deviations from the official look, even in components that were not included in the trousseau. Costume jewellery, for example, was not allowed, nor could pantyhose be anything other than "beige silk." Shoes had to be "classic," and only "black or dark blue." The hostess's coat, the wrapping on the present, needed to be "navy or petroleum blue raglan, weighing of 630 grams exactly, [with the] Air France seal on the middle of the left arm."[60] Clearly hostesses' uniforms bore huge significance and symbolic meaning, even before they became a global fashion sensation.

In 1962, Air France executives turned to the lauded couture house Christian Dior to design updated uniforms for hostesses, setting off what one writer described as a "veritable revolution" in fashion.[61] The choice of Dior was extremely significant. Christian Dior himself had saved the French fashion industry with his 1947 New Look, effectively returning the centre of global fashion to Paris after its temporary removal to New York during the Second World War, so it was appropriate that his house should set the standard for the chic French *ambassadrice*. In its own history, the airline lauded the uniforms by Renal and Trèze, but went on to state, "the old uniform no longer suited

1.4. This hostess is sporting the Christian Dior uniform, a collaboration with the storied fashion house that was designed to associate hostesses and French couture in passengers' minds. The look was so popular that women the world over sought to emulate it in their everyday dress (1963). Courtesy of the Air France Museum.

the active role Air France executives wanted hostesses to play."[62] Thus as the job of hostesses expanded into informal diplomacy, the airline wanted them to wear clothing that reflected the prestige of the entities they were representing: Air France and the state. In 1962, designer Marc Bohan, the head of Dior at the time, created an outfit meant to whet the appetites of all women. As writer Hélène Kernel breathlessly reported in the on-board magazine for Air France, "Coming from Europe, the Americas, Africa, or Asia, the women of the world – the whole world – have only one very specific goal: Paris … Even in the airplane, Air France hostesses give them a taste of Parisian elegance. Marc Bohan, Director at Dior, recently designed a new uniform with them [and here it is unclear whether 'them' refers to the hostesses or all 'women of the world'] in mind."[63] He incorporated a new colour, a new pillbox hat, and a new attention to detail that typified couture design.

The uniform even had a required hairstyle, one that would set off the hat to maximum effect, and the coiffure, dubbed the "mid-air tambourine," became famous in its own right.[64] *Le Monde* deemed the uniforms perfect, arguing that Bohan had achieved a balance between the "fleeting" trends of fashion with the "permanence of elegance."[65] The 1962 uniform combined hostesses and fashion to send a message to the world: France abounded in beautiful women swathed in elegant apparel. Bohan even designed an outfit for female passengers travelling to Paris, based somewhat on the 1962 uniform, so that they could blend in with the French aesthetic – the most superior, cultivated one in the world. *Air-France Revue* published a photograph of models in the two outfits, with this description from Kernel: "Symphony in blue of two elegant women, a blue that, much like the taste in travel, never goes out of style."[66] According to Kernel, Paris never goes out of style, France never goes out of style, French fashion never goes out of style, and Air France hostesses are the embodiment of these eternal maxims.

Hostesses themselves were not immune to the lure of couture. René Philippe's fictional hostess Sylvie described the uniform as a grand perk for having endured the rigours of hostess training: "the uniform," according to Sylvie, was "a detail, sure, but not a small one! ... and a very attractive one at that."[67] In René Puget's novel *The Long Haul*, when asked by a passenger why she became a hostess, the character Jacqueline de Valbon simply replies, "I fell for the uniform."[68] Similarly, the real-life hostess Marie-Josée Dragon, when asked whether she preferred her own clothes or the Air France kit, equivocated momentarily, and then spoke about the emotional response she received from others, saying, "people give me a big smile when I'm in uniform."[69] And Odette, the hostess interviewed for Claire Andrée Roe's juvenile series about careers, enthusiastically cited the uniform as her big draw for initially entering the profession as well. Odette explained, "[I] love the trips, the prestige, the uniform is pretty ... actually, they showed us our new winter uniform, which is even better than the summer one: navy blue suit, and very warm coat because it gets cold, believe me, on the runways! And high boots in navy blue goatskin – that makes you wish for winter!"[70] The element of glamour symbolized in the fabric of an Air France uniform was a powerful draw.

These tests and trials and trainings and trappings all seem amazingly rigorous and detailed, and for good reason, because the airline was not simply putting hostesses on airplanes but was creating *ambassadrices* to represent the country across Europe and the world. The training more closely resembled that of an official political diplomat, whose words and understandings of particular global regions would reflect directly back upon the metropole. The women Air France juries chose needed to be flawless exemplars of French femininity. Each stage of the examinations and training checked and perfected some aspect of the hostess's person: physical, intellectual, sartorial. Once complete, they could begin to perform.

On the Plane: Service with a Smile

Air France Personnel Manual, 1954: Air hostesses' welcoming attitude toward passengers "MUST BE THE PERPETUAL CONCERN OF ON-BOARD PERSONNEL THROUGHOUT THE FLIGHT."[71] (original emphasis)

Now visions of physical and intellectual perfection, hostesses could finally board Air France airplanes and interact with passengers. These interactions were not spontaneous, however; from the side of the hostess, they were carefully managed, so as to convey the best possible impression of themselves and France at all times. The hostess was constantly described as a perfect *maîtresse de maison*, but in the skies. Indeed in its first article about air hostesses in 1947, an industry publication, describing the head of hospitality of Air France showing the new recruits around their planes, wrote that M. Jourdan was introducing them to their new "homes."[72]

A gentleman could expect to board a plane and be taken care of in the same way as he was at his own home, or likely better. His every need would be seen to by a solicitous, beautiful, smiling hostess. The company explicitly mandated that male passengers receive almost fawning treatment. In 1948, the hostess manual called on hostesses to learn passengers' names, as "a man is always flattered by being called by his name."[73] If he had any trouble at all, the hostess's responsibility was to see to it, and quickly. On night flights, for example, she was required to patrol the cabin every 15 minutes to "assure passenger comfort."[74] The manual announced the presence of a sewing kit on every flight, and it specified that if a man asked for it, the hostess must complete all repairs for him. No such offer was to be made to a woman passenger.[75] Attesting to the success of these amazingly attentive policies, as well-known writer Hervé Lauwick put it in an aviation magazine in 1956, "the purest place in the world right now is the airplane ... Primarily due to the air hostesses, because these young women are perfect. They are nice, honest, serious, full of energy, they really have every virtue, and I propose that we add a definition to the Larousse [the famous French dictionary] that is not there right now but is definitely merited: "AIR HOSTESS: Woman you would want to have in your home ..."[76] The following section will explore Lauwick's definitional statement using several criteria, including emotional labour, maternal instincts, and overall wifely suitability.

Smile

Air France Personnel Manual, 1954: "Learning to smile while speaking facilitates conversation and gives an agreeable air to the dialogue."[77]

In 1948, the French National Assembly held a vociferous floor debate on determining the Air France budget. In arguing strongly for generous funding, Deputy Pierre Beauquier, representing the northeastern town of Belfort, urged his colleagues to remember that Air France was a symbol of French prestige, and that they needed to "extend its rise" even further to ensure French aviation domination. Beauquier extended special thanks to Air France personnel, singling out air hostesses, who "brought to the world a piece of French prestige and also some of France's smile."[78]

The smile was key to the hostess's bearing, important for attracting passengers the world over, and the demand for her emotional labour came directly from the company. "Do everything with a smile" became a sort of *de facto* motto for air hostesses.[79] Alix d'Unienville depicted her Air France smile as unique among her other expressions of emotional happiness; it held a "commercial" quality to her.[80] Describing how to load passengers on board, for example, she wrote, "smiles, welcoming words of encouragement, promise of a quick departure, more smiles, and everyone is seated in ... the cabin."[81] In *France-aviation*, the company newsletter, aviation journalist Robert Savreux exhorted all Air France employees to remember that they had a role to play in making sure that Air France airplanes were full. Targeting hostesses particularly (the article was accompanied by a large picture of a hostess serving food), he urged them to remember that "the smile of the hostess is part of our sales pitch."[82]

In her work on affective labour, sociologist Arlie Hochschild has argued that the exercise of some emotional control is part and parcel of everyday life. All people, she notes, do some "surface acting," or behave in a certain way that does not necessarily reflect or impact one's deep self.[83] The real crux in the case of flight attendants, though, and particularly Air France flight attendants, is the involvement of the company, and by proxy, the state. Hochschild argues that "something more operates when institutions are involved, for within institutions various elements of acting are taken away from the individual and replaced by institutional mechanisms."[84] Thus in the quest to create perfect *ambassadrices*, the airline controlled not just hostesses' bodies, but also their innermost selves. The 1948 hostess manual reflected this directly when it exhorted hostesses that they "must take criticism with grace and apologize on behalf of the company," never betraying their actual emotions.[85]

Over many years, advertising for Air France consistently promised passengers that they would be treated to the smiles of hostesses, making the smile a

1.5. A reassuring, constant smile was integral to the air hostess's demeanour – and job performance. Here, a company poster from the 1950s reminds hostesses to "always say it with a smile!" (1950s). Courtesy of the Air France Museum.

hallmark of Air France service.[86] In 1959, an ad featuring a beaming hostess lured passengers with the slogan, "Always say it with a smile!"[87] In a 1969 advertisement aimed at French business travellers, the copy promised "the smile of an Air France hostess who tends to you through the whole journey."[88] Hostesses affected the mood of an entire flight, according to Air France publicity. In 1956, an ad appeared proclaiming "Everyone smiles on board an Air France flight!"[89] It was accompanied by images of beaming hostesses and passengers. An air hostess's smile could cause everyone around her to do the same. A 1969 ad designed to attract American customers to Air France sold the experience of flying with the company as "a few hours of luxury and rest in mid-air, a hostess, a smile."[90] In advocating for Air France, the company sold their hostesses as a distinctive perk for air travellers, and for a hostess, as for all its female workers, a smile was her most important feature.

Company literature also reflects the importance of the female smile to the overall success of the airline. In his first interview with an internal publication for Air France workers, newly named company president Joseph Roos tried to inspire workers to go the extra distance for clients and boost sales. It was not simple timetables, he said, that prodded people to choose Air France, but also intangibles like "the smiles of our air hostesses."[91] In an article designed to spur an improvement in customer service among its women workers, a company writer urged Air France's receptionists to recall hostesses' "legendary smiles" when dealing with clients. Even though they were working on the telephone, the writer asserted that all receptionists should put on a "smiling face" when taking calls for Air France.[92]

Media took up the description of the Air France hostess as constantly smiling, making the ad campaigns' promises come true. A reporter for *Sud-Ouest* newspaper, Jacques Vulaines, reminded readers of the importance of hostesses to their travel experience, describing how a hostess's "charming smile and constant devotion count a lot toward the enjoyment of a flight."[93] In another article in the same newspaper on how to become an air hostess, the author reminded hostesses that their smile was an effective tool in calming anxious passengers and creating an "atmosphere of comfort" on board. It reminded potential hostesses to be especially vigilant that their smiles appear "in no way commercial, understand!"[94] This unintentionally ironic command demonstrates the extreme, and often absurd, nature of the emotional labour that hostesses were expected to perform.

Even children's literature emphasized a hostess's smile. In the 1965 book *Martine en avion* (*Martine on a Plane*), a part of famed children's author Gilbert Delahaye's series about a little girl's life, Martine embarks upon a trip to Rome with her mother. The reader accompanies Martine through all of the steps of air travel at the time: buying a ticket at an airline bureau, going to the airport, and so on. A constant in this whole process is the friendly expression of the air hostess, who acts as a guide through the book, always "smiling at Martine."[95] The hostess plays nearly the exact same role, "guiding" Caroline through the process of flying with "smiles" in Pierre Probst's *Caroline en avion*, published in 1957 as part of another series about the adventures of a little girl.[96] And in Catherine Beaumont's children's book, she describes the job of the hostess as "she must know, without ever losing her smile, how to serve, direct, care for, and counsel passengers." Her description of the steward's job held no such prescription for smiles.[97]

Often in descriptions, the hostess was reduced to nothing more than her smile. In a 1959 article for *Sud-Ouest*, reporter Jacques Vulaines wrote about the longest-serving Air France employees. He described their dedication to France and to the company, and he detailed some of the work they performed. One such employee was Nicole Moucot, the first air hostess to get her 10,000-kilometre cap, whom Vulaines described as a wonderful "*ambassadrice*." Vulaines further wrote, "And she hasn't yet finished walking that smile through the aisles for Air France."[98] In a stunning bit of synecdoche, Vulaines equates Moucot, clearly an excellent hostess, with her smile alone. Another article in the same newspaper performed a similar feat of physical reduction. Discussing the hostessing tryouts, the writer detailed the constant loss of hostesses to marriage. Because of hostess depletion, he said, Air France "periodically needs to revive [its] precious stock of femininity and smiles."[99] Again, the hostesses are not people in this description; they are their womanliness and their smile. In 1958, the Air France company newsletter published a large photograph of new hostesses all posing in front of a plane. The caption for the photo read: "A fresh bouquet of smiles!"[100] When Chief Hostess Solange Catry penned a piece for Air France's on-board magazine, *Air-France Revue*, on the role of hostesses from the beginning of their tenure at the company until her writing in 1961, she also distilled hostesses down to their smiles alone, perhaps reflecting the deep internalization of Air France's policies regarding deportment. She called the piece "New Smiles," suggesting that there were always new tricks to learn, but the hostess's smile itself firmly remained as a symbol of Air France – and France itself.[101]

Even when the flight was not going well, hostesses were expected to remain smiling. In former pilot René Puget's bestselling novel *The Long Haul*, which was also translated into English and German, a retired pilot and flight instructor, Gilbert Marnier, remarked that the smile was the hostess's only "weapon for dealing with panic." He argued that her smile was the primary reason to have an air hostess on board at all. "Eight men and one woman," he mused, "Was there any real value in having a woman aboard the team?" Responding to himself, Marnier reasoned that a hostess's smile could calm anxious flyers and provide the right measure of "charm" for long trips.[102] When the plane experiences mechanical trouble, Marnier finds himself proven right, for the air hostess Jacqueline de Valbon:

> introduces, organizes, making up and unmaking groups, watching over their harmony, mixing with some for a few minutes, then escaping to liven up others whose spirits are flagging, or to moderate those who are too boisterous. With her easy manner and the experience and authority of a woman of the world, she gives this chance gathering of strangers the atmosphere of an ambassador's reception. She is where she should be at the exact moment: she is hostess of the air. She makes sure that passengers receive the comfort that the company has promised them. Her friendliness and warmth are included in the fare. No one but her colleagues can know the anxiety behind her amiable smile.[103]

On a later flight depicted in the novel, the passengers experience extreme weather en route to Jakarta. Again, it falls to the hostess, here a woman named

Mireille Daniele, to relax and bolster the frightened flyers. As Mireille roamed the cabin, she "looked around with a smile," reminding the passengers to "Keep calm. Breathe deeply."[104] Later, upon takeoff from Cairo, Mireille calmed sick passengers again, "soothing their anxiety with a smile and a few words."[105] In the novel, the flight turns into a harrowing ordeal, including a landing in Paris with only two of four engines functioning, but Mireille never loses the appearance of calm and good cheer. "Impeccably turned out in uniform, with fresh make-up and hair dressed," Puget writes, "Mireille was at her post near the door, looking as spic and span as she had been on departure from Saigon. She had a smile and a word for each of her passengers."[106] In René Philippe's novel *Sylvie, Air Hostess*, one passenger, having experienced a bump, asks Sylvie if she has ever felt any fear on the airplane. Sylvie mentally responds, telling herself that only in the airplane, with her "tranquil smile," did she truly feel "marvellously useful." When the airplane later shakes violently, the result of an on-board fire, Sylvie does feel a pit in her stomach, but she reminds herself to remain steady: "'You don't have the right [to fear] Sylvie ... the uniform that you're wearing, did you forget it? ... You must smile, Sylvie ...' She smiled."[107]

Odette, the real-life hostess in Claire Andrée Roe's career book, recounted a remarkably similar experience to that of Sylvie. Odette had earlier argued that smiling and a calm demeanour were actually a hostess's best weapons in the often tense atmosphere on board an airplane:

> not only can you never allow yourself an impatient word or gesture, but, tired or not, you always must be alert and smiling. When everything's going well, it makes the trip more pleasant for the passengers. And in difficult moments, they feel more reassured. Their eyes turn instinctively toward the hostess. If she smiles, it reassures them or at least prevents them from losing their heads. That's the only way that you can hold the necessary authority over them. They don't want to show less courage than a young girl![108]

Odette's anecdote reveals the power of gender norms in shaping people's behaviour. She continues to recount how, on a flight from Agadir in Morocco, the plane encountered bad weather, and Odette was thrown to the floor, losing her shoe. In the aftermath of that violent jolt, Odette described, "there were several seconds of panic. I got back up and laughed, as though it was the funniest thing in the world; the passengers calmed down and finished attaching their seatbelts."[109] She then made a joke about how she was like Cinderella with only one shoe and everyone laughed and even applauded her. Meanwhile, internally, Odette was utterly terrified.

This kind of emotional labour – to have to keep an unceasing smile upon her face, no matter the circumstances – could be very taxing for a hostess. Alix d'Unienville recalled in her memoir that "on short flights, a smile and a bottle opener are the two weapons of a hostess, but one is nothing without the other."[110] D'Unienville, who lasted only a couple of years in the position, chafed at the company's expectations that she could deny her true feelings. Recalling a testy interaction with a passenger, she described how, when she returned to her seat, she wanted to "be hot in peace, perspire like the others, be in a bad mood like the others, not be obligated to always show that things are going well, when everything is going poorly, have the right to be ugly ..."[111] The disconnect d'Unienville felt was echoed many years later, in 1969, when psychiatrists tested the mental health of pilots and hostesses of Air France. Hostesses, they found, were seven times more likely to face grounding for "mental reasons." The cause, they hypothesized, was the "forced gaiety" hostesses were expected to project at all times.[112] In her later writing on affective labour, Arlie Hochschild describes this as the very real "cost" of emotional work, that it "it affects the degree to which we listen to feeling and sometimes our very capacity to feel."[113]

Indeed the main conceit of René Philippe's *Sylvie, hôtesse de l'air* had to do with Sylvie's panic and dread about having to go up in the air and maintain a positive mien after an in-flight incident. At one point Philippe describes Sylvie as "terribly weary, hurt, like she was about to get the flu when she was a little girl and her ears were ringing. And she cries."[114] This woeful description reads nothing like what the company would have its passengers think of its hostesses. Ultimately, after flying in medicine to save the life of a friend's child, Sylvie looks upon her work with newly appreciative eyes. When she wakes up in the morning, she feels a sense of "joy." Still a bit groggy, she tries to remember why she has this feeling. Then, Philippe writes, "all of the sudden, she remembered; and she tossed her pillow up in the air, like she had done when she was a little girl. She got out of bed. She threw open the curtain of her wardrobe. She took out the blue uniform. She touched, with her finger, the wings of gold."[115] On the airplane, serving the passengers, whom she considers "her children," brings her intense satisfaction. She feels needed, for the passengers "were depending on her ... for their own reassurance."[116] In Philippe's account of her idealized emotional transformation, Sylvie, having tapped into her maternal instincts, is able to overcome fear and regain her composure.

In demanding not just placid demeanours but also constant smiles from flight attendants, the airline and the state created a system that negated the actual feelings of women themselves. One hostess, identified as Annick in an interview, grumbled about this disconnect between popular perceptions of a hostess's life and the grimmer reality: "Despite what everyone thinks, air hostessing is not such a happy job, you know ... at the beginning, you don't realize it, but then all of a sudden, you crack, and it's a lot of depression."[117] In the symbiotic relationship between the state and Air France, the former consistently reinforced that air hostesses were vessels for France, and whatever empowerment they enjoyed in the skies was boxed in by the needs of the state.

One anecdote in particular highlights just how effective this emphasis on smiles proved to be in the long term. In 2009, Solange Catry, then retired and 79 years old, was featured in a profile in *Versailles Magazine.* Catry, a longtime resident of Versailles, talked at length about her memories of her time in the air and how much she had loved being a hostess. The author, in the very last line of the article, described how Catry "made everyone around her feel like family, [a family] that she enlarged by giving out her smile … like a calling card."[118]

On-Board Nurturing

If in postwar France a perfect woman on the ground was a patient, caring mother, in the sky she could be no different. Air hostesses also took on that maternal role, caring for juvenile passengers. In fact in early company literature the airline presented this child care service as a major perk of being an Air France passenger. In 1948, the company told mothers to sit back and relax upon entering an airplane. "The hostess is there, cultivated, friendly, like a good 'maîtresse de maison,' to be there for passengers and take care of children," so mothers need not worry.[119] In one of the very first issues of the on-board magazine, an article about passenger "comfort" was accompanied by a picture of a hostess, sitting with a baby on her lap, spoon-feeding the child.[120] The airline even put out a line of bookmarks, presumably to distribute to mothers upon boarding, that they would use in books while relaxing on the airplane. The bookmarks featured pictures of pretty hostesses holding smiling children, and the text on them read, "Your time off [*congé*] begins on board the Air France Constellation!"[121]

Hostesses, in their guise as on-board mothers, entertained children in a variety of ways. Often, they escorted children to the cockpit to visit the pilots and see the instruments. It was rare, one hostess reported, not to have "several children on any given flight."[122] Odette, the Air France hostess in Claire Andrée Roe's career series, touted the services available to mothers as well as the hostesses' expertise with children. "On board," she began, citing the entertainment on planes for children, "we have games and books. In general [the children] are very nice and wise. I remember a little boy of six or seven years old who didn't want to leave me; he hung on my neck: 'You'll write me, right? You'll come and see me? You promise?'"[123]

Many airlines of the time used wing demonstrations and cockpit visits to attract and entertain children, but Air France executives went the extra mile. They recruited the famous children's author, Pierre Probst, to use his popular Caroline character as the protagonist of a series of colouring books about how much fun it was to fly and how nice and beautiful the hostesses were.[124] In 1960, in an effort to attract passengers, Air France published a pamphlet entitled "Your children travel …," with the cover featuring a hostess smiling

1.6. Hostesses' duties included caring for children on airplanes, and the company – and passengers – demanded that they do it with a smile (1970). Courtesy of the Air France Museum.

gently, hugging, and playing with an overjoyed young boy. Inside, the message was clear: "Madame, the Air France hostesses will help" was the inner title of the pamphlet, which went on to explain the many ways in which hostesses would attend to children, whether or not their parents were on the plane.[125] Ironically, the 1948 hostess manual reveals that the company's motivation was not quite as angelic as it would originally seem. "Women with babies must be especially cared for," it reads, "as the child may cause damage and discomfort to other passengers."[126]

Children's literature abounded with portrayals of the air hostess as maternal helper and even surrogate mother. In Delahaye's *Martine en avion*, Martine is having a blast on her trip to Rome, at least in part because of the hostess, who has already walked her through the entire process of buying a ticket and boarding the plane. "The air hostess is so nice!" the book proclaims, continuing, "the children who are travelling on the plane love her very much. To help them pass the time, she introduces the children on the plane."[127] It was not simply her geniality or social skills that endeared her so much to Martine, though. It was also the small touches she provided throughout the course of the flight. For example, when it came time for lunch, Delahaye described a delightful repast: "Now it's time to eat. The meal is ready. The table is not very big, but it has everything you need ... Look, someone even put a small bouquet in Martine's place. Who thought to put it there? The pilot? He has too much to do ... Yes, you guessed it. It is the air hostess."[128] In Pierre Probst's *Caroline en avion*, the "always attentive" air hostess performed similar in-flight feats of maternal kindness in the eyes of the young protagonist, offering "souvenirs and candy to the young passengers."[129]

René Philippe's novel treats the adult passengers themselves like children, and Sylvie, the air hostess, as a mother to them all. He describes how Sylvie was constantly pelted with passengers' questions, from "what's the name of that river?" to "will we arrive on time? My husband hates to wait." For her part, Sylvie tends to them with care and looks upon them with a maternal gaze: "They are like children. They like to seem unconcerned, but Sylvie knows they are vaguely worried. How she loves them, the passengers! *Her* passengers!"[130] Odette, the model Air France hostess in the children's career book, described herself as similarly devoted. Once the doors close, she explains, "they are *my* passengers. When they close the doors of the airplane and we're about to leave, I look at them and I am happy. I tell myself: 'For a few hours, they belong to me, and I want to give them a good memory of this trip.'"[131]

Passengers who were mothers fully expected a high level of maternal service on Air France airplanes, and often they received it. In an interview about her experience on board, one such mother, identified as Mme Louis Lapierre of Paris, heaped praise upon the hostess who had accompanied her and her three daughters to Africa. Lapierre referred to the airline hostesses as a "precious" commodity for mothers because of their "gentle" care of children.[132]

Sometimes the company's active marketing of hostesses as stand-in mothers led to misunderstandings. Alix d'Unienville remembered an especially distasteful interaction with a mother on an early Air France flight. The woman asked d'Unienville to prepare a small meal for her children, suggesting perhaps steak or eggs. In response, according to d'Unienville: "I explain[ed] to the lady that an airplane is not a flying restaurant, that the menus are not à la carte and that, further, we have no way to make food on board." The mother then "archly" retorted that she had heard that "'air hostesses were perfect *maîtresses de maison* and that children would have whatever they wanted.' 'But, madame, with the best will in the world ...' She turns away from me."[133] Even Solange Catry, who was generally extremely positive about all aspects of working for Air France, recognized the misunderstandings that company advertising caused in mothers' expectations of hostesses. She often flew between Paris and Mauritius, serving the wives of military officers and functionaries. These women had high expectations of their hostesses: "Used to being served by 'boys,' these mothers did not modify their attitudes vis-à-vis hostesses. They asked us to change the infants, prepare bottles, make them drink, distract them … They lost sight of the fact that, in the face of two dozen toddlers, which was commonplace on the 'colonial' lines, the hostess was basically a bottle warmer!"[134] Serving on that line, she wrote, "taught me the real meaning of fatigue."[135] Despite the logistical and emotional difficulties it presented for the hostesses, the image that the airline continually cultivated was one of a naturally maternal woman who would occupy the children on the airplane with skill and ease.

A hostess's nurturing also extended to the adult men on board, where they acted as surrogate wives in an idealized vision of charm, nurturing, and sexuality. Reflecting on the hardscrabble early days of flying, famed humour writer Hervé Lauwick scolded the unappreciative younger flyers of the postwar years. He had flown often on the prewar Paris-London line, little more than a tin can in the skies. "Today," he wrote, "you find it natural that a ravishing hostess rushes toward you with a little plate of food, lays it across your lap with care, arranges everything for you, props up your head, and looks after your children."[136] Now, it appeared, the traveller had become accustomed to sumptuous, relaxing service from an attractive air hostess.

The air hostess was like a super-wife, never complaining, always looking her most attractive, and ready to see to the slightest needs of her passengers. Many publications used the word "solicitous" to describe her. In his novel, René Puget describes an Air France hostess, Jacqueline, as a perfect woman in the skies. Despite a long flight, he wrote, in the cabin, the atmosphere was that of a "small, busy cocktail bar." As boredom set in for the passengers, "the hostess intervenes: she goes from group to group, seeking a fourth for bridge, a partner for chess, a friendly interpreter. She takes orders, hurries up the stewards. She fetches a Paris newspaper and a London fashion magazine. She recommends a liqueur for the ladies, gives the address of a good hotel in Saigon and the estimated time of arrival at Hong Kong."[137] Even flying overnight from Pakistan to Saigon in rough weather conditions was no match for Jacqueline's good humour: "There was no trace in Jacqueline's bearing of her long hours of anxiety, of the fatigue after a second night running with no more than two or three hours' sleep" as she came to serve breakfast.[138] When asked in an interview if she ever tired of passengers' incessant demands, hostess Marie-Josée Dragon responded forcefully, "A hostess never loses her patience!"[139]

Publications depicted air hostesses' innate predilection for service; it extended even outside of airplane settings. In Puget's *Long Haul*, he described the crew eating together in Pakistan, discussing the potential weather problems ahead. As they did so, the air hostess, Jacqueline, was "passing around the hors d'oeuvres."[140] Later on the same trip, a different hostess, Mireille, joined the crew for dinner in the South Pacific, with similar results: "Laughing, joking, passing quickly from hilarity to a serious technical discussion, Mireille set the tone of the dinner … as if she were mistress in her own house. For coffee she led the way to a quiet corner of the hotel garden. There the animation that had accompanied the meal gave way to complete relaxation."[141] At one point, she even provided musical entertainment for the group, singing in "an untrained voice, but with a crystal clarity and remarkable versatility that followed not so much the score as the inspiration of the composer."[142] Mireille both literally and figuratively hit the perfect note of femininity on and off the airplane.

The natural quality of hostesses' care most certainly had more to do with company demands than biology. In 1948, the hostess manual called for hostesses to "predict even the smallest of desires" in flight.[143] Once the plane landed, the pilot could rest, but the hostess's work continued. The company demanded that she spend her free time researching her destinations, going so far as to mandate that "they must know the name of a good hairdresser in Tehran if asked."[144] In its 1954 manual, Air France executives again called on hostesses to see to the needs of passengers at all times, no matter the circumstances. "Personnel must not consider their work to be done" upon landing, the company advised. Hostesses must aid the welcome crews on the ground, "bid a gentle adieu" to passengers, or just generally act as a calm and friendly presence, well after the flight was done.[145]

Romance/Marriage/Sex, Not always in that order …

In the Puget novel *Long Haul*, the hostess Mireille serves the protagonist coffee in the middle of the night: "'Dreaming, Monsieur Marnier?' All the lights were dimmed, and in the semidarkness Mireille was at his side with a tray of coffee. 'No. Thinking about airline crews.' 'And here's one who's thinking about you,' she said, fixing the tray to the arm of the seat."[146] At the end of the novel, Marnier and Mireille acknowledge that the long series of flights they have taken together has in fact been a sort of foreplay. Marnier confesses his affection first, to which Mireille responds that if she were not in uniform, "I would throw my arms around you and kiss you."[147] Interestingly, here, the uniform acts as a prophylactic barrier for the hostess, reminding her that her first physical duty is to the company and the state.

Romances between passengers and hostesses spawned a whole subcategory of commentary from a vast variety of sources. The company did not permit married hostesses for many years, which prompted regular exoduses of cabin personnel. Max Hymans, president of the airline, stated in 1954 that the average tenure for Air France hostesses was three years.[148] René Philippe's novel actually concludes with Sylvie finding love with a pilot, Philippe Gambier: "The motors sang, as did her heart." This true love likely spelled the end of Sylvie's flying career, but in a culture in which marriage was promoted as women's ultimate fulfilment, the author portrayed Sylvie's coupling as indeed the happiest of endings. The very last line of the novel reads: "She lets herself be whisked away by happiness."[149] While happiness had once meant her career, now happiness meant the love of a pilot. Finding love on the airplane was not uncommon, but romantic love was meant to fulfil all of a woman's dreams, and it was her career that bore the brunt.

The company itself theorized why certain hostesses did not marry, a puzzle since they were consciously designed to be alluring. Indeed Solange Catry, who remained single throughout her career, attributed her rapid rise to the top of in-flight service administration to the high attrition due to marriage. As she later put it in her memoir, the rate of marriages was not surprising, for "the selection criteria for hostesses coincide[d] with those of the ideal spouse in the mentality … of the time."[150] Max Hymans had a different theory, arguing that the women were in fact solely devoted to Air France. For these women, he wrote, "it has become more than a job. It has truly become a calling, a need, something inseparable from their daily existence." Their ambition, for Hymans, played no role in the rationale for working for the company: "they have no desire for a sudden promotion," he explained. Hymans presented these women almost as though they were devout nuns, but rather than marriage to the Church, they gave themselves to Air France and its passengers. This complicated discussion of women's motivations for work reflects some of what historians know about women and work in the postwar period, that work was an exigency for women, but one rarely seen as being as important and pressing as it was for men.[151]

In reality the rationale for keeping hostesses single likely had more to do with maintaining the heteronormative illusion of romantic and domestic perfection, an illusion that would be shattered if it involved another man's property. It also had some basis in the French Civil Code, many of whose provisions still applied to women. Legally, married French women had been considered minors until 1938. More applicable in this case, married French women could not work without a husband's consent until 1965, and similarly paternalistic provisions of the code would continue until 1970. Air France and the French state were perhaps not keen to challenge patriarchal authority within the home. Rather they created a team of pretend wives and mistresses in the air.

Air France required that air hostesses resign their positions upon marriage, a rupture not always easily accepted by hostesses. Early resistance took creative forms. One hostess, who had "courageously" lost 10 kilos to qualify, ended up writing a love story in which a hostess rejects a pilot in favour of a soldier.[152] Still, many hostesses accepted the restrictions. In Puget's *Long Haul*, the first hostess portrayed, Jacqueline, described her sadness at leaving her career to become a wife. She would miss the camaraderie and the work, she said, but, alas, "marriage disqualifies us."¹⁵³ The company promoted the transition as a fun new opportunity, arguing that married air hostesses could now work on the ground as "welcome hostesses" for the company, greeting and seeing to the needs of arriving and departing passengers. If "an air hostess desires marriage," the headline of a trade magazine read, "she will become ... a welcome hostess!" Of course the reality of the new position likely did not reflect the excitement promoted by Air France. In that same article, the company acknowledged that the position was far less "spectacular" than being up in the skies, but it was still "important." And then they added that for single women who did not quite measure up to the air hostess standards, specifically because they "weigh too much," they, too, could take up the company mantle, but only on the ground.¹⁵⁴

In fact in the early 1960s Air France air hostesses sued the company to have the unmarried requirement removed. They faced many obstacles, even from within the ranks of other Air France workers, who, in 1960, had voted to deny any benefits to hostesses forced out of work by age and marriage requirements. According to *France-aviation*, the vote tally came out to 62 against and 29 for, but an article assured readers of the aviation trade journal that the vote against would have been unanimous if not for some extraneous personnel issues that had been tacked onto the ballot.¹⁵⁵

In 1961, Air France hostess Anne-Marie Domergue married and became Anne-Marie Barbier, in direct conflict with Air France's policy that all hostesses must remain single. She sued the company for wrongful termination, but lost her first trial, for several reasons. The company argued that hostesses who married would not be able to be proper wives to their husbands, "because of their necessarily errant and disruptive existence."¹⁵⁶ It purported to worry that hostesses' children would be "semi-orphans" living in "part-time homes." The mothers, home perhaps "three or four times a month," would not recuperate sufficiently to be able to go back and perform their work for Air France. Barbier's lawyer also used the rhetoric of motherhood and respectability in his arguments. He asserted that the perpetuation of the ban on married hostesses would lead to immoral living arrangements, including a flood of illicit cohabitations and secret marriages.¹⁵⁷

In the first verdict, the court agreed with the company, finding the prospect of married hostesses troubling both to the company and to the nation. The life of a wife and mother, it ruled, was subject to myriad unforeseen schedule disruptions, prompted by pregnancies or various sicknesses, which "risked disrupting the general functioning of aviation services." Not only that, but the "activity of the hostess" was difficult to "reconcile with family life."¹⁵⁸

A lot of newspaper ink was spilled in France – and beyond – as a result of the Barbier decision. One of these was an Associated Press article by Pulitzer Prize–winning *San Francisco Chronicle* journalist Stanton Delaplane that appeared in newspapers across the United States, from Nebraska's *Lincoln Star* to the *Salt Lake City Tribune*. Proclaiming shock at the backwardness of France, Delaplane described waking up in Utah that morning to the "low blow ... that La Belle France has put an official knock on marriage." He described Barbier as an "Air France angel who succumbed to love and marriage." Delaplane put no stock in the company's argument that home life would suffer if hostesses married. "This seems as old-fashioned as chivalry," he wrote. "In these jet-powered days, a stewardess can put the roast in the oven and fly to New York and be back in time to carve it rare." Alas, Delaplane continued, "France will keep its flying tigresses unringed."[159]

The "flying tigresses" of Air France had to wait only a few years, for Anne-Marie Barbier persisted with her case, and she ultimately won on appeal. The court agreed with her lawyer's argument that the clause likely led to immorality in hostesses' lives. It also ruled that other companies overseas successfully employed married women.[160] The court did not want women to have to live in a state of what it called "concubinage" just to work at Air France.[161] Additionally, the court ruled that women now worked in many industries, all of which faced the possibility of women becoming pregnant, and these industries had managed to cope with any resulting disruptions.[162] Barbier was awarded 10,000 francs in damages, as well as 3,900 francs in back pay. In response, the newspaper *Sud-Ouest* lamented the verdict, arguing that the old policy had at least kept the stock of hostesses "young and fresh."[163] The quote – and the case – reveals an interesting aspect of the hostess job, implying that there needed to be a semblance of sexual availability – real, imagined, or even manufactured – for the hostess profession to be successful. Air France considered air hostessing as an exceptional category of women's employment; as the face of France, all parts of the hostess required perfection, and that state of perfection did not include a pregnancy bump. According to the *The Guardian* newspaper, Barbier gave birth to a son as the courts handed down the appeal decision.[164]

The law was beginning to change in terms of the restrictions on women's work lives, thanks in part to shifts in women's own views of what ought to be possible, and air hostesses were at the fore as agitators on their own behalf. The company, in hiring air hostesses, had not foreseen that creating a cohort of ambitious women would provide opportunities for their collectivization.[165] However, in many cases, air hostesses were not initially disposed to organize. In her memoir, Solange Catry recalled not even considering the company's age clause (Air France hostesses faced mandatory retirement when they turned 35) when she signed her initial contract, for she was certain she would be married by that time anyway.[166] In an article about how to become an air hostess, the newspaper *Sud-Ouest* brushed off any concerns candidates might have about the age limit, blithely proclaiming "how it seems so far away to you now ..."[167] Ultimately, Catry and two other hostesses led a successful campaign to raise the maximum age to 40, and it was raised again to 45 not long after. Still, hostesses continued to worry about their futures. As one hostess, Annick, recounted, when your "career ends at 40 … what's to become of you if you are single?"[168] Even so, the relationship between hostesses and labour organization engendered complicated feelings. Catry herself described her work life as her marriage. She felt married to the company, she wrote in her memoir, and she was willing to "fight for [her] husband."[169]

Despite the legal battles, at least in terms of promotion, marriage had been and continued to be seen as the pinnacle of an air hostess's career. As Solange Catry wrote, the company fully expected hostesses to meet their husbands on board: "It seemed that in the mind of the employer, the job of air hostess was akin to a sort of quest for a husband."[170] I would argue that it was Air France executives' fear of the hostesses losing their attractiveness after a few years that prompted this mentality. The mindset of temporary employment was still in evidence in 1972, almost 10 years after the Barbier decision. Odette, the air hostess profiled in Claire Andrée Roe's series about careers, had met her fiancé, René, on board a flight returning to Paris from New York. She looked forward to marrying him the following summer, and she envisioned that her Air France career would cease almost immediately. Asked if she would continue to work after marriage, Odette responded: "You can in principle; but there are not a lot of married hostesses. It's difficult to have a home life if you're constantly away."[171] Odette's answer betrays the chasm that often exists between legal and cultural change; even though the law was clear, any number of pressures – from her fiancé, from the company, from her family, even from herself – may have worked to render the legal question moot.

Assumptions about the duration of air hostesses' careers extended beyond the employer and employee; the broader public also expected that marriage would continue to end hostesses' careers. As a writer in *Sud-Ouest* newspaper put it, the job of air hostess was a dangerous one. Most hostesses lasted "3 to 5 years" in the air, facing many perils during their tenure, not just "air catastrophes," but also "other risks. Principally matrimonial ones!" Even despite the recent ruling by the Court of Appeals, "few hostesses professionally survive a honeymoon." Air France, the article continued, "periodically need[s] to revive their precious stock of femininity and smiles." And what an exciting prospect for these young women. First they would travel to exotic places like Rio, and then "they marry the inevitable lonely diplomat, to whom they will have served French champagne and Soviet caviar … Far from the miserable parties and small-time flirts of their little hometowns, they are air hostesses! Even more, they are '*la femme*.'"[172] In the French language, the word *femme* means both woman and wife, and it seems to carry that dual sense in the article. In being first an air hostess and then a wife, hostesses perform femininity and wifeliness in both roles. Either way, women (married or not) across France were entering the professions in increasing numbers during the time period covered in this book, but they still faced barriers to achieving success. As historian Claire Duchen put it in her study of women's work lives in the postwar period, "Combining family and paid work became a fact of life for Frenchwomen in the 1960s, but this does not mean that anyone made it easy for them."[173] The case of air hostesses emphatically illustrates Duchen's point: at nearly every turn, hostesses encountered both formal and informal barriers to their work aspirations.[174]

Outside of the realities of work and marriage, the fantasy of the air hostess as the perfect wife or girlfriend was a prominent feature of Air France advertising campaigns. In 1958, Air France advertised for "Fall Tours" of various places throughout Europe. The background photo of the ad included an Air France hostess standing at the bottom of Rome's Spanish Steps, next to a gentleman giving her flowers. Both parties were smiling at the camera.[175] In some sense, the advertisement equates the luxury vacation and the adventure of going to Rome with the romance of falling for an Air France hostess, all of which could be part of an exotic European vacation. In the 1960s, the message shifted a bit, as seen in one campaign that consisted simply of beautiful air hostesses holding flowers and smiling at the viewer. The text at bottom of the ad repeated the Air France motto of the time, "À votre service" (At your service).

The flowers here carry at least two meanings. First, as seen above, hostesses' act of adorning food trays with flowers was taken as a sign of their hospitality and the overall sophistication of flying Air France. Second, the modern context for flowers is often a romantic one, linked as flowers are to dates, weddings, anniversaries, and other special occasions. Customarily different types of flowers have been used to communicate specific messages: roses are associated romance, daisies with happiness, and so on. In Air France advertising, the hostess smiled at the viewer as though she had just received the flowers from that person. In an ad from 1967, one hostess held an iris up to her mouth, head turned toward the camera, and smiled; this particular woman, blonde and blue-eyed, also featured on timetables and tourist pamphlets from the late 1960s.[176] A few years later, in 1971, another shot portrayed a hostess smelling a pink rose and smiling at the camera.[177] In floral parlance, pink roses symbolize a first love. The red rose symbolizes love in general, but does not connote the of innocence of the pink rose. So here, the symbolism is romantic and yet a bit opaque. This sensual nebulousness would soon shift.

In 1970, the hugely famous French singer Jacques Dutronc released a single entitled "The Air Hostess." In the song, he equated the freedom of flying with sexual freedom. "All my life I have dreamed of being an air hostess … / all my life I have dreamed of high heels / all my life I have dreamed of having my ass up in the air." As the plane is at altitude, he continues: "loosen your seatbelts / free up your inhibitions … / wait for your adventure … / change your attitude / everyone strips [se dénude]."[178]

1.7. Air France capitalized on hostesses' perceived amiability and availability with its "At Your Service" campaign, which featured smiling hostesses prepared to see to passengers' every need (1960s). Courtesy of SJAdvertArchive/Alamy Stock Photo.

As sexual mores gradually loosened across Europe and the United States over the course of the postwar period, portrayals of air hostesses reflected shifting societal norms with a more overtly sensual image. As Sarah Fishman has argued, although cracks in the foundation of conservative gender roles were appearing, the 1950s were not as repressed in France as scholars had thought, and the 1960s were somewhat less liberated than the popular narrative of the time would suggest.[179] Within that ebb and flow of loosening mores, the air hostess, as emblem of Frenchness to the world, operated in a potentially difficult space, not unlike that *maîtresse de maison* who must both attract and serve her husband, while maintaining an upstanding reputation to the outside world. In some ways this mirrors the particular tension of the postwar French project of attracting tourists; the French government needed to maintain the overall respectability of a great power, while reinforcing France's long-standing image as a nation that embraces sensuality, and "soft power," to uphold its greatness.

If the nurturing quality seen in hostesses' portrayals first held a maternal and romantic aspect, with much discussion of marriage and wifeliness, it soon took on a more sexual character as the company matured, which had consequences for hostesses in terms of their lives and their bodies. In some ways, because of hostesses' aggressive availability, proffered via official advertising and portrayals since the 1940s, the company was ahead of the "sexual revolution" curve. As early as 1947, Air France's monthly bulletin called the hostesses' service "literally heavenly joy" infused with "pleasure."[180] In a humour article for the onboard magazine *Air-France Revue* in 1950, well-known writer Georges Ravon recalled an exchange with his child on an airplane in which the child used the saucy word "pin-up" in other people's company. Ravon immediately scolded the child: "such language"! The child retorted, "But that's what you said about the air hostess when we boarded!"[181]

Air France hostesses' powerful allure, depicted across various types of media, as the song by Dutronc evidences, was often tinged with a sense of danger. In 1964, the famed New Wave director François Truffaut released *Soft Skin*, a film that was nominated for the prestigious Palme d'Or at the Cannes Film Festival and won the 1965 Bodil Award for best European film. The film tells the story of a famous writer and literary critic, Pierre Lachenay (played by famed French actor Jean Desailly) who embarks on an affair with an irresistible air hostess, Nicole (played by Françoise Dorléac, elder sister of Catherine Deneuve), with disastrous results. The two first lock eyes on an Air France flight between Paris and Lisbon, and a tumultuous, passionate relationship quickly begins. Eye contact with a tempting hostess is again the hook for an attached man, but of a different stripe, in Robert Daley's 1969 novel about a priest who falls in love with a French air hostess, *A Priest and A Girl*. In the novel, Daley, who married a French woman, describes the mysterious connection that could happen on a plane: "Again she turned those eyes on him, and he didn't know what he felt – rattled, mostly. Maybe she put something in the coffee, he thought. A love potion or something."[182] The hostess is so enticing that she prompts the priest to give up his profession and reject his religion and his family. In 1973, the well-known British singer Clifford T. Ward released the song "To an Air Hostess," in which he recounted a failed love connection with an Air France hostess:

> There was nothing unexpected
> Until she appeared looking calm and collected.
>
> I fell in love with an air-hostess
> Together we flew the skies with "Air France"
> I wanted to give her a copy of my record
> But I did not have the self-confidence.

Again, the air hostess is so attractive and alluring that she leads a promising man – even a well-known singer – to question his worthiness.

The image of the air hostess as sexualized creature reached its anglophone apogee of popularity in 1967, with the publication of *Coffee, Tea, or Me?*, a purported memoir by an air hostess of her sexual exploits. But in France, the parallel erotic novel *32 Stops of Love* (*Les 32 escales d'amour*) actually appeared one year earlier, in 1966. A major success, it was quickly translated into both English and German, and was reprinted in 1968 in France. The novel was written pseudonymously by Nadine B., ostensibly an air hostess who travelled the world and had erotic adventures between flights – or sometimes in the middle of them. It included explicit scenes depicting Nadine in flagrante, often completely unclothed except for her hostess hat or official heels. One vignette about Marseille detailed a liaison with a local man, whom Nadine "could not refuse what he asked me to do, with that accent," and she went on to describe their actions in detail. Encounter after encounter, Nadine expressed an unrelenting sexual appetite, until, lured home, she returns to "my original lover, Paris."[183] *Coffee, Tea, or Me?* was later revealed to be the product of male fantasy about flight attendants' sexual adventures, written as it was by two men. It would be unsurprising if Nadine B. proved similarly sprung from male fantasy.

Given all of this highly charged cultural imagery, it was not uncommon for passengers' sexual expectations of their hostesses to cross into the territory of physical and verbal harassment. The line between these expectations of romance and constant availability and outright unwanted attention could be porous. Solange Catry recalled making what she referred to as a mental "cataloguing" of passengers on board, including the inevitable "would-be seducers."[184] In one case, Catry remembered being asked to dinner by a businessman; she did not want to go alone, so he agreed to take the entire air crew out, which she found very "munificent" of him – until he spoke about sexual positions and his wife for the bulk of the meal.[185] Catry also related the story of another hostess, who was being solicitous during a layover, as mandated by the company. She was conversing with a Central American general, a VIP according to the New York desk, when, in the middle of the conversation, he stopped, looked the hostess over, and said: "Darling, if I give you a thousand dollars, will you follow me to Guatemala?"[186] Still another hostess, Madeleine Thiplouse, remembered how a passenger had asked a captain on one of her flights if he could purchase the hostess. The captain laughed it off, saying he was not "authorized to sell 'company goods.'"[187] In his *A Priest and a Girl*, Robert Daley wrote about the immediate attraction the priest had toward air hostess Michèle Moreau. The moment the priest crossed into the territory of flirtation, though, Moreau became more closed off. Moreau's reaction to this interaction was so automatic that it led the priest to wonder: "Did *every* unattached man on every flight try to pick her up?"[188] Once they arrive in Nice, Father McCabe runs into Moreau outside of a bakery and successfully convinces her to go out with him. As a priest, everything about the date is new and exciting to McCabe: "They went to a restaurant, where he ate *canard à l'orange*, which he had never tasted before, and sipped a château bottled wine he had never tasted before, beside a girl he had never known before."[189] In the construction of that sentence by Daley, the air hostess appears as one part of a menu of tastes and pleasures laid out in front of the priest. As such, it is unsurprising that, due to awkwardness or ill intent, interactions between hostesses and passengers were often less than smooth.

Not only did hostesses face potential complications between themselves and passengers, they also ran into turbulent air, so to speak, in their relations with other Air France employees. Many hostesses reported that, at least in the early years, a significant number of pilots and other on-board personnel were resistant to their presence at all. As Solange Catry recalled, the Paris-London pilots were friendly, but the Paris-Algiers pilots barely tolerated her. They resisted having women on the planes as part of the staff, viewing women as "dead weight coupled with an element of discord."[190] Essentially, hostesses represented too much potential female drama, not enough actual labour value. Hostesses' general attractiveness blunted some of the difficulties, though, especially with the younger pilots, who appraised new female colleagues as "potential spouses or girlfriends, or at least a female hand to fix a uniform or sew on a button."[191] In *Long Haul*, René Puget describes Mireille as infinitely attractive to her air crews, but all of them had to hold themselves back from approaching her romantically, as she had lost her fiancé in Indochina.[192] For Mireille's male colleagues, their respect for her dead partner, her standing as another man's woman (albeit a deceased one), and also for her love of flying preclude their desire for romantic attachment.

On the other hand, Catry, who described herself as plain and provincial, felt she needed to rely on charm to ingratiate herself with the crew. She remembered one pilot on a Paris–New York flight who took one look at her and radioed into the tower, right in front of her, "What the heck is this hostess that someone stuck us with?" When they landed in New York, he asked her to lunch, intending to "see if I was as stupid as I was poorly dressed." At lunch, she worked her charm, in a successful effort to make "him laugh enough to be adopted by his team."[193]

The bias that hostesses faced as they approached the company's upper age limits for the profession was intense. The older hostesses became, the more subject they were to both ageism and sexism. Catry, who in her memoir is generally positive about her experience working for Air France, even referred to the company's management as "misogynist" and "male chauvinists," exposing some of the gender-based tensions throughout her career with the company.[194] As Catry approached the maximum age of 35, she found herself subject to critical observations from passengers and fellow crew alike. After she had just turned 34, as Catry put it, "some oafs took it upon themselves to remind me that I wasn't 20 anymore." One passenger jokingly approached her, saying, "Hello mademoiselle. I feel like I've seen you somewhere before … Wasn't it in the Dardanelles in 1917?"[195] Nor were crews particularly kind to the women they referred to as the "*anciennes*." "Catry, you're still flying?" she recalled one pilot as joking. "I thought you were in the Museum! Laughs."[196] Even in a 2003 interview, Catry, who fondly "adored" flying with Air France, chafed at the "misogyny" she faced from some pilots.[197]

Conclusion

Narratives of decline characterized French political life in the 1950s and 1960s. The two foci of decline, decolonization and waning status as a global power, ultimately led politicians, and social and cultural commentators, to engender a new politics of prestige. A defining element of that prestige was monetizing and promoting France's long-standing reputation as a sensual, even sexy place, and women, in their guise as agents of welcome, formed the vanguard. The difficulties of working as an Air France air hostess, while attractive to many young women, were myriad. First, a prospective hostess went through layers of assessment, both physical and psychological. The toil and ultimate product paid off: French air hostesses were considered the global gold standard. Due to its success, the program began to expand in significant ways over the course of the 1950s and 1960s. The state, aglow in the light of hostesses' global conquest, decided to replicate the air hostess program, but this time on the ground. Hostesses now staffed tourist booths, train stations, major business centres, and important events, like World Expositions and the Olympic Games. Anywhere the French government could put a carefully cultivated female face on an international interaction, they did so. This expansion of hostessing and the reception of hostesses – in the air and on the ground – are the subject of the following chapter.

Chapter Two

Hostessing beyond the Airplane

Air France created the position of air hostess not just to further the company's interests but to reflect well upon the industry and the nation as a whole. Attractive and cultured women were thus recruited to fulfil these objectives. As such, air hostesses quickly found themselves working in a variety of capacities, as ambassadors of French genius in whatever form it took.

Technology, intellectual innovation, and the arts were only a few of the fields where hostesses stood at the foreground of Gallic ingenuity. As this chapter will show, hostesses were present at all types of events, whether they were related to air travel or not. The most beautiful, cultivated, and expertly curated women in France were placed at the centre of all French successes, putting a lovely face on French achievements and reminding the world that France also excelled at beauty, fashion, and allure. Such displays often took place within France, for a largely French audience, but they also occurred abroad at international events, whether small – presenting flowers to the US First Lady, for example – or large – working the Brussels World Exposition in 1958 as French information representatives. As such, hostesses truly acted as *ambassadrices*, female diplomats in the service of the *patrie*.

The main rationale of crafting perfect hostesses was to display them to foreign consumers, and in the 1950s and 1960s in France, the most important of these were Americans. In 1949, American tourist spending in France was equivalent to four-fifths of French exports to the United States, meaning that American tourism was just as important to France's economy as its exports. As Christopher Endy pointed out, from 1945 to 1949, "Americans spent at the very least $214 million in France, the equivalent of roughly 9 percent of France's $2.4 billion share of Marshall Plan aid."[1] That means that tourists were injecting almost another 10 per cent of the entire Marshall Plan's value through their spending, making them a crucial component of the country's economic health.

French tourism professionals endlessly debated how best to lure Americans back to France, eager as French government officials were to capitalize on the

2.1. Hostesses quickly became so ubiquitous – and so associated with glamour and success – that various companies sought to capitalize on them. Here, a hostess promotes French Camembert cheese – illegally, as the company never gave permission for the brand to use her image (c. 1950). Courtesy of the Air France Museum.

potential of the tourist market. One of the most common subjects of debate was French friendliness, or more precisely its absence in the presence of tourists. In 1959, France's Economic Council presented a report on tourism in which it laid out the importance of expanding the tourist industry in the country and proposed a three-pronged plan to do so. The plan called, first, for a focus on modernizing sites and locations tourists were likely to visit, including monuments and hotels; second, for a renewed emphasis on *accueil*, which directly translates as welcome, and meant putting a warm face on France for tourists; and third, for a propaganda campaign to publicize all of the improvements, human and infrastructure alike, to prospective tourists. The council emphasized the importance of Americans to the success of the plan, reporting that the whole project of increasing tourism "almost exclusively depends on developing touristic flow from North America," later repeating in the same report, "*It is on [Americans] that, at the end of the day, the success or failure of our tourist policy depends*" (original emphasis). If implemented properly, the council forecast, the plan could net up to 570 million dollars.²

The human part of the plan, *accueil*, depended on French citizens putting a friendly face forward for tourists, and when it came time to determine the specifics of that face, the government looked to air hostesses for inspiration, mostly because of their proven success. The government sought to capitalize upon the triumphs of air hostesses by expanding the program, taking the hostess out of the airplane and into the airport, and the train station, and the tourist welcome booth, and even into the general population of France, until all French women were, essentially, hostesses.

French hostesses' superiority became a source of pride for the nation, in government circles and beyond. As hostess Solange Catry described in her memoir, at the end of the war France was "mutilated and impoverished," and, somewhat shamefully given its storied aviation history, no longer constructing its own planes. The French industry was forced to buy from American companies, like Douglas and Lockheed, in order to begin competing in the postwar civil aviation market.³ Ultimately, French aviation would thrive, but in the intervening years, French citizens could always turn to hostesses as a source of national pride.

This chapter will first explain how air hostesses took early steps off of the airplane, but still remained air hostesses. It will also explore how Americans, French tourism officials' primary targets, viewed French hostesses. It will then examine how the figure of the air hostess first transitioned to the Air France ground hostess and then later moved outside of the aviation industry to the tourist industry and beyond, creating a cadre of feminine faces to front French international affairs.

Air Hostess as Ambassador, aka "How Delightful to Travel *à la française*"⁴

On 4 April 1957, French radio and television broadcast a special program from the Théâtre de Paris called "C'est ça la France!" or "*THIS* is France!" Hosted by early French television figures Michel Péricand and Maurice Hutin, the program received a glowing promotional article in *Le Monde*, advertising it as one hour of presentations dedicated to "the magnificent French achievements in the realms of economy, science, technology, culture, arts, etc." The program would be full of luminaries who brought distinction to France, people like "scientists, engineers, builders, technicians, professors, artists, etc." It would also feature performances from actors and singers, as well as displays by the French fashion and film industries. Air France would also feature prominently in the program, for its "planes will bring objects symbolizing our brilliant successes back from the four corners of the globe, where so many French people work, all of which will be presented by an air hostess."⁵ Here, the celebration of Gallic achievements was literally carried in a basket and presented to the French people by an air hostess, not on the basis of her own achievements but in a decorative sense, the wrapping paper on the present of French success.

Air hostesses' duties extended well beyond service in the airplane cabin. They attended all manner of official state functions in their guise as *ambassadrices*, always to promote sectors of French society tied to Gallic prestige. The vast range of events they attended reveals the shifting requirements of representing France and French femininity. When Queen Elizabeth visited France in 1957, a reporter for *Le Monde*, Jean Couvreau, described in detail her descent from her airplane, calling the new monarch "majestic and simple," and then continued on to note the "staircase dressed in blue velvet, with large red swaths of fabric, which the wind swells." Presumably, the decorations of the staircase celebrated both British and French traditional colours. Then, as Couvreau described it, Elizabeth reached the end of the staircase, "at the bottom of which [stood] two flight attendants in reseda uniforms, hands covered with white gloves."⁶ Just as the colour scheme can act symbolically for France, so too the hostesses work as almost inanimate representations of the country. Similarly, when American debutantes landed at Orly before attending their coming-out ball, they were met by French elites and an air hostess, who carried a bouquet of flowers from an "unknown French admirer."⁷ Here, the hostess was a romantic go-between, working in service of love and romance. When the film *The Spirit of Saint Louis* premiered in April 1957, Air France hostess Françoise Lagarde made the trip to New York to represent the company, a reminder of the historical connection between France and the United States, as well as the two countries' distinguished aviation histories.⁸ For this prestigious, symbolically laden trip, the company entered unknowing candidates into a fierce competition to determine which of them embodied the "ideal" hostess, a process which culminated in seven finalists participating in a popular French television program to assess their beauty and likeability.⁹ The rigour of the contest suggests the high stakes that the company – and its parent, the state – attributed to such events, and the need to send the most elite hostess is indicative of how important these women were to Air France and the reputation of France itself.

Air France hostesses also often served as feminine complements to the masculine French technology that historian Gabrielle Hecht has argued was so crucial to the restoration of French confidence and global standing in the postwar era. Indeed I would argue that the presence of the women reinforced the very idea that technology was masculine, powerful, and active; the women, as the opposite or complement, represented a correspondingly analogue, passive, and domestic vision of femininity. The very first Air France Paris–New York flight in 1946, carrying a multitude of dignitaries, was a major event that emphasized the company's aviation capabilities. The company's general manager, Henri Desbruères, gave a statement upon arrival in New York in which he praised Air France and expressed his happiness at "this new link between our two countries." The press coverage touched upon his official statements, but it homed in on the flight's hostess, Madeleine Thiplouse, and her diplomatic function. Immediately after arriving, Thiplouse travelled on to Washington, DC, to bring a "sheaf of Picardy roses," a symbol of French welcome, to First Lady Bess Truman.[10] The gift was reciprocated that same year when an Air France air hostess, Mlle Chamereau, brought orchids to Madame Suzanne Bidault, wife of France's president, as a gesture from the mayor of New York. An Air France personnel newsletter, *Terre et ciel*, documented the moment with a large photograph picturing the two women, Mlle Chamereau smiling and resplendent in her uniform.[11] Twenty years later, when New York and Paris organized a celebratory luncheon in honour of the anniversary of the flight, it was Chief Hostess Solange Catry who represented Air France at a luncheon at the St Regis Hotel in New York City, emphasizing some of the continuities of the feminine diplomatic mission.[12] Other new service routes received similar treatment, despite their lesser prestige (Paris–New York was most coveted by the airline, which sought US dollars, and by the hostesses, who generally loved being in New York City). In 1967, Air France held a cocktail party to celebrate new Bordeaux-Geneva direct flights, and they tapped the "charming" Air France hostess Mademoiselle Duphil to represent the company.[13] Again the publicity for the new service route in the newspapers was strategically accompanied by a prominent picture. Traditionally masculine pursuits also received the Air France hostess treatment in the press. When the French rugby team travelled to Dublin to take on the Irish in the rugby world cup (in which they were demoralizingly defeated), the *Sud-Ouest* newspaper published a large picture of the team surrounding a pretty Air France hostess on the tarmac before takeoff. The image of many men, whether they were in industry, sport, or tourism, surrounding one or two of the most beautiful women in France was eye-catching, and it also told a story about what France had to offer the world, a combination of feminine sexuality and masculine technology.

Other new technological advances received the enhancement of Air France hostesses. In 1961, to fete its new renovations, Orly Airport sent out hostesses to greet passengers from the first planes, which were arriving from Tokyo, Beirut, and Casablanca. Each new passenger "received, from the hands of a gracious air hostess, a medal commemorating this first use."[14] When King Hussein of Jordan came to France in 1963 to look at airplane purchases, he was welcomed by dignitaries of all stripes – and a "charming" hostess.[15] In 1957, when the first Caravelle plane – a sleek new French design that bolstered national pride – flew to Los Angeles, a columnist (and later renowned travel editor) for the *Los*

2.2. Hostesses could be called upon to put a beautiful feminine face on official ceremonies, as they did here at the unveiling of the Concorde airplane (1967). André Cros – Ville Toulouse, Archives municipales de Toulouse. Used under a CC BY-SA 4.0 licence. Photo courtesy of Wikimedia Commons.

Angeles Times, Jerry Hulse, described the fast plane and its wonderful service ("naturally" champagne flowed"), but he also emphasized the warm greeting travellers received upon arrival. "On had [*sic*] to greet the passengers were scores of persons," Hulse wrote, "including a tall, willowy French girl [the AF hostess] who pinned red carnations to the lapels of male passengers."[16]

This widespread marriage of technology and sexuality complicates the idea that masculinity was the most important driver behind the government's quest for prominence on the world stage in the postwar period. The famed francophone Canadian writer Jacques Godbout, writing for the political journal *Liberté*, made the connection direct and explicit. Travel was difficult, he said, and sleep on planes was especially challenging. But travel with Air France proved the exception to the rule. Godbout explained, "Of course the planes are attractive, solid, comfortable, and reliable; of course the hostesses are attractive, solid, stimulating, and reliable." With this parallel comparison, Godbout rhetorically links the actual aircraft with the hostesses, animating the mechanical while depersonalizing the human, all while sexualizing the women themselves.

In the United States

Air France hostesses, in their guise as the best hostesses/women in the world, travelled frequently, particularly to the United States, to represent French femininity in all its glamour and beauty. In order to gin up business, Air France officials sent hostesses to all manner of places, with the idea that the hostesses themselves constituted an irresistible attraction, which would then translate into more passengers and visitors to France, where they would spend their valuable dollars. For example, in 1965, the company hosted its third annual Air France Day at the Oakbrook Polo Club in Illinois, an event that the *Chicago Tribune* covered in detail in a lengthy article. The accompanying photo, which was oversized, featured a smiling Air France hostess sitting sidesaddle on a "polo pony," with onlookers staring at her.[17] The entire point was to use the figure of the hostess as a point of entry for the communication of French glamour and sophistication, and thereby attract people to France. As a company executive "rhapsodized" to an Atlanta newspaper in 1962, "when I see 100 [Air France hostesses], I see 100 different worlds."[18]

All of the promotional work done by hostesses meant little if American consumers were not buying, either metaphorically or literally, what Air France was selling. Americans were indeed buying. In her work on the American flight attendant profession, *Jet Sex*, historian Victoria Vantoch argues that American aviation companies competed to make themselves the most "French," equating Frenchness in their hostesses with "mystique and allure ... Paris was still the epicentre of fashion and cuisine, and Americans considered French fashion designers the arbiters of taste. 'Frenchness' served as a paragon of high culture – French fashion, cuisine, and champagne were deemed the apex of luxury production." French hostesses were the visual representation of French sophistication and charm, and Americans, even American hostesses, wanted access to that world. As Vantoch asserts, "this fascination with French culture" led some American hostesses to sew "French labels into their own clothing ... [and] in 1965, National Airlines boasted that stewardesses were trained 'to serve and pronounce Quiche Lorraine'" while Pan Am promoted its hostesses as capable of correctly serving wines like Châteauneuf du Pape.[19] If France could be characterized as chic and tempting, stylish and charming, in American eyes, then French air hostesses were the living embodiment of that vision of Frenchness. The superiority of French air hostesses represented a rarity in the postwar era, an arena in which the French were clearly besting their American counterparts.

The belief in French air hostesses' ability to attract customers ran deep on both sides of the Atlantic. In 1956, the head of Pittsburgh-based Allegheny Airlines, Leslie O. Barnes, inaugurated a new program in which 15 French air hostesses would work on Allegheny planes for a few months. The hostesses were specially chosen from a select applicant pool.[20] Barnes argued that the program would be beneficial to both Air France and his own company. Allegheny at that time carried only stewards, no hostesses, and the airline itself viewed the French women as an attraction for passengers. As one article in the *Washington Post* emphasized with a wink, these "mademoiselles" are now "gracing National Airport ... A tip for travellers: They'll serve on 'Executive' flights in Middle Atlantic states."[21] On the French side, the hostesses would act as salespeople for the benefits of French travel, and show how "Air France personnel cater to travellers."[22] The company also hoped they would learn about the particular needs of the American traveller, so crucial to France's economy.[23] Further attesting to the diplomatic nature of this enterprise, Barnes revealed in an interview that a randomly assigned seatmate on an airplane, who just happened to be a State Department employee, first gave him the idea.[24] Even more striking, Barnes referred to the program as "Project Lafayette," in honour of the French military officer and revolutionary hero on both sides of the Atlantic, attesting to the importance afforded to hostesses.

The program of exchange air hostesses (one- or two-way) caught on with other airlines as well, as Air France hostesses cemented their reputation as the world's best. As early as 1949, TWA decided to hire primarily French air hostesses to run its European routes after a two-year trial program which the airline declared a "marked success." The airline's assumptions about French femininity drove this decision as well: "French girls are polite, they work hard without complaining, and they have a national tradition of ably taking care of guests."[25] Such assumptions continued and even intensified over time. In 1962, the *Boston Globe* reported that Northeast Airlines was running a special program by which it imported Air France hostesses to serve on its airplanes, with the stated purpose of "stimulat[ing] more international travel to and from the U.S. using the combined facilities of Northeast and Air France." As part of the exchange, each participating aircraft was renamed in honour of a French chateau, to symbolically meld the "luxury" of air travel and France and associate it with the airline, and on the airplanes themselves, Northeast served a "special French menu." Finally, the newspaper noted, on select planes, passengers would be tended to by Air France hostesses, "to give U.S. passengers a first hand [*sic*] sample of their cabin service."[26] United Airlines partnered with Air France in 1969 for an exchange program to promote international travel as well; passengers on United, the *Atlanta Constitution* reported, were greeted by "an attractive, smiling girl in a powder-blue Balenciaga uniform – with an Air France emblem on her cap."[27] French air hostesses also directly trained prospective American counterparts, further demonstrating the equation of sophistication and service with French femininity. In 1962, French hostesses participated in a question-and-answer session at Boston's Bay State Academy, responding to queries from students in an air hostess class there.[28]

As noted in the previous chapter, hostess uniforms were a major focus for the company, blending key traits of French womanhood, international prestige, and the French economy. As such, the uniform serves as an excellent test case for the effectiveness of the air hostess enterprise in its prime target, the United States. The combination of Air France, femininity, and fashion proved hugely attractive to Americans in the postwar period, and Air France moved quickly to capitalize on it. At the end of the Second World War, aided by the French government, French designers had worked tirelessly to amplify their impact on the American market. If the success of Christian Dior's New Look had reinstated Paris as the fashion capital of the world, French industries, including fashion and aviation, still sought American interest and capital. In 1946, Jacques Fath designed a look he called the "Air France," but rather than a hostess uniform, it was a high-fashion vision of what a regular woman ought to wear on an airplane. Consisting of a voluminous coat, large pockets, and a fedora-style chapeau, the outfit was an acknowledgment of the connection between fashion, aviation, and femininity. If a French woman were to board a plane, she would be on display, and as such, she needed to be appropriately attired.

Air France played a crucial part in the export of French fashion. The company worked with American department stores to promote French fashion, linking it to a sophisticated, high-end lifestyle. As early as 1948, Bonwit Teller and Air France teamed up for a promotional flight between New York and Bar Harbor, Maine. On board the flight, they showcased French Riviera fashions. An article in the *New York Times* reported: "While Air France's ship, The Golden Comet, winged its way from New York to Bar Harbor, Bonwit Teller showed the press, aboard for this special flight, a nine-piece wardrobe ideal for any air traveller but selected with a fortnight's holiday in Paris and the south of France in mind."[29] In the same paper 10 years later, in 1958, the society and fashion reporter Agnes Ash described the rush buyers faced to board Air France planes carrying French fashions in their quest to be the first to see and touch the prized garments. As Ash described, "THE first runway that French fashions hit when they make their American debut is not red-carpeted. It is a cement strip at New York International Airport, Idlewild, Queens." Immediately upon arrival, Ash continued, "almost before the propellers stopped turning, the brokers went to work."[30]

French fashion was highly sought after by Americans in the postwar era. In 1962 in American *Vogue*, Dior and Air France published a three-page ad that featured depictions of women awaiting takeoff on an Air France jet for Paris. All of the women were drinking champagne, wearing Dior, and ready to embark on what promised to be a fabulous adventure. The images reflected a high level of glamour, likely unattainable for most women, even readers of *Vogue*, and were probably intended to reflect the aspirational quality of French fashion.[31] In 1957, Neiman Marcus did a massive 35-page spread in American *Vogue*, touting that "Neiman Marcus Brings France to Texas, Everything from A to Z!" The advertisement featured the familiar hallmarks of French sophistication, including perfume, literature, and wine. But the very first symbol of France, standing in for A, was Air France.[32] It was clear that Air France had become a sign of French sophistication in the American mind, along with fashion, food, and sensuality.

The exchange of buyers and fashion was not always one-sided; at times Air France brought prospective clients directly to Paris. In 1960, the company held a promotion by which any woman travelling from the United States to Paris on a first-class fare between October and December would automatically receive a ticket to a couture show.[33] In 1965, the airline again held the promotion, which was lauded by the *Los Angeles Times*, which argued that people clamour to go to Parisian couture shows "for good reason."[34] In fact the company weaponized American fashion buyers' anxiety that they would be late to find the latest French fashion. In 1961, the company put an ad in *Women's Wear Daily*, the fashion trade magazine, called "Paris Ben?" The ad features a photo of a businessman holding a sheet of numbers and speaking on a telephone. The businessman is speaking to a fellow buyer named Ben, ramping up Ben's anxiety by saying he is going to miss out on fabric sales by not going to Paris. The businessman rubs it in, telling Ben that he would think of him on his way to Paris, "when I'm leaning back with a drink in my hand, relaxing, being served by a pretty French stewardess."[35] The state mobilized to maintain American interest – and spending – in French fashion, so crucial to French prestige and the French economy.

Air France also regularly invaded local department stores in major cities, where they more directly wedded hostesses' beauty to French fashion. In Atlanta in 1960, Davison's held a major event to promote the latest French fashions. Interestingly, the models were actually not Air France hostesses; rather they were local women who, the store promised, would sport the latest designs "from Paris with an Air France Flair." In addition to the spectacle of the fashions, Davison's also promised to have an actual Air France hostess on hand to answer any questions its chic shoppers had about Paris and travel.[36] Similar events took place in Boston, New York, Los Angeles, and Washington, DC, where ads for the event screamed "MEET AIR FRANCE HOSTESS IN-PERSON TODAY."[37]

American newspapers also reported extensively on French hostesses' uniforms, reinforcing hostesses' place at the fore of the fashion world. When the Dior redesign was introduced in 1962, the *Christian Science Monitor* described it as "chic and comfortable."[38] The *New York Times* referred to French hostesses as "smartly dressed," while *Women's Wear Daily* described the uniforms as quintessentially French and sophisticated, calling them "L'Air de France."[39] Reinforcing the link between sophistication, France, and French hostesses, a writer for the same magazine stated that "Air France, of course, could abide nothing less than uniforms by Dior."[40] The *LA Times* printed a large picture of two hostesses sporting the summer and winter models; the newspaper also called the new uniforms "chic," referred to their designer as "the talented Marc Bohan," and cited them as evidence of how "the French airline has long been conscious of fashion and how it makes the world go round."[41] Ultimately, American airlines followed suit, tapping famed designers like Pucci for their own hostess uniforms and setting off what one travel journalist called "the fashion race in the sky."[42] The praise held strong when Air France changed uniforms again in 1968, this time selecting a different designer, but still showcasing French genius. As fashion writer Eugenia Sheppard argued in the *Los Angeles Times*, "Air France stewardesses will go right on upstaging the others. They've been wearing Dior, but Balenciaga has just designed their new uniforms."[43]

The allure of the French hostess – and really the French woman, for whom the hostess acted as stand-in – extended from her clothing to other parts of her appearance. Stores in cities across the United States held clinics where local women could learn new hairstyles from the most successful French coiffeurs, who were often accompanied by an Air France hostess. In Boston, Marcel Maggy, the head of the French coiffeurs' union, held an event at the Filene's department store at which he told reporters of how he longed to expose Boston's women to the height of French hair fashion. The *Boston Globe* ran the interview, along with a sizable photograph of Maggy, a Filene's manager, and a smiling Air France hostess.[44] Maggy promised to make the American women look more like their French counterparts through hairstyling as a means of attracting and maintaining men's interest. "The French woman," Maggy announced in another article by reporter Rebecca Blake, "prefers to go home looking like a new woman than have her husband go out searching for a new woman."[45] Maggy did similar appearances in New York, where the Abraham & Strauss department store promised free consultations and the chance to win an Air France flight to Paris.[46] Maggy was joined in his coiffeur-related diplomacy by Alexandre Raimondi, another very famous French hair stylist. Raimondi visited the United States again in the early 1960s, where he was feted for his vision – and accompanied by an Air France hostess. The *New York Times* covered his arrival at Idlewild (now JFK) Airport, on an Air France jet; the paper announced: "ALEXANDRE RAIMONDI, whose comb has crowned some of the most publicized royal and commoner heads with glory, arrived at Idlewild yesterday afternoon from Paris, bubbling with news about coiffures and diplomatic messages for American hairdressers."[47] A few days later, the *Washington Post* reported on a luncheon given in his honour by the French ambassador's wife, linking French aesthetics with official diplomacy once again.[48]

Air France's aesthetic standards were rigorous – and compelling for the American audience. In 1962, the style editor of the *Atlanta Constitution*, Frances Cawthon, wrote a piece describing beauty rules for hostesses of various airlines. She concluded the piece with a look at Air France hostesses, whom she deemed the gold standard in their field. To understand the rigorous criteria behind their success, she interviewed the US South's head of operations for Air France, Paul Doassans, who offered a narrow definition of appropriateness for the airline's hostesses. Within the article, Doassans characterized the French hostess as "neat": "This is very much watched, and there are frequent inspections. And never, never too much makeup. Always the simplest, the most natural." Doassans then expanded his observations to apply to all women of France: "It is a mistake … to think that French girls go for heavy makeup anyway. They are always very discreet."[49] In that way, the air hostess represented all French women, a model for American women to emulate.

At times the commercial link between French hostesses, fashion designers, and sales became quite concrete. In 1956, the Christian Dior couture house released a line of stockings, called "Fashion in Flight." Advertised heavily in high-end department stores, the company promoted the new line by telling consumers that if they bought six pairs, they would receive an Air France hostess travel bag as a free gift.[50] Further, in 1965, the Dior house named a shade of stockings "Air France," described as a "misty olive" in colour in one advertisement.[51] Dior placed an ad in American *Vogue* featuring the "Air France" colour, using only a hostess's calf and shoe stepping on a rose. The ad referred to the "Air France" shade as "fashion's newest color … a heavenly taupe-in-a-mist."[52] Similarly, for a fundraiser gala event in Washington, DC, guests would "land" at "Orly Airport" – actually the Washington Sheraton Park Hotel – and be greeted by "attractive" Air France hostesses holding Molyneux and Dior perfume.[53] If French fashion was a hook to catch American dollars, then French air hostesses were the bait.

Outside the Airplane

Buoyed by the evident success of Air France in attracting American tourists, which many commentators attributed to its hostess program, the government aimed to expand its hostessing goals. The expansion began with welcome hostesses at airports, and then moved far beyond that, until every official town in France had a tourist booth staffed by a pretty, well-trained, English-speaking young woman. The hostessing program even extended beyond interactions with travellers; now hostesses played key roles at major diplomatic events, like the Brussels World Exposition in 1958 and the Grenoble Olympics in 1968, the subject of the following chapter. The idea that a hostess was crucial for success spread to private industries as well, and theories and classes sprang up to codify a hostess's proper appearance and behaviour.

To some extent, an Air France ground hostess was essentially an air hostess, holding similar physical and emotional responsibilities. In a competitive global

2.3. Like their counterparts in the air, Air France welcome hostesses provided smiling, friendly service in an attractive package. Here, a hostess helps a customer at Air France's headquarters at the Invalides Station in Paris (1950s). Courtesy of the Air France Museum.

civil aviation market, Air France distinguished itself by its service, both on and off the plane. As early as the 1940s, the company made sure to provide travellers with friendly, female faces at each point of contact with Air France. In 1947, *Échos de l'air*, an aviation trade magazine, published an article, entitled "Air France Comfort," about what the company's passengers should expect. First of all, the article noted, there was the "sumptuous" atmosphere provided by welcome hostesses at Air France's Invalides Station in central Paris, where passengers would await further transport to or from Orly.[54] Buses, another journal reported, left regularly, and upon arrival and departure from Invalides, customers could count on gracious service and, along with amenities like banking and hotel help, an "on-demand welcome" from the hostesses there.[55]

That welcome could take on a nationalist, and romantic, tone. In 1966, the airline adopted a program by which all foreign travellers arriving on Air France at Orly Airport would be greeted by ground-based hostess holding either "a rose or a bottle of perfume," depending on the sex of the passenger.[56] In that interaction, Air France offered the traveller "French" products: romance in the form of the rose, French luxury beauty items in the form of perfume, and fashion and femininity in the form of the hostess herself, making the exchange tangibly and symbolically meaningful.

Ground hostesses performed a wide variety of duties at airports around the globe, providing information, seeing to ticketing needs, and assuring general comfort and a positive experience for travellers. A trade publication described one hostess in Amsterdam not only as a "charming angel" and a "conscientious shepherd," but also rhapsodized that Air France's passengers "will keep the memory of her farewell smile as one of their favorite Amsterdam memories."[57] Like the air hostess, the ground hostess catered to the needs of her clients. In London, one observer remembered, an "angel" of a welcome hostess took care of all of the travelling men's needs, even in some cases taking over the care of their families, so that the fathers could simply sit back, have a smoke, and relax.[58]

Company literature from the time emphasized that these welcome hostesses, like their celestial counterparts, needed to put on a good face for Air France. In 1967, Robert Cusin, the chief press secretary for the company, dedicated an entire article to welcome hostesses in *Air-France Revue*, the on-board magazine. He linked hostesses' job performance to travellers' impressions of whole countries; while he was general in his application, Cusin was clearly referring to visitors' impressions of France. For visitors, Cusin wrote, there were only two options when they disembarked from a long flight: they were returning to a country where they had been before, or they were there to discover it for the first time. Either way, it was crucial to make a good impression: "If the welcome is poor or even disappointing, you have a passenger who is going to hate a whole country based on a fleeting impression or who, having loved it during previous visits, falls back to earth and will prove all the more unrecoverable psychologically and sensibly because he had been seduced." The decisive force in determining a visitor's positive or negative image of a country, Cusin went on to argue, was the welcome hostess who greeted him at the airport. She was the face of the country on the ground, and thus crucial to foreigners' first impressions.[59] Cusin advocated that all ground hostesses undergo smile training, to ensure that their greeting sent the correct message of charm and pleasantness to travellers. The smile, according to Cusin, ought to say "We are very, very happy that you have come *chez nous* ... [And] the people of our homeland are ready to do everything to prove this to you."[60] The article was accompanied by several large images of ground hostesses serving passengers, and also of one such hostess applying makeup. Cusin's caption for the photo informed the reader that the hostess was not preparing "for some banal date." Rather, he wrote, "her prince charming is the just-arrived Air France airplane that she will now greet; and, no matter the age or sex of the passenger, she reserves her most charming smile for them. It has become a ritual for all of these young Air France girls to put on their best behaviour – and their makeup – before going to serve in the departure and arrival halls, or anywhere in the airport where visitors might be, for their task is to welcome, guide, inform, and help."[61]

Despite the similarities in their tasks, ground hostesses themselves, along with the company, were aware that their position was a step down from that of the air hostess, the ultimate symbol of glamour for Air France. In 1947, the company bulletin announced that if an air hostess wanted to marry, or perhaps she was single but "weigh[ed] too much," she could certainly become a welcome hostess.[62] One ground hostess wrote in to a company newsletter to report that she was happy to be employed by Air France, for the moment: "One year ago, Air France took me under its wings and I now work as a commercial agent and welcome hostess at Berlin Tegel Airport. I really like this job, but I strive to be an air hostess. That is why I have the intention to present myself at the next competition. This is, I believe, my most important future plan."[63] In the same newsletter a few years later, in 1966, a welcome hostess, Gisèle Dardour, wrote that she was currently working in the company's Champs-Elysées flagship ticket office in that capacity. There were aspects of her work that Gisèle enjoyed, including "constant contact with the public," which she found "nice and interesting," but what she really wanted was to be in charge of long-haul ticket delivery as a commercial agent.[64] Similarly, *Terre et ciel*, a journal for Air France employees, feted the new welcome hostess career in 1947, while acknowledging that the ground hostess "dreams every night of a celestial career to which her diurnal functions undoubtedly prepare her."[65]

Becoming a ground hostess was also a career step that air hostesses could take after "aging out," a move tied to general perceptions of their attractiveness by both themselves and the company. As Solange Catry wrote, the possibility of becoming a ground hostess allowed older air hostesses to feel "provisionally secure," but she still wanted to be in the air. She thought her experience "compensated well for the freshness of [my] younger years."[66] In 1969, Air France capitulated to hostesses' demands for an increase in their upper age limit, from 40 to 50, in order to avoid a strike. For their part, hostesses of a certain age agreed to "set up a mixed commission [company and union] that will judge on the 'attractiveness' of the older hostess. In cases where they are less than pleasing to the eye, they may be asked to take ground jobs."[67] The union itself shot back – albeit with some ground ceded – arguing that "it is not fair for the airline to take the best years of a girl's life and then discard her when her sex appeal diminishes."[68] Meanwhile, by 1969, many American airlines had no such age requirements at all. The attractiveness of the air hostess remained paramount to her duties in France; as she aged, her acquired skills received a lukewarm welcome on the ground.

Hostesses beyond Air France

In 1960, France played host(ess) to a summit of leaders from the United States and the Soviet Union for the purpose of easing Cold War tensions. Eisenhower and Khrushchev, as well as Charles de Gaulle and the UK's Harold Macmillan, were to meet in Paris and discuss critical issues like the arms race and political tensions in Berlin and Cuba. Ultimately, the summit collapsed after just one day, owing to the Soviet downing of an American spy plane.

Despite the summit's unexpected brevity, French officials had prepared two different corps of hostesses to tend to the visitors, most notably the large numbers of journalists in attendance. The first group of hostesses consisted of students selected from the most elite French families – one was the niece of a former prime minister, Antoine Pinay, for example. Identified by their "smart … [and] trim navy-blue, white-edged suits, specially created by a Paris couturier," according to one columnist, Tania Bothezat, writing for the *Baltimore Sun* newspaper, the hostesses adhered to a very "strict code of conduct" when dealing with the attendees. These rules included accepting no food or drink and offering scripted responses to various types of queries: "the three cardinal virtues they had to embody in their general behavior were politeness, efficiency and discretion." The second group formed part of a new, official cadre of hostesses, full-time employees of the French Tourist Office. These women were professional hostesses, sporting the official royal blue dresses that were emblematic of their position. Normally, Bothezat continued, "they are detailed to meet important visitors as well as ordinary tourists at the main Paris railway stations, and help them if they are in difficulty or merely need information about France and Paris. Whether help is wanted or not, they are there with a welcoming Parisian smile." Bothezat even interviewed one such hostess, Marie France Pilon, whom she described as "typical" of the type, taking "her work in stride with calm philosophy and good humor." Bothezat then departed from her discussion of hostesses at the summit and described the contours of this new French profession, writing, "in addition to the 'Hostesses of France' and the 'Paris Hostesses', every town has its own team of young, helpful girls in uniform whose job it is to take care of foreigners … [further], today big firms and industries are also recruiting their own teams of hostesses for public relations work." Bothezat concluded her observations on the ubiquity of hostessing by writing that "a new profession is open for young and attractive girls in this country."[69]

The 1950s and 1960s witnessed an expansion of French hostessing, from hostesses working within planes and in direct affiliation with Air France to hostesses staffing all major sites associated with the country as a whole. The transition off the airplane was directly related to air hostesses' success. The famed author André Maurois alluded to the link in a piece on new professions, writing, "far better than men, [women] know how to ... make a pleasant space ... Their courage and their good humour do much to ensure the tranquillity of passengers during long journeys above the seas. Their success has led to the birth of an analogous profession: that of Paris hostesses, charged with informing and guiding visitors."[70] Maurois went on to describe the Paris hostesses in strikingly similar terms to their airborne counterparts, calling them "young," "cultured," and "nice" in the face of unending tourist questions.[71] It was "a new world," according to Maurois, one to be welcomed – with a friendly female face, of course.

In 1959, the French Economic Council put out a call to significantly increase the number of hostesses in the tourism industry across the nation. "It would seem quite opportune," the council's report stated in a large-scale plan to attract more tourists, "to increase in big cities and train stations the number of our welcome hostesses."[72] Just one year later, in 1960, the same council asked all municipalities to contribute to funding their own welcome hostesses, essentially calling "the case of the hostesses" and their importance to engendering warm feelings about France a national enterprise in which all French towns and people had a stake.[73] According to François-Xavier Aubry, professor of public law at the Sorbonne, as of 1972, "happily," about 60 per cent of all towns in France were staffed with a welcome hostess, meaning that they had "made some effort in favor of *accueil*."[74]

Welcome hostesses represented some of France's ground troops at the front, an army of women mobilized to fight the country's new war for money and prestige. In the eyes of tourists France was seen as less than welcoming, and the government decided that the most effective ambassadors to counter that reputation were attractive young women. In 1963, the well-known journalist Nicole Bernheim publicized the government's call in *Le Monde*, writing: "If you are of age, have passed the bac, can type, are single, nice to look at, if you are under 25, if you speak fluent English and a second language (preferably German), if you are a 'smart cookie' able to face any obstacle, and if you are able to control your nerves in a room where 22 telephones are ringing, you can become a Paris hostess." And these women truly were on the front lines for France. In 1965, France's secretary of state, Pierre Dumas, announced an official campaign of friendliness and welcome, to be fronted by a new cadre of hostesses. Dumas identified 35 places around Paris where contact with tourists was likely, and his ministry placed a hostess at each and every one. In addition, the ministry identified metro stations in Paris most frequented by tourists and staffed them with hostesses.[75] Every foreign tourist would be greeted by a hostess's smile. As a testament to the program's success, in 1971 *Le Monde* reported that *hôtesses de France* in Paris alone interacted with around 300,000 tourists a year.[76]

Like their skyborne counterparts, welcome hostesses travelled the world in the name of France, promoting French tourism via their very bodies. In 1961, for example, the French tourism board sent hostesses to Australia to amplify the French presence at the Sydney Trade Fair. There, Australians could study models of Paris that depicted major landmarks like the Notre-Dame Cathedral, all under the helpful guidance of a *hôtesse de France*.[77] In 1954, the French had created a French exposition in Montreal, hoping to drum up tourism numbers from francophone Canadians. Right at the entrance, organizers stationed Jacqueline Bonnet, a *hôtesse de Paris*, who was supposed to "offer France's smile to the Montrealers." Tellingly, they made sure to parade Bonnet out at a press conference prior to the exposition, in an effort to demonstrate the splendours of France.[78] In these instances, hostesses performed an exercise in nationalist marketing in which they sold France in commercial displays and with their own bodies.

Tourism hostesses were apparently quite effective – too effective, according to one report from the World News Service. It recounted the story of Christian Marin, a business traveller who was so "entertained and distracted" by French tourist hostesses in the Vienna airport that he had to dash off at the last minute to catch his plane. Delayed by the "too kind" hostesses, Marin completely forgot not only his luggage, but even his coat and hat.[79]

In 1972, the government again expanded the hostess playing field by putting out a list of state-related hostess positions that were currently in existence and to which young women could aspire. The pamphlet claimed that these days a hostess could show "many faces." These faces, apparently in order of prestige, started with the air hostess, and then went to include airport hostess, marine hostess, train station hostess, private hostess/interpreter for tourists, roadways hostess, Paris hostess, spa hostess (*hôtesse de cure*), and rural hostess.[80] Starting from the profession's beginnings as an elite force dedicated to airplanes, the transition was fast and unequivocal: France now had a hostess for any and all situations.

As hostesses transitioned from the airplane and the airport to the greater world, they would require a new set of regulations. Here again, the state and other regulatory bodies, formal and informal, stepped in to ensure standards for these new French ambassadors. As early as 1950, a reporter from the *Chicago Daily Tribune*, Henry Wales, described a system designed to create the optimal experience for the American traveller. Train travellers arriving into the Gare Saint-Lazare in Paris would be handed folders that contained useful information, as well as a photo of a hostess on duty in the station. Once they disembarked, travellers could seek out the hostess, easily identifiable in her distinctive uniform. The hostess would readily provide the traveller with important information, from ratings and prices of hotels to recommendations for restaurants serving all kinds of cuisines, although they apparently only guaranteed excellent service at the French restaurants. If the hostesses were meant to provide tourists with a happy travel experience, then American reporter Henry Wales was a satisfied customer. He even recommended that the tourist hire one of these hostesses as a guide "to escort him around the city," citing just how "attractive" they were. Yes, Wales continued, "their uniforms do much to glamorize their slim figures. A large beret perched alluringly over the right eye helps to frame their pretty faces." Wales was fully aware that the hostesses were like bait on a fishing line, and the tourists – especially male ones – were the fish. He went on to write that "the alluring appearance of the hostess is all part of the hostess scheme. The Paris city officials want tourists to get a good impression of the city right from the start. They figured pretty *demoiselles* would go a long way toward that end. However, the girls have to be more than shapely and pretty. They must know English."[81] Several years later, the *Christian Science Monitor* cheekily acknowledged the attraction of this same genre of welcome hostesses, publishing a large photograph of several hostesses smiling and waving at the camera, captioned only "When in Paris …"[82]

The conflation of hostessing with beauty and a warm welcome was actively cultivated in order to maximize tourism and profits. For example, the SNCF, France's national train company, held competitions to determine the most welcoming train hostess crews in France, rewarding the winners with prizes like couture uniforms designed by Jacques Heim. Vincent Bourrel, the secretary general of the SNCF, reminded hostesses that a "commercial welcome" was unacceptable on the train. Instead, he told them, hostesses needed to make trains feel "familial," so that passengers could enjoy the "better welcome" France could offer them.[83] A later article in *Le Monde* revealed that a hostess from Châlons won the grand prize. As a bonus to the winner and the three runners-up, the newspaper reported, they would be sent to Brussels to represent the SNCF and France at the world exposition, thereby further aligning France's reputation with welcoming femininity.[84]

Hostesses acted as aesthetic diplomats at key international events as well, emphasizing the French government's desire to put a good face forward to the world. When the city of Bordeaux held a major festival, the local newspaper, *Sud-Ouest*, published a giant image of seven welcome hostesses on the cover of its special edition. The caption, which also featured small blurbs about each hostess, read "Whether you are French, Spanish, German, English, Italian, or Danish … Seven Smiles to Greet You!"[85] In this statement, the hostesses, much like their Air France counterparts, were essentially reduced to their smiles, their superficial expression of welcome. At times this synecdoche took a suggestive turn. In covering the Paris-Nice bicycle race, one sportswriter described how, while many people go to Holland to see the tulips, the Dutch racer Leo Duyndam "only had eyes for the carnations offered by the Paris-Nice hostesses after his victory in the sprints."[86] What is interesting here is that French women were not only associated with tulips, a product synonymous with the Netherlands, but that the allure of French women was so powerful, it could even make a Dutch man forget his natural, and national, allegiance.

Other major diplomatic events received similar treatment, endowing public representation of France with a feminine presence. When the Danish king and queen visited Paris in 1955 for an official state visit, *Le Monde* trumpeted that they were met at the train station by three Paris welcome hostesses "delegated by the City of Paris." The paper went on to describe the women as "three svelte young women in becoming royal blue uniforms,"[87] clearly highlighting their physical appearance. Similarly, when the Peking Opera Company arrived in Paris, "*hôtesses de Paris*" distributed red roses to all of the company members as they disembarked at the Gare de l'Est. The company, in turn, applauded the young women.[88] When Paris held its annual business fair, organizers listed "*hôtesses de Paris*" as a perk available to international businessmen, along with a bar and a currency exchange centre, among other amenities.[89] And when a major university played host to a global chemistry conference in the southwest of France, "three charming *Hôtesses de France*, dressed in their attractive blue uniforms," were deployed to help "welcome, inform, and guide the attendees."[90]

Aesthetic directives for hostesses originated largely within the government, but they could also be found in new school curricula and industrial programs. In 1964, "a group of French experts" published an extensive review of the "new professions" in the tourism industry, a field that they argued had been revolutionized following the Second World War and the rise of mass tourism. One of them, Dr. Hubert Delestrée, the head of France's travel agency union and an important postwar tourism figure, focused on the position of the hostess, saying first, "Hostess, what a wonderful job!" (Quel beau métier que celui d'hôtesse!).[91] He immediately rescinded that statement, however, arguing that being a hostess was not a job, but rather a "calling at which young girls are marvels." Delestrée thus explicitly connects femininity itself with the profession. Delestrée continued:

> True vocation springs from a foundation of generosity. In this case, that it is for the purpose of the public good. Whoever her interlocutors, the hostess will have the same desire to serve, and because of that desire the same smile, the same softness of voice, and in the expression of her thought, all while knowing how to adapt to please each and every person. In effect, she is but the satellite that reflects the radiance of a great work of art [oeuvre] and that lights the path for the person calling upon her services. This is why the designation of hostess *of various functions* immediately attracts the goodwill of the masses.[92]

The hostess, according to Delestrée, put a feminine face on a grand achievement, regardless of the field in which she served.

The hostess's ability to front an enterprise, public or private, was in Delestrée's eyes a crucial international service that she provided for the nation. She was an ambassador, perhaps not in the most traditional, political sense, but nevertheless important: "The hostess most often acts as a useful, efficient facilitator in international relations. She plays her role in contemporary international life. In that role she also deserves esteem, respect, and sympathy."[93] But her role required a massive investment on the hostess's part in terms of appearance, comportment, and knowledge.

The hostess's capacity to please, Delestrée noted, was essential. "This," Delestrée argued, "is why hostesses have become the best public relations representatives. This is why industry, commerce, tourism, and transportation are searching to create friendly and graceful female ambassadors to the public, to facilitate contacts and make social and business relations and exchanges of information effortless."[94]

The hostess's essential, natural femininity was the definitional component of her work, according to Delestrée. Men, he contended, were simply far too busy to bother with the small, personal touches that appealed to clients of all stripes. Male workers therefore required hostesses to "do the grunt work" of pleasing. But, he warned, hostesses must never make their jobs look like work, either to their boss or to the client. Rather hostesses should act like a helping hand, not an impediment or annoyance. It was for this very reason, the ability to please clients and act as though they truly enjoyed their work, that the career of hostess must, Delestrée argued, belong to young women. The work of hostessing is a "delicate mission," and the people "capable of accomplishing this task with a great deal of gentility and friendliness" are "gracious, intelligent young girls."[95] Regardless of training and work requirements, a hostess's feminine presence could delineate a space. "By definition," he went on, hostesses display "generous hospitality [and] an active altruism that reflect the assistance and care that you can rely on. Her very existence creates a warm reception space that is welcoming and attractive."[96]

Over the following few years, hostess schools began springing up across France to train prospective employees. The government wholly approved of training as many young women as possible in the profession. On the floor of the French Senate n 1969, the secretary of state for tourism, Marcel Anthionoz, lauded hostess preparatory schools, going so far as to call them "high-quality institutions" that would allow officials to place more and more people in jobs across the hostessing spectrum. These schools and their students, Anthionoz argued, were "an indispensable element of [France's] welcome" to the world.[97]

In 1971, the two directors of one such institution, Marie-Josée Salin and Jeanne-Marie Laporte, wrote a guidebook for the young women interested in becoming hostesses. In *Welcome Hostess: Guide to the Perfect Young Woman*, the heads of the Bordeaux hostess school laid out a roadmap, one not so dissimilar to that of Delestrée in 1964. They first encouraged women's interest in the career, noting that it is a perfect fit for women, as "the job showcases essentially feminine qualities." Still, they cautioned, the work was "difficult" at times, both "physically and morally," and so it was important for young women to arm themselves with the authors' combined knowledge and directives. The goal of their book, Laporte and Salin wrote, was to address both the external and internal qualities prospective hostesses needed to meet the requirements of potential employers. The authors promised to help the reader "learn to take care of your exterior appearance, which will give you a welcoming manner and friendlier reception"; as for inner beauty, they would "help you stay charming, modest, adaptable in all circumstances without succumbing to snobbishness or excessive social contingencies."[98]

Both guides emphasize that the welcome hostess had no value if her appearance failed to please in any way. Her exteriority was the initial point of contact with the client, and thus was critical to impressions of whatever institution she represented. In terms of dress, Delestrée argued for mandatory uniforms, stating that sartorial diversity detracted from the hostess's work, and that by 1964, the uniform had become synonymous with hostessing. In the case of some events, like the Brussels Exposition, the "iconic" uniforms of welcome hostesses became symbols of the events themselves.[99] Laporte and Salin called being well-dressed "the golden rule" of hostessing, advising women that "you must be pleasant to look at."[100]

While Delestrée advocated uniformity in clothing, Laporte and Salin's guidance was more general, targeting hostesses of all industries and stripes, and thus their directions for clothing focused on the most minute details in order to avoid potential fashion pitfalls. Laporte and Salin listed innumerable rules to follow when wearing and caring for hostess garments. Hang the uniform up immediately when not wearing it, they directed, and always be ready to iron. Then, starting at the top, they worked their way down, offering directions on the appearance and care of each garment, always emphasizing how a hostess's tenue began with her clothing. They advised hostesses to take extra care with hats, ensuring that they do not collapse upon removal. Always wear gloves, they counselled, as a sign of your elegance and good taste, but remember to keep them "always white, impeccably white ... be intransigent: neither stain nor hole." As for hosiery, a hostess should "never be surprised by a run ... always have in the bottom of your bag an extra stocking or pantyhose, it takes so little space!" Shoes must be practical but attractive, according to Laporte and Salin: "classic [designs] are the most appropriate, with heels around 40mm" (~1½ in.).[101] The height of the heel had little to do with hostesses' comfort after long hours of standing; rather, the authors warned, a hunched appearance would cause them to seem like an "old woman [with] tired features," the opposite of the image of an energetic ingénue that the hostess needed to present. Similarly, the authors told their readers not to wear boots, even in winter, for these would give hostesses "an unattractive gait," a faux-pas in a profession where appearance reflected on important institutions and not the hostess alone.

A hostess's accessories also needed to be unquestionably tasteful, according to Salin and Laporte. When choosing a bag, they advocated for a shoulder bag, but they cautioned readers to "wear it without looking too military." Bags were sometimes better left behind, for as Laporte and Salin advised, "with free hands, you will have more supple, elegant gestures to guide or accompany the people you're helping." Similarly, a scarf could be "very useful," it was important to select umbrellas in "discreet colours," and jewels "complete your appearance very well … You again need to know how to choose them judiciously and wear them at the correct times."[102]

With these detailed instructions, the authors are indicating a need for representational perfection on the part of hostesses. An "unattractive gait," or a stain on a glove, or an unstockinged leg on a hostess signified a potential flaw at the heart of Air France, the SNCF, or even France itself. The power that hostesses held, then, was aesthetic, not individual (unlike that of a man), and that distinction is important because even though the profession elevated women and gave them a purportedly crucial role, the role itself, as envisioned by powerful state and private interests, did not empower the women who played it, regardless of their individual reactions and experiences.[103]

The beauty regimen of the hostess also warranted attention from hostess experts Delestrée, Salin, and Laporte. In fact Delestrée warned that the absolute worst – and most common – character flaw of the hostess was not a lack of intelligence or warmth, but rather "overconfidence in one's physical beauty." Delestrée expanded on this further, arguing that "physical appearance certainly plays a major role" in a hostess's work. For him, "the attraction of beauty is an element of success. It applies particularly to hostesses."[104] Thus the success of the overall institution depended on the perception of beauty on the part of that institution's hostesses.

The scrutiny of hostesses' bodies, from their makeup to their hair to their teeth, was intense and meticulous. Starting off an entire instructional section on beauty, Salin and Laporte, like an unkind relative, asked, "Maybe nature didn't bless you with as many good features as you would have liked?" The authors presented a woman's lack of beauty as a solvable problem.[105] They assured anxious readers that, with a combination of charm and some detailed attention to their appearance, they could still achieve success as a hostess, despite any physical shortcomings.

The hostess's appearance also necessitated a general bearing that would appeal to all people. The hostess trainers, Laporte and Salin, included advice on sitting ("few people sit with grace" but please do not simply plop down), her silhouette (avoid sugar, exercise a lot, and remember to look "elegant" – for which a trim figure helps immensely), her voice ("Cultivate [your voice], for it gives an extra charm that shouldn't be neglected," and make sure it is neither too high nor too low), and even her laugh ("don't laugh too loudly or for too long," but "laugh gently, cheerfully, in a way that makes your whole entourage participate in your gaiety") among other morsels of wisdom.[106]

Hostesses also needed to shape their personalities to be as appealing to as many people as possible. Delestrée laid out the intricate roadmap of hostess behaviour. He wrote: "[her] uniquely feminine charm gives the hostess all the power of her action without having to impose it. The interlocutor should think he is driving the conversation. The visitor should have the certitude … that he is receiving the exact satisfaction that he wishes."[107] In some sense, the encounter between hostess and client or coworker took on romantic overtones; through her personality, her "charm," the hostess would attract, even titillate the object of her attentions, albeit with the goal of making him think he was leading the dance.

The prevailing directive for hostesses' personalities was that they should be eternally upbeat and positive; in the words of Laporte and Salin, the hostess should be "maîtresse de [ses] sentiments" (mistress of her emotions). The emotional labour of the hostess, as seen in the previous chapter, entailed heavy lifting on her part. Here again, the hostess's own feelings were suppressed in favour of a public face onto which the public could write any emotion. Laporte and Salin addressed this issue directly, negating the hostess's access to her own inner life: always be in "a good mood; your face should never in any case reflect the least contrariness. You might be tired, irritated, preoccupied by personal problems; those whom you are showing around should never be able to guess. You need to ensure their well-being and their comfort and they will often need to have a calm and smiling face around them."[108]

Despite the insistence on the part of experts that hostesses required no high-level training, the same experts also expected hostesses to speak other languages and to have at least a cursory knowledge of history, politics, and culture. Delestrée went further, arguing that in order to perform their work satisfactorily, hostesses needed to have a deep, anthropological comprehension of the society of the people they were serving. "Knowing a language well isn't enough," Delestrée insisted, "they also need to understand [foreigners'] way of life."[109] In order to deal with Americans, then, the hostess should be able to speak English, but she should also be well versed in all aspects of American life, an intellectual mission that could take years. Similarly, Laporte and Salin encouraged prospective hostesses to undertake an education in "music, painting, literature, sports, travel, current expositions, etc. … It is your responsibility to draw from all of this [press, TV, radio, etc.] the essentials to perfect your cultural knowledge and to use it wisely."[110]

The cumulative effort that prospective hostesses were expected to expend in order to perform adequately within the hostessing profession belies its imprint as unskilled, temporary work. The money they had to spend to look the part must have seriously cut into their earnings. Makeup, skin care, and hair care products were expensive. Still, women responded to calls for beauty vigilance. According to a 1968 industry report, sales of beauty products in France increased by 126.9 per cent from 1960 to 1966, and an industry growth analysis projected a continuation of the trend.[111] Indeed the same report showed that France, in 1968, had the "highest per capita consumption of cosmetics in Western Europe," and it remarked on French women's recent uptick in hair and beauty products and services.[112] In the postwar beauty industry, production rates in France skyrocketed as well; French suppliers outpaced their German counterparts and obliterated the British industry, leading that same report to label France "the most important cosmetics exporting country," especially taking into account the "invisible exports" – beauty products purchased by tourists while in France.[113] The definition of female labour as unskilled and nonessential in the broader scheme of the family income also likely capped hostesses' pay at relatively low rates, despite their often heavy workloads and their actual value in terms of company profits. In 1962, French women generally earned about two-thirds of what their male counterparts in the same job would earn, a fact that ignores the reality that more women worked in lower-paying positions than men.[114] The gender-based salary gap was likely greater if one factors in women's work-related expenses in terms of keeping up their physical appearance. And no statistics about income or spending could possibly reflect the expenditure of time and energy that women were required – informally or formally – to ensure their appearance met industry standards.

It is important to remember that these hostesses, even as late as the 1960s and 1970s, had a relatively short shelf life in terms of work tenure. In a section on the future of hostesses, Delestrée argued for an important distinction to be made between the future of the individual hostesses and the future of the profession as a whole. The future of the profession, he argued, was robust, but individual hostesses were not likely to last long. He cited the statistic that "nine-tenths of hostesses" will leave because of marriage, because in many cases being married is "not at all compatible" with their work. Also, as hostesses aged, they presumably lost the attractiveness that was part and parcel of their work. "Prettiness," Delestrée stated, "goes away to some extent with the years. The profession of hostess is foremost *a young woman's profession* and … the *average number of years women perform it is five*" (original emphasis).[115] Echoing both Delestrée's commodification of hostesses and their impending expiration dates, one hostess training school advertised to prospective employees that they were available not only to train hostesses, but also to "ensure the recycling of your welcome personnel."[116]

The prospects for former hostesses were limited. Delestrée offered that some could perhaps work in non-public areas in offices, where they were unlikely to be spotted by the general public. Or, in a happier outcome for Delestrée, "others finally become excellent spouses and mothers, the qualities that they wielded in their youth finding very natural application in their home."[117] In a way, then, all hostesses were temporary placeholders, waiting for the next set of younger, prettier women to take over.

Conclusion: Every Woman a Hostess

In her book aimed at educating young people about the air hostess career, a book in which Air France is expressly thanked for its help in contributing content, Claire Andrée Roe quotes one hostess as saying: "Hostess training teaches you so many things. [My fiancé] says that all young girls should have this kind of training."[118] And in the Air France company magazine, one retrospective on hostessing, in honour of its twentieth anniversary, took the question of universality and influence even further, stating (apparently quite accurately) that one day scholars would study how hostesses created "a new vision of women's roles in public opinion." The article acknowledged that the women themselves had begun to move away from the "mistress of the house" model of hostessing, but noted that this development occurred much to their male passengers' chagrin. "Even women passengers," the author stipulated, could not help but be aware (*sensibles*) of the "charm" and "presence" that hostesses steadfastly modelled in the plane, hinting that the hostess model of femininity, while somewhat flexible (partially due to the actions and attitudes of hostesses themselves), remained faithful to many of its roots, at least in the official literature. In that, at least, there was a remarkable continuity over the decades since the profession's introduction in France.[119]

The difficulties that the French nation faced in terms of fighting stereotypes of rudeness – particularly among Americans – were a major concern of early Cold War governments. Christopher Endy has written about how tourism disputes became proxy wars in the 1960s between the United States and France, where diplomatic frustrations about Cold War politics and government leadership erupted in accusations of rudeness on both sides. In this context, Endy argues, hostesses took on extra importance, as a "premodern and feminized" face of the nation. Even more, Endy continues, the government hoped that *all* French women would take a lesson from hostesses, in providing what he calls "an ideal of courtesy" for the French people to emulate in their dealings with tourists.[120] I would argue that there exists a further exigency created at this time: not only should all French women *act* like perfect hostesses, thereby imbuing tourists' images of France with warmth and gentility, but as this chapter has shown, they also ought to *look* like perfect hostesses at all times. Appearance was integral to hostessing, which in and of itself was an exercise in aesthetics. French officials, then, subscribed to a narrow, heteronormative vision of femininity, in which, as stated above, all French women "should have this kind of training," and employed it as a way to lure money and attention to the nation, all at a time when hard power measures of French success were waning. The next chapter will demonstrate how, in high-visibility moments, the French government turned to hostesses, in effect "all young girls," to act as *ambassadrices* to the world.

Chapter Three

Hostessing Global Events

When major events of the postwar decades drew the world's eyes toward France, the French, usually under the auspices of the French government, consciously put forth their women to capture, maximize, and monetize that global gaze. French officials had many moments to capitalize on global attention; this chapter explores two one-off events: the 1958 Brussels World Exposition and the 1968 Grenoble Olympic Games. At each of these international gatherings, various industries, in the case of Brussels, and even the government itself, in the case of both, carefully chose a specific type of woman to front their entire operations, to the point that the hostesses selected became emblematic of the entire event. Much like her skyborne counterpart, the ideal international event hostess was glamorous, elegant, fashionable, beautiful, welcoming: a model of perfection. She both emblematized French femininity and unattainability.

This chapter will explore how the French government deputized women to represent the entire nation in each instance – but only for aesthetic purposes. In the case of Brussels, this chapter will explore the intent and process behind the selection of hostesses, and in the case of Grenoble, it will delve into the question of their international reception. In each case, French officials were acutely aware that the world was watching, and that the event represented an opportunity not only to shape the global image of France, but also to capture an outsize share of the tourism market. The selection of the Brussels and Grenoble events for my in-depth analysis was not random. In this chapter I wanted to show change versus continuity over time (in this case 10 years) between two somewhat similar one-off events: both ushered in massive international attention and representatives from many nations, and in both the French heavily utilized their now-acclaimed hostesses.[1]

Anxieties about losing out on tourists, especially Americans, to other countries penetrated the highest levels of government. In 1959, the Economic Council published a report in which it sounded an alarm about French tourism, during what it called "a particularly delicate period" for the industry. Looking at data from 1955 to 1957, the council noted that tourism seemed to be "losing steam," a frightening prospect for the second-largest sector of France's economy. The council went on to ask the government and related businesses to be thoughtful, to make good choices, and to "set France on the right path." Alarmingly, American tourism was, in the council's words, "particularly falling." In order to push back against this trend, the French government and various industries once again turned to femininity, a now-familiar commodity, to affirm French greatness and bolster the economy.

Brussels

At the onset of the Brussels World Exposition in April 1958, an envoy for the major newspaper *Le Figaro* described the arrival in Belgium of a "battalion" of 12 French hostesses, serving as forerunners of French participation in that major event. The writer, Henri de Linge, continued the near-militaristic language, depicting how a "mob" of their "Belgian sisters" swarmed out to meet the French hostesses. The encounter ended peacefully, Linge continued, with an event at which the two nations' hostesses "formed a delicious tableau, the red of the Belgians mixing with the blue uniforms of the French." Linge wrote of a pleasant evening, but he also warned that more French women would soon arrive. The "avant-garde" of hostesses who were already there, he reported, would soon be joined "in just a few days by Paris hostesses and information hostesses." The Belgians, he went on in a sort of pep talk that may reflect more anxiety than the reality of Belgians' feelings, were "unanimously agreed" that the "French pavilion would be the most beautiful in the whole Exposition. This same unanimity also decrees that the French hostesses are the most graceful." To emphasize just how esteemed French hostesses were already, Linge noted that "even the Belgian hostesses affirm that [opinion], the compliment comes from them."[2] In preparation for a major international exposition, France activated some of its most important representatives – hostesses – to set expectations for French superiority on the world stage.

The year 1958 saw two major France-associated, tourist-related events captivate the world: the Brussels World Exposition and the centennial of the Virgin Mary sightings at Lourdes. At the outset of official preparations, the French government was determined to capitalize on both the proximity and the enthusiasm of these events.[3] Much of the motivation behind the intense efforts was economic: the government wanted to make money and minimize trade deficits: as one newspaper put it, "an 'invisible' export like tourism is not being neglected by the men who sit and count in the Ministry of Finance."[4] However, within the government, there were serious concerns about France's readiness to profit from the major events of 1958, and officials noted the French reputation for brusque dealings with tourists. In February 1958, the Minister of Tourism,

Édouard Bonnefous, addressed these concerns in the French Senate: seeing that the nation's "accueil" preparations were "a delicate problem ... for Brussels, a special effort has been made. The French tourism stand will have an information desk available, staffed by 'hôtesses de France,' girls who will be provided by the senior management of tourism."[5]

Some of the earliest representations of the French welcome hostess saw life around the time of the 1958 Brussels World Exposition. French officials, hoping to capitalize on the proximity of Brussels as well as the exposition's concurrence with the centennial of the Lourdes religious visions, decided to implement what they referred to as a "friendship chain," a series of telegraph offices and lines that would connect tourists with friendly hostesses who would answer questions and provide information about France and French travel. The hub of this enterprise was an office on the Champs-Élysées, in the centre of Paris; it was externally decorated by an enormous two-storey banner that read "WELCOME," in English, another sign of the power of the anglophone, and particularly American, tourist in postwar Europe. It was accompanied by a smaller sign below, in French, that read "Accueil de France" (France's Welcome). The face of the "friendship chain" was female, as these offices were staffed by friendly and knowledgeable young women sporting fashionable blue uniforms. Like their aerial counterparts, the welcome hostesses in the friendship chain were young, pretty, and fluent in English, and ideally one other language as well. The original experiment was so successful that the government then made the program, which was supposed to last for six months, a permanent one.[6]

The French government viewed the Brussels Exposition, held from 17 April to 19 October 1958, as a serious opportunity to showcase the glory of France. In touting the record 4,305,000 tourists who visited France in 1956, for example, Minister Bonnefous predicted that France, and Paris in particular, would "turn the heads" of most of the 30 million expected visitors to the Brussels Exposition.[7] Success was almost inevitable, as a reporter for *Le Figaro* noted, for it was France that invented the entire concept of a World Exposition.[8]

In the planning stages, Pierre de Gaulle, Charles de Gaulle's brother and a prominent political figure in his own right, was named head commissioner of the French task force, in a show of just how seriously the government took this promotional opportunity.[9] In an interview with the major newspaper *Le Monde*, Pierre de Gaulle characterized France's showing in Brussels as a "national advertisement," and "propaganda" the likes of which the French tourist industry had never wielded. The French presence there, he contended, ought to act like a "window display" at a grand department store, advertising the contents within and whetting tourists' appetites to experience France for themselves.[10] In another interview with the media, he pointed out the most important goals of the French display: "Putting our country in its proper rank among the nations

3.1. Pierre de Gaulle, organizer of France's entry into the 1958 World Exposition, held an event at a Parisian restaurant to publicize French efforts. At the event, he surrounded himself with one of the main attractions: beautiful French hostesses (1958). Courtesy of Keystone Press/Alamy Stock Photo.

of the world," de Gaulle argued, "is doing indispensable work for France's present and future."[11]

Government officials eagerly promoted French grandeur at the exposition, often echoing the high-stakes language used by Pierre de Gaulle. Indeed one official referred to the French display as the "climax" of the event, and a newspaper argued that while the exposition was billed as having seven wonders, the 1958 French pavilion in Brussels would inevitably count as the eighth. The government responded with serious financial support, first approving 75 million francs in 1955, and then one year later upping the national budget for the event to 2 billion francs.[12] France and Paris would have separate pavilions, a source of Gallic pride in and of itself for, as *Le Monde* proclaimed, Paris stood "alone among all the world's capitals" as holder of a unique display.[13] Still, one newspaper assured its readers that the two pavilions would work in tandem to showcase "French prestige," along with displays on the Maghreb and other colonial holdings "in order to present the full picture of our nation,"[14] a bold –

but not surprising – assertion in the midst of the Algerian War. Pierre de Gaulle later wrote that the French wanted to demonstrate to the world "an idea as complete as possible about the role played by France today in technological progress and the intellectual evolution of humanity."[15] France's entire display would cover three hectares out of 50 for the entire exposition, a percentage often touted by French officials prior to the exposition's opening.[16] René Coty, the French president, even visited the exposition, spending a few hours at the French pavilion and lending it some official pomp.[17]

In the lead-up to the Exposition, a writer for *Le Monde* stirred up excitement about French architectural contributions while alluding to anxieties about prestige: the Soviet Union and the United States might have the largest pavilions at the Exposition, the paper conceded, "but everyone is talking about how France will have the most elegant one."[18] Writing on the front page of *Le Figaro*, a reporter sang the praises of the proposed design: "Pavilion is not the right word. In truth, there may be no words to describe it. Is it an immense hall, a superhuman tent of glass and steel, some unknown vessel? It is, in any case, an amazing project in that it is the most audacious gift that our age could possibly imagine."[19] And in case the building itself failed to capture attention, French officials adorned their pavilion in tricolour flags, catching even the King of Belgium's eye.[20] "We must tell the truth," a writer for *Le Monde* proudly proclaimed in a preview piece about the exposition, "the French pavilion is striking [*saisissant*] in its audacity."[21] Another writer discussed how the French and Parisian pavilions worked beautifully together: "Via their architecture, their technological achievement, their beautiful shape, their decoration, their hardiness, and their newness they constitute a lesson in and a witness to French prestige."[22] Still another reporter for *Le Figaro*, Raymond Cogniat, reassured the paper's readers that "at the risk of seeming immodest – the French pavilion is by far the most interesting from all vantages." Offering anecdotal evidence, Cogniat took pains to assure his French readers that they need not take his word alone, for "this is certainly the opinion expressed by the vast majority of the early visitors. We will all be talking about it."[23]

The French pavilion's architecture was meant to present a vision of France that was forward-thinking and technologically advanced, but the organizers also paired it with a feminine aspect in the form of French hostesses. The special envoy for *Le Figaro*, Henri de Linge, lauded the hostesses' presence at the pavilion. Unfortunately, he said, the building was positioned in the middle of the US and USSR exhibits, but not to worry, France was a notable presence. For Linge, what made the French elements stand out were the "graceful *hôtesses de France*" who stood at the base of the pavilion and whose role was to "explain the technology" of the building to the crowds. Dressed in "sky-blue uniforms with delicate little white hats," the women of France had become, as Linge described it, an attraction in and of themselves. He again depicted the women as soldiers for France, using the word "troops" to describe the teams of hostesses. The demand for access to the women led to a scarcity in their number: "the curiosity of the visitors is very high," Linge reported, and there are "barely enough women" to do the job.[24]

The grandeur of France appeared not only in masculine technological forms like architecture at the exposition. Pierre Balmain, the famous designer and then-head of the union of couturiers in France, gave a major speech at the exposition in June of 1958 in which he linked the nation of France with the very root of feminine elegance. He spoke of his recent stroll down Fifth Avenue in New York City, where he noticed that the windows of the most chic department stores contained French-themed displays. One, he recalled, was a series of French-inspired hats, which Balmain argued would likely not pass muster on the streets of Paris, where styles were more refined, but the display nevertheless was clearly a tribute to France. Another window display consisted of imported French couture shown in a sea of mini–Eiffel Towers, which for Balmain married the concept of elegant couture directly to the reputation of France itself. Balmain went on to expound upon how foreigners could capture for themselves a bit of this sophistication. Balmain cited artists like Picasso, who, according to the couturier, was Spanish but expressed his genius most freely in the *patrie*, as well as queens like Florentine-born Catherine de Medici and the Austrian Marie-Antoinette, whose adoption of French fashions contributed to their overall reputation as regal, elegant women. Balmain marvelled that the current group of organized couturiers numbered only 24, employing 4,500 workers, and yet "that seems so small when you think about the enormous influence of Parisian couture across the entire world." Balmain encouraged people, especially Americans, to visit Paris in the hope that a bit of that French feminine elegance would rub off on them as well.[25]

French women's elegance was also displayed at the exposition in practical ways. The information presented by the various industries of France at the Brussels Expo was meant to impress tourists, but the presence of French women served as the decoration to entice them in the first place, another example of the combination of hard and soft power deployed by the French during the 1950s and 1960s. In discussing the Brussels Expo on the floor of the French Senate, for example, Édouard Bonnefous sought to convince sceptical politicians that France was putting its best face forward to the world. "We are placing special emphasis on our welcome," he asserted, and as evidence he cited the centralization of information about France at the French pavilion. Booths there, he reassured the politicians, would be staffed by the elite "hôtesses de France," who would be vetted by the national tourism ministry, ensuring that they were the highest-quality specimens, both inside and out.[26]

Various government divisions sent hostesses to Brussels, eager to wield French femininity as a promotional tool for the industries they oversaw.[27] Hostesses of train cafés, which the SNCF had introduced in order to make train travel more enjoyable, competed unknowingly in a competition to represent the organization at the exposition. These hostesses, dressed in gray Jacques Heim–designed uniforms, would first serve train clientele and then provide them with an evaluation card, to rank their performance. In the lead-up to the Brussels Exposition, an "anonymous committee" travelled across France by train, searching for exemplars of the profession. Four hostesses – from Châlons, Strasbourg, Épernay, and Paris-Montparnasse – were chosen as the best-performing, most beautiful women in the job. The SNCF reported that, for their prize, it would send them to Brussels "to represent French female grace."[28] The women would never have known that they were being surveilled, which, *ex post facto*, would likely have made them wonder who was watching them at any moment.

Emphasizing how essential hostesses had become to public exhibitions, entire French industries hired hostesses to represent them. The French press, for one, combined forces for a show of greatness at the Brussels Exposition. They developed a theme, "Liberty, Diversity, Multiplicity of the French Press," and commissioned a poster from the most prominent *affiche* artist of the time in France, Paul Colin. They also had their own kiosk for displaying their publications. But the most effective way to lure onlookers, one newspaper reported, was with the eight hostesses selected to represent the French press for the exposition. One newspaper described the women's tenue in Brussels: "Dressed by a Parisian designer, with very becoming navy blue suits, and topped by a ravishing beret in the same colour, stamped with a white feather whose edges form the word 'press,' with exquisitely tasteful shoes and makeup, these delicious *ambassadrices* will be the most attractive part of the stand." The article went on to say, tongue in cheek, that the government's information minister worried that the girls were so alluring that "visitors to the exposition would come to admire this octet of French beauty than to read the newspapers there." At the very end of the article, the writer reported that all of the girls knew at least three languages and "received a solid education that would allow them to respond to any press-related queries."[29] Hostesses' linguistic abilities allowed them to practise more traditional diplomacy as well. When a group of Flemish nationalist protestors demonstrated at the French Pavilion, decrying a lack of Flemish-language translations on display, Pierre de Gaulle himself came out to address the group's concerns. He was accompanied by a *hôtesse de France*, who, reporter Pierre de Vos scoffed, translated his words "in a Flemish more perfect than that of most of the Flemish journalists" at the Expo.[30] The French press felt they needed hostesses in order to be successful and attract attention, and by any account they were; they won the International Grand Prix, awarded to the most successful display.[31]

Air France's participation at Brussels combined the elements of feminine elegance and technological innovation that had come to characterize the image France chose to present to the world. The theme that the company selected for its presentation was Air France's outstanding technological advances. To support this theme, the aviation section of the French pavilion featured a giant planisphere, measuring eight by five metres, showing all of the flight destinations of French airlines. The purpose of the display was to demonstrate that Air France had the largest network in the world, a fact that then reflected favourably on the industry and the nation. Air France officials, in a company magazine, argued that the wide network was a display of French "progress." The company also displayed large models of its most popular and advanced airplanes, including the new Caravelle, which, the magazine reported, attracted "mobs" of visitors.

The personnel chosen to represent the company at the French Pavilion had a decidedly feminine cast. The large photo accompanying the trade magazine's piece, about the Caravelle plane, was dominated by an Air France hostess, who was herself seemingly entranced by its technology. Air France selected some of its best hostesses to sell visitors on the luxury and excellence it offered. As a trade publication, *France-aviation*, reported, the big "attraction" of the exhibit was the "charming" young woman, "dressed in an Air France uniform." The magazine remarked with surprise on how well-versed this hostess seemed to be in highly technical aspects of aeronautics. All was explained, however, when she was asked how she could know so much about technical details: although she admitted to not having any training, she had "asked for all the information from an SNECMA [a French aerospace engine manufacturing company] engineer who had come from Paris." This anecdote reveals the representational quality of the power that hostesses held. Their appeal lay solely in aesthetics, not in the domain of technical knowledge or skill; the hostess's knowledge was shallow, propped up by the real skills of one of Gabrielle Hecht's "men of action." There were more such company "attractions" at the Air France exhibit. The article described two exceptional young women: "ravishing in their blue suits ... performing beautifully as hostesses and ambassadors for the company ... taking care of visitors, giving them information ... reserving return seat assignments and even selling some tickets. Between them, these two young girls speak six languages: French, English, Spanish, Dutch, and Swedish."[32] The company's expertise and service, hallmarks of its brand, wore a fashionable, friendly, and above all feminine face for the world at Brussels 1958.

The French government viewed the Brussels Exposition as an opportunity to display the bounty of France to the world, with grand displays and talks about subjects as diverse as technology, fashion, and intellectualism. These were enhanced by a sheen of heteronormative femininity, provided by the French hostesses who abounded at the Expo. Hostesses fronted industries' presentations, as well as the entire French Pavilion, the wrapping on the gifts France provided to the world. The Expo was a smashing success for the French, who won 1,141 prizes out of a total of 3,861 awarded.[33] For the closing of the Expo,

French officials threw a grand ball in celebration of French design, titled "Le Bal de Paris." Pierre de Gaulle viewed the ball as an opportunity for one last display of French superiority. In anticipation he invited 40 ambassadors from nearly every participating country, the Belgian royal family, and European high society. In a fitting turn, for the ball, the French government sent its most attractive debutantes, sponsoring a special train and 15 Simcas (a French car) for the trip to Belgium. The cars and train would carry the girls, their dresses, and hairstylists, to ensure they would be at their most most glamorous. The debutantes' dresses originated with some of France's most prestigious couture houses: Lanvin, Yves Saint-Laurent (at the time the head of Dior), and Nina Ricci.[34] Famed designer Jacques Heim crowed that the ball would be a marvellous opportunity to display the "heavenly hands" of French fashion work, which, he argued, have contributed to the great "prestige of French couture across the globe ... this couture that ... continues to seduce all the women in the world."[35] The debutantes, then, were to be the vessels of French couture genius, much in the way that hostesses fronted French industries and added to their prestige. Well-known journalist Hélène de Turckheim claimed that the girls, whom she actually deemed "French elegance" itself, were also bringing "French luxury, charm, and beauty in their suitcases," while the newspaper *Figaro* billed the ball as the "number one event of the season."[36] Thus the Brussels Exposition, at least for the French participants, ended in the spirit in which it began: with French femininity on display as a measure of French worthiness.

Grenoble 1968

"It is likely," a journalist boasted in France's premier sporting newspaper, *L'Équipe*, in 1968, "that these Games of the Nineteenth Olympiad will completely eclipse anything that came before them."[37] In many ways the events in Brussels were but a dress rehearsal for France's big show a decade later: the 1968 Grenoble Winter Olympics, which combined an existing quest for relevancy with an intensely Gaullist assertion of national greatness. Indeed President Charles de Gaulle, who took the post just after the Brussels Expo, famously proclaimed the Grenoble Olympics to be "les jeux de France" (the games of France).[38] Designed to showcase French accomplishments and spur tourism and development, the Grenoble event was the largest Winter Olympic Games to date, with 1,355 athletes from 37 countries (Innsbruck, in 1964, was second-largest, with 1,111 athletes from 36 countries).[39] French grandeur was consistently front and centre at all times from the moment the International Olympic Committee (IOC) awarded the Games to Grenoble in January 1964. Maurice Herzog, famed athlete, de Gaulle ally, and Secretary of Youth and Sport, crowed that the selection proved France's "considerable estimation in the eyes of the world."[40] Other political figures acknowledged the risks inherent in taking on such a massive global event. The president of the French Olympic Committee and a member of the IOC, Armand Massard, emphasized the Games' reach, saying, "The prestige of France is at stake in the eyes of the world."[41] An American visitor to Grenoble in 1967 commented on the country's obsession with itself: "Everything is prestige, saving face, looking good all the time."[42]

Despite the early hopes for self-promotion, things did not get off to a good start for the French organizers. First, their initial goal was that Lyon would be named host of the 1968 Summer Olympics, but, in an embarrassing turn, France lost out to Mexico for those Games.[43] The awarding of the Winter Games to Grenoble thus came as something of a relief. However, during Grenoble's preparation, it became clear that the region was in no way ready to support the Games. Early organizational efforts, rendered more complex than usual due to the constellation of sites hosting events, fell flat and had to be remanded to the state.[44] In terms of practice runs, the French organizers held a series of "International Weeks" over the course of the winter of 1967.[45] Sparing no Gallic feelings, *Sports Illustrated* writer and editor Jack Olsen called the pre-Olympic competitions in Grenoble a "debacle," while a columnist for the *Boston Globe* labelled them a "fiasco."[46] Olsen directly attacked the French, writing, "if ever a nation lost face and prestige simultaneously, it was France at the pre-Olympic meeting." According to a columnist in the *Washington Post*, the Swiss, Austrians, and West Germans all "snootily" quit the competition, citing poor accommodations.[47] Olsen then listed a litany of problems and complaints. The weather was too warm and then too cold. The bobsled and ski runs were unfit for racing. The French sport newspaper *L'Équipe*, summing up the disastrous experience, issued a challenge to the Olympic committee: "The situation is very serious. It has been abundantly exploited outside our country. In the face of this scandal, this incident must at least show that a great deal of work remains to be done. There is not a second to lose."[48] For its part, the committee labelled the problems as "unfortunate incidents."[49]

International embarrassment was not to be borne in the 1960s in France, where the entire goal of winning the games was to promote the grandeur of France – and international tourism – and the rocky start to the Olympics was met with outrage from the Elysée Palace. Charles de Gaulle infamously upbraided the officials in charge of the Games about the shame they had brought to the French nation. He then ordered that organizers not only ensure that the country be ready in 1968 but that the Games to be "the most spectacular of all Winter Olympics" ever.[50] The French committee responded with vigour, bringing in experts from across the country to manage the situation in Grenoble and to ensure a successful outcome. They also dramatically increased the number of people working on the Games. In winter 1967, at the two sets of International Weeks, official personnel numbered 151 and 133, respectively. One year later, at the Games themselves, that number had ballooned to 1,910.[51]

The French organizers also enlisted the help of their armed forces by way of an October 1967 agreement, assigning more than 7,000 soldiers and 1,000 pieces of military equipment to the Games.[52] The extra attention ultimately resulted in what one historian has deemed a "rigidly planned and programmed" Winter Olympic Games.[53]

The *grenoblois*, who had won the Games under a Gaullist mayor and subsequently elected a left-wing slate of candidates, were not necessarily excited at the prospect of hosting the Games.[54] The cost of the Games was enormous, almost 225 million dollars, which far exceeded the original bid from the city and represented a breathtaking 1 per cent of the entire national budget.[55] The secretary of state of the interior, André Bord, delivered a speech on the floor of the French Senate in which he acknowledged the overspending, but urged his colleagues to recall that all of the extra expenditures were necessary "so that the Games might honour France."[56] In the Grenoble region, people did not seem convinced by Bord's argument. Disparaging quotes from townspeople were reported widely in American newspapers, a major publicity target. Comments such as "We survived the wars only to be destroyed by the Olympics" and "the city's in debt up to [our necks]" dominated the coverage.[57] A journalist for France's main sports newspaper, *L'Équipe*, published a major exposé in which he reported that for only one day of use, the speed skating rink cost 250,000 francs in maintenance, the skating arena 1 million, and the bobsled venue a whopping 3 million.[58] Worse still, 16 workers preparing for the Games were killed in the run-up to the opening ceremonies.[59] The government embarked on a campaign to convince the *grenoblois* that they, too, had a crucial role to play in promoting France, papering the region with 3,000 posters and placards that read: "A smile wins the day – 5 rings, 3 roses [the official symbol of the Grenoble Games] and YOUR smile."[60] The government demanded the full participation of the region's population as a symbol of the Games themselves, as well as a sign of French welcome.

De Gaulle and the organizing committee were determined to sell the Games both within France and beyond the borders of the metropole. A modern press centre dominated the Olympic village, expressly designed by the official committee to provide "representatives of the press all possible and rapid contacts with the athletes, the venues, the town centre, and the ice sports staff."[61] Press representatives were helicoptered to and from venues, and they were grouped with other journalists from their time zones to ensure that no one missed a deadline.[62] They also were provided with rooms where only their language was spoken.[63] To sweeten the experience further, the Official Committee offered journalists "elaborate" food as well, in order to win them over and to provide another platform for expressing Gallic greatness. Each day chefs treated the press to a special meal that represented one of France's provinces. This meant journalists had access to dishes like trout *à la grenobloise*, lobster thermidor, and Alsatian choucroute.⁶⁴ In addition to these perks, the Official Committee distributed a new gift to accredited press personnel each day, all of which were presented by sponsors – who themselves were no doubt looking for positive coverage. These gifts ranged from perfume and Cognac to razors and scarves.⁶⁵

There were large numbers of press personnel at the Games, but the largest contingents by far were the anglophones (551) and francophones (510), with the German- and Russian-speaking press ranking a distant third and fourth.⁶⁶ Clearly the the Games meant nothing without an audience, especially of the English-speaking variety; organizers hoped that spectators would be so captivated that they would bring their money to France in the near future. For the French press "no fewer than 1,300 technicians of the government-run radio and television networks" were brought in, *New York Times* columnist Lloyd Garrison observed. "To the captive French audience," he went on, "the accent will be on grandeur, and in France, grandeur is synonymous with Charles de Gaulle."⁶⁷ Added to all of this French television technology, the government also rented out movie theatres in cities across France to ensure citizens' access to what promised to be a glorious moment for the *patrie*.⁶⁸ American television coverage, from the ABC network, was also comprehensive, spanning more than 26 hours of live broadcast, not including re-runs. One columnist called it "the most ambitious, most expensive coverage of a sports event in the history of a home screen."⁶⁹ Indeed ABC spent over 5 million dollars and sent 40 cameras and over 200 staffers for their non-stop, wall-to-wall coverage. Additionally, for the very first time, the Games would be broadcast in colour, adding another technically innovative element to the coverage.⁷⁰ The French and the American markets were watching, to say nothing of the rest of Europe and world.

Reporting on the opening ceremonies, *L'Équipe* heralded them as "the most spectacular Winter Games" ever seen.⁷¹ The opening ceremonies of the Grenoble Olympics were breathtaking for the time, as befit a country anxious about its prestige and hoping to make a splash on the world scene. The Official Committee explicitly stated that they wanted to give a "particular brilliance" to the opening ceremony and outdo those of Tokyo and Innsbruck, and by all accounts they succeeded.⁷² "Spectacle followed spectacle" was how a columnist for the London-based *Guardian* newspaper described the experience.⁷³ "Wondrous it was," reported Fred Tupper of the *New York Times*, explaining how the ceremony was a departure from the small gatherings on mountains of Winter Olympics past. President Charles de Gaulle, "hatless" in the frigid alpine air, officially opened the Games.⁷⁴ When he came into the stadium, one columnist reported that his "entrance was as unobtrusive as a burglary," while another referred to him as the "featured actor" at the ceremony.⁷⁵ The most colourful description, found in Arthur Daley's column for the *New York Times*, called de Gaulle "the most grandiose figure to do the job since Nero handled the assignment about 1,900 years ago. Or maybe even since the first Olympic show was put on the road in honor of Zeus in 776 B.C. The chances are that Mon General would rather be bracketed with Zeus than with Nero. Nero wasn't even a God."[76] De Gaulle apparently "stylishly" arrived three minutes late, having alerted photographers to be prepared for his 3:03 pm arrival.[77] He then uttered "I open the tenth winter olympic [sic] games at Grenoble," with, according to one columnist, an extra emphasis on the word "Grenoble," and then presided over the pageantry while "beaming with pride" at the sights before him.[78]

As the celebrations began, thousands of French schoolchildren, bedecked in ski attire, paraded through Grenoble's temporary stadium, waving to the approximately 65,000 onlookers.[79] The *Los Angeles Times* described how soldiers from the alpine region carried in the Olympic flag, and then nine cannons fired loudly "at five-second intervals to mark the arrival of the Olympic flame." The crowd boisterously cheered Alain Calmat, the silver medal winner in men's figure skating in 1964, as he carried the flame through the stadium while loudspeakers blasted a pre-recording of his heartbeat.[80] And then French runners lit torches from the main Olympic flame, following Calmat's lighting, and raced out of the stadium to each of the locales used during the games. Fred Tupper summed up the over-the-top ceremony: "This was a huge extravaganza, conceived by a film director and run on Hollywood proportions. It had everything. Parachutists leaped out of the sky and landed on five Olympic rings in the stadium infield. Cannons exploded tiny Olympic flags that veered, off direction, over the end of the stadium. Then 30,000 perfumed paper roses dropped obligingly into the laps of 60,000 spectators. Planes tumbled out of the horizon to form the five colored Olympic rings in smoke."[81] Not only that, but, as another columnist reported, "Fireworks exploded. Bands played. Choirs sang."[82] The general consensus, reported the *New York Times*, was that the ceremony was "spectacular."[83] As writer and leftist thinker Jean Bastaire relayed in the French magazine *Esprit*, at that moment, France's "success was total." Bastaire marvelled at how even the weather seemed to cooperate with the nation: "at the designated time, glorious sunshine overcame a sinister wet snowfall that fell that morning; the region's familiar gusts of wind did not even show up to snuff the torches."[84] France was ready to take centre stage in the eyes of the world.

The icing on the cake of the Olympic Games, even the opening ceremony, came in the form of a group of attractive French hostesses. According to Fred Tupper, after the planes traced the Olympic rings in the sky, just before the athletes began to march into the stadium, "300 beautiful French hostesses came down a carpet of stairs and vanished into limbo."[85] A report from the Associated Press depicted the hostesses' entrance as a highlight of the ceremony: "One of the loudest roars heard at the opening ceremony of the Olympics today was for 350 Olympic hostesses who came over the rim of the stadium and marched in formation onto the infield. Labeled bunnies because of their red rabbit fur coats and tight-fitting blue ski pants, the girls are serving as interpreters for athletes, newsmen and officials. When President Charles de Gaulle sat down in the Stadium, one of the bunnies rushed over and tried to place a blanket over his legs. But De Gaulle brushed her away, refusing the blanket, and the girl stepped aside."[86]

These "beautiful French hostesses," a climax of the theatrical component of the opening ceremony, consisted of a cadre of carefully selected young women. There were three categories of hostess: Olympic hostesses; welcome hostesses; and Grenoble welcome hostesses, all of which performed similar functions for different – but often overlapping – groups.[87] One of the aforementioned experts trucked into town to save the Games was none other than Solange Catry, now chief hostess at Air France, who was placed in charge of welcoming tourists, dignitaries, and press. Indeed *L'Équipe* somewhat cheekily labelled Catry "the super-chief-hostess of the Games."[88] In discussing the run-up to the Games, one American columnist for the *Boston Globe* described massive preparations undertaken by the French in hosting the event. After detailing infrastructure and housing improvements, she went on to include hiring and training hostesses in her laundry list of pre-Olympic tasks: "Air France has loaned its chief stewardess to head a crew of young hostesses," thereby equating the importance of hostesses with other aspects of the preparations.[89] The French Olympic Committee called Catry "an obvious choice" for the task.[90]

Solange Catry had a specific vision of the ideal hostess for the Winter Olympics, one that, unsurprisingly, derived directly from the ideal Air France hostess. All hostesses, for example, needed to be at least bilingual, if not trilingual. One newspaper report attributed France's hiring of multilingual hostesses to a general fear of hard feelings due to miscommunication, a problem that had plagued the Innsbruck Games in 1964.[91] Indeed one article in *L'Équipe* quoted one Colonel Neyme, in charge of operations in Grenoble, as placing the welcome of visitors at the top of his priorities: "We want the foreigners who come to us to be considered not as foreigners," he said, "but as guests who come to France for an event marked by a spirit of brotherhood."[92] Another article posited that in hiring so many girls "the French are taking no chances."[93] Still, in one interview, Catry argued that while the language requirement was non-negotiable, as the women would be dealing with visitors from all over the globe, other considerations bore equal weight in her decisions. Catry ticked off a familiar laundry list of qualifications: "charm, poise, beauty, and personality." She reported 1,500 prospective hostesses, a number she whittled down to a far more exclusive 350 over the course of eight competitions.[94] Prospective hostesses travelled to Paris, where they faced a jury composed of Catry and two other chief hostesses associated with the Press Centre, as well as a representative from either the French Olympic Committee or the Ministry of Sport.[95] Many of the prospective hostesses already worked in the profession, as airport hostesses for Air France or welcome hostesses in French cities. According to one television news interview, these hostesses considered their selection for the Grenoble games a major "step up" on the hostessing ladder.[96] Once selected, the hostesses submitted to intense training, including studies at the University of Grenoble, where they learned about Olympic history, Grenoble history, regional geography and economics, and French politics.[97] Finally, Catry helped assign the hostesses to all of the locales where Olympic events were occurring, as well as to train stations and airports as far away as Lyon.[98] In addition, at least two hostesses served as press liaisons from 6:30 am to 2 am every single day of the Games.[99] If hostesses made any misstep, directors ensured that they would be subject to even further training. One hostess, apparently mistaking a local official for a cook, announced her desperate "need for the necessary," while another misspoke to a prefect, saying, "at your service," rather than a less innuendo-heavy offer of help.[100] The organizers made every effort to guarantee that the hostesses were perfect in every way.

Grenoble was the first Olympics to have an official mascot, a skiing bobble-head named Schuss, but in reality hostesses came to represent the Games in the eyes of visitors, precisely because they confirmed expectations of what France represented, at least in terms of women and femininity. The writer Will Grimsley reported that France was "sell[ing] the Winter Olympic Games with the commodities it knows best – charm, beauty, sex, and mademoiselles."[101] The young women, Grimsley went on, were a virtual painter's palate of femininity: "There are tall ones and short ones. Blondes and brunettes. A smattering of redheads. Small, dark Asiatics and tall, Nordic blonds." The vast majority (285) of the hostesses were French, but some (87) came from other countries because of language ability.[102] Still, it was their beauty and ubiquity that drove international coverage, with another columnist writing that "France's prettiest girls with multilingual talents" were everywhere helping in the early "confusion" of the Games.[103] A French report described them buzzing around, "going and coming, everywhere distilling their charm."[104]

Hostesses' service to the Games and to France was so evident, sportswriter Will Grimsley argued, that he felt compelled to dub the hostesses the "pride of the Games," observing that they had become more synonymous with France in Grenoble than even Charles de Gaulle. Indeed Fernand Albaret, writing for L'Équipe, lamented de Gaulle's absence from a VIP function, where luminaries like members of the royal families of Greece, Spain, Afghanistan, and Sweden, as well as tycoons like Henry Ford, would receive their first impressions of the Grenoble Games. However, Albaret went on, readers could take heart, for 40 hostesses would be at the event, attending to every need, so "everything will no doubt go beautifully."[105] The hostesses' hospitality was not limited to elite guests. Grimsley also commented on their welcome for all attendees: "they meet every plane. There's a language and a smile for every athlete, official and dignitary from each of the 38 countries [sic] competing. The girls are everywhere. They are stationed at all the buildings. They swarm all over this mushrooming snow and ice capital, turning a veritable babel into a friendly little village."[106]

The Grenoble hostesses' uniforms captured much attention. There were several versions for Grenoble hostesses, including one designed by French celebrity Sylvie Vartan, a singer and one-half of France's foremost celebrity couple at the time (the other half being singer Johnny Hallyday). This particular outfit, one writer reported, was popular with the men, for at its unveiling, a "mischievous gust of wind slipped under the skirt of one of the girls [modelling it] and exposed more leg than even the most scandalous of mini-skirts."[107]

One uniform in particular came to symbolize the women who wore it, and even the Games themselves. The distinctive costume, created by the designer Pierre Balmain, consisted of red fur coats from Chombert, a noted clothier, paired with blue stretch pants and fur-lined boots.[108] Indeed, one newspaper report indicated that the particular hue of the pants, dubbed "Olympic blue," would be the "star" of 1968, and that the French skiers should consider adopting it.[109] In Grenoble, women who sported this red and blue uniform were commonly referred to as "bunnies," allegedly because of the coats. After the Games were over, a fashion columnist at the *Boston Globe* reporting on trends in skiwear, wrote "and now furs, everything from skunk to mink, are considered superchic on the slopes."[110]

The uniforms were crucial both for their role in identifying the hostesses and for their ability to attract tourists. Raymond Darolle, writing for a Bordeaux newspaper, stated that this fetching uniform "will charm tourists and help them forget all their troubles and worries."[111] Apparently it worked, for in another dispatch, Will Grimsley described the hostesses as a "sexy corps of Olympic bunnies – multilingual beauties in rabbit fur and boots."[112] And Gwen Morgan, writing for the *Chicago Tribune*, described the hostesses as "tucked into [their] blue and red ski outfits."[113] The term "bunnies," likely derived not only from the fur they wore but also from the term "snow bunny," denoting a woman who does not participate in winter sports, but rather is a decorative element, prized for her appearance.[114]

Like their counterparts in the air, hostesses for the Grenoble Olympics were required to be constantly pleasant and keep their true feelings under close check. One French correspondent for the Games, Jacques Belin, described the hostesses he encountered as "charming … extremely amiable, deploying vast reserves of patience, understanding, and friendliness," even when faced with trying situations and aggravated clients.[115] *New York Times* correspondent Lloyd Garrison described the women as "pretty, red-jacketed 'bunnies,' the ever-smiling, ever-pleasant Olympic hostesses who translate, find tickets, and have been known to help fix your car and do just about everything but a visitor's laundry."[116]

With this combination of enforced friendliness and availability, romances – wanted or not – often occurred. Prior to the Games, Solange Catry acknowledged the temptation on both sides of romantic entanglements, saying to one reporter that "the pressure on [the hostesses] for dates is tremendous ... You can imagine these girls thrown among strapping young men from around the world." Still, she continued, her rules for comportment were clear. The girls were welcome to go out for dinner or dancing, but they needed to heed their 10 pm curfew. Just as important, Catry insisted, was that the hostesses "act the lady at all times ... The girls can't smoke or drink while in uniform."[117] The French Olympic Games were a female-led show for a world audience, and the main actresses needed to play their parts to perfection.

Hostesses sometimes chafed at the regulations governing their behaviour and the emotional dissonance they entailed. A reporter for *L'Équipe*, Robert Colombini, hinted at the difficulties of this labour, noting the hostesses' beautiful smiles, but speculating that they hid "tears ... and even a degree of bitterness." One Grenoble hostess, "a pretty blond" speaking off the record to Colombini, expressed frustration at being under such a behavioural microscope, grumbling: "It's untenable. Up at seven, back at nine. At ten, there's a bed check. We're forbidden to smoke or drink alcohol during the Games. Even our fingernails are inspected every day. Like we're in barracks! ... I didn't come here to take the veil." Analysing the discontent between hostesses and management, Colombini superciliously labelled it a "tempest in a bottle of fingernail polish." For her part, Catry emphasized that her hostesses had undergone rigorous training, they knew what they were signing up for, and the vast majority of hostesses were "very happy with the program."[118]

At times the copious charms of the Olympic hostess could backfire; a reporter recounted how one hostess had "learned to say no in nine languages."[119] In another case, *L'Équipe*'s Robert Colombini joked about the pamphlets circulating throughout town, which contained directions for CPR in the event of an emergency. He wrote that the pamphlets were thorough and informative, except for one key detail: they did not "precisely state whether or not a beautiful hostess would be the one administering mouth to mouth."[120] Indeed Catry asserted that her strict regulations for the hostesses actually served to protect them from unwanted attention of male athletes, calling the nighttime checks in particular "highly necessary." Every day, she argued, "a significant number of suitors" pursued the women, and she would rather have the hostesses follow her rules than have to pry them from the arms of an athlete "in the nearest dancehall." Based on his observations, Colombini ultimately agreed. For the average hostess, he wrote, "underneath that beautiful uniform beats a heart that, if not totally full, is at least satisfied."[121]

A story from the bobsledding hill reveals the level of seductive power the hostess could hold, at least in the eyes of athletes. In this instance, several bobsledding teams staged a protest after their hostess was reassigned from Alpe d'Huez to Grenoble. The hostess, whom one newspaper winkingly labelled "nice (too nice, according to some gossipmongers)," had allegedly embarked upon a romance with an Italian bobsledder, in violation of Catry's strict rules.[122] When she was reassigned, teams from Italy, Romania, Spain, and England, enraged, stormed the organizers' offices and demanded her reinstatement. At first, tourists and athletes alike were amused by the incident; however, according to the paper, events grew more tense when the bobsledders carried the car of the French team's coach, a full-size Renault, into the offices and deposited it there. They then proceeded to light stacks of paper on fire, all while calling for the hostess's reinstatement. Finally, "they threatened to boycott the event if they did not, in the greatest haste, see the return of the smile of their hostess."[123] Happily – for the bobsledders, anyway – the hostess took up her place at Alpe d'Huez once again. For not arresting the bobsledders, one American journalist awarded the French police the "Maurice Chevalier Award," named in honour of the debonair French Hollywood star – who had recently written a popular memoir detailing his many romantic exploits.[124]

The hostesses worked hard to ensure the smooth running of the Grenoble Games, at times to the detriment of their own health. Fernand Albaret, writing for *L'Équipe*, described a veritable plague of exhaustion among hostesses in Grenoble, starting at the very top, with the woman he referred to as "General Catry." Indeed Solange Catry became so ill during the Games, "just as everyone who saw her [work pace had] predicted," according to Albaret, that she had to take to her bed in the early days of competitions. Albaret further reported that hostesses did not have the time to take meals, leading to a very public fainting spell for one, as well as near breakdowns for several others. Still, like well-trained soldiers, Catry's army pulled together to function for France. Albaret pulled no punches when relating their importance to the Games' success, writing "if the hostesses give out, the entire Olympics will fail."[125] The article makes clear that, like an army battle, the hostesses would fight to bring glory to their nation at the Grenoble Games. Indeed, their general, Solange Catry, was decorated for her service with the National Order of Merit for her work in Grenoble; 10 years later she received the Legion of Honour for her service to Air France as well as for her work in Grenoble.[126]

At the very end of the Games, during the closing ceremony, two French women dressed in regional alpine clothing solemnly handed the Olympic flag to two Japanese women dressed in kimonos, a symbolic, and distinctly feminine, national exchange. As an exercise in international ambassadorship, the

3.2. "Good luck Sapporo": At the end of the 1968 Olympics, hostesses from Grenoble, dressed in traditional regional clothing, passed the Olympic rings to their counterparts from Sapporo (1968). Courtesy of the International Olympic Committee.

French organizers considered the Grenoble Olympics a rousing success. In the official report, the French Olympic Committee concluded with a simple message to the next host city: "Good luck Sapporo."[127] No doubt this was an expression given in good faith, but in light of the immense effort the French had put into the Games, it may also have felt like a challenge.

Chapter Four

Selling Postwar French Femininity

The postwar construction of French women as singularly welcoming, beautiful, elegant, and sexy may have found amplification in the halls of the French government's aviation ministry through its promotion of air hostesses, but it quickly and profoundly expanded outward. The idealized narrative of a beautiful French woman as hostess was deployed by government officials to attract tourists and money to a nation struggling to rebuild its economy, infrastructure, and prestige at the end of the Second World War. In order for the narrative to be take hold, it needed to be as appealing as possible, and its targeted audience – in this case primarily Americans – needed to believe in it and literally buy into it. This chapter explores the commodification and expansion of the notion of French femininity beyond hostessing and beyond French borders.

Key to the dissemination of this model of French femininity was a group of people I call translational figures, who acted as intermediaries between France and the United States. These figures ranged, as this chapter will show, from authors and travel writers, who explained French mores to American readers, to French government officials selling femininity through heavily funded tourism campaigns, to people like Brigitte Bardot, one of the most famous people on Earth for a time in the late 1950s and early 1960s, someone who, we shall see, was deemed France's most important export by key government figures. Not technically hostesses themselves, translational figures still served a crucial purpose: modelling, explaining, and/or selling idealized French femininity to its intended audience. They are examples of what philosopher Sandra Bartky has deemed disciplinary characters; they show us how the formation of femininity can be "institutionally unbound," meaning not necessarily originating within the halls of schools, churches, or governments, but rather in more casual cultural settings.[1] As this chapter will demonstrate, these translational figures actively expanded both the understanding and consumption of France's purported superior femininity.

As a caveat, there is much work to be done on French masculinity and its portrayal in the United States. In my limited reading of primary sources on the topic, I saw how French men were sometimes depicted as romantic prodigies, other times as lecherous, and still other times as insignificant or even feminine. This book, though, focuses on French femininity as a valuable commodity in the United States. The purpose of this section is to challenge the ostensibly natural, effortless nature of that femininity by examining the rationale and work behind it and examining also how it spread. While French masculinity is a worthy scholarly pursuit by any measure, this section concerns itself with what seems to be a far more profitable commodity: the unattainable perfection of the French woman.

Officially Marketing French Femininity and Romance

Following the Second World War, the French government hesitated to allow imagery of French women as sexually free and as an attraction in and of themselves; however, that pause quickly morphed into a full-bore campaign that made French women and their milieu reason to visit the country. Starting in the early 1950s and lasting well into the 1970s, the government, via the Ministry of Tourism, sponsored poster campaigns that featured French women juxtaposed with major French attractions, natural or man-made. These posters usually came in two languages, French and English, suggesting that the women and the other attractions displayed on the posters served a dual purpose: first, to attract French people to travel more within France and spend their money in the metropole,[2] and second, to entice anglophones to visit. Campaigns targeted men and women differently, as the chapter will show, but in all cases the message was undergirded by a gendered foundation that emphasized an ideal of French femininity.

In a 1961 piece he wrote for Air France's on-board magazine, *Air-France Revue*, the commissioner general of tourism, Jean Sainteny, expounded on what he believed was the role of advertising in attracting visitors to France. Sainteny is an interesting historical figure in and of himself, having served in many high-ranking positions in the French government. In addition to his tourism post, which he held from 1959 to 1962, Sainteny served as the minister for war veterans and war victims for the French during the Fifth Republic.[3] Earlier in his career, he had been the official liaison for France at the surrender of the Japanese in Vietnam, where he then attempted to return Vietnam to the French empire. He served as the French commissioner for Tonkin and North Annam from 1945 to 1947, and then as French delegate-general to North Vietnam from 1954 to 1957. A personal friend of Ho Chi Minh, Sainteny became a key figure in peace negotiations between the Vietnamese and the Americans at the end of the Vietnam War, meeting with Richard Nixon and Henry Kissinger to share impressions and information at the top-secret talks. At one point, he even hosted Nixon and the North Vietnamese in his Paris residence. According to one contemporary scholar, Sainteny downplayed his role in an interview with her, saying, "I showed them where the whiskey was and then withdrew."[4] In addition, Sainteny was elected as a government deputy in 1962; he actually led Air France from 1967 to 1972, and served on the elite Constitutional Council until 1977. I think this background on Sainteny – his high positions in government and his importance to the protection of empire – reveals the stakes of how seriously the government took tourism in the postwar era.

According to Sainteny, France was already esteemed for its beautiful monuments, its idyllic countryside, and its illustrious history and people. Tourism marketing, Sainteny pronounced, must therefore take another tack to find potential tourists. "Tourism advertising ought to reveal that which might be hidden," he wrote, "so that no one can possibly ignore it, and then, if they have the taste for it, they can go off to discover it."[5] Under Sainteny (and of course the president, Charles de Gaulle, who appointed him), the French government increased its advertising budget and shifted the focus of its advertisements from history and monuments to images that would, in the words of historian Christopher Endy, be "consistent with Gaullist diplomacy's search for international prestige."[6] How interesting, then, that many of those advertisements – both before and after the new campaign – centred on selling women and femininity. The confluence of prestige and femininity suggests that French women had become a sought-after commodity on the world market, that the French government was aware of their value, and that the state was eager to exploit that commodity.

At times the attractions the Ministry of Tourism featured remained man-made, despite Sainteny's search for a new publicity direction. For example, in this 1961 poster of the famed cathedral in Reims, the traditional site of the coronation of French kings, the photograph shows the cathedral relatively far in the background. The image that dominates the poster is that of an attractive young woman, smiling and looking slightly off camera.[7]

Another, similar poster from 1968 shows a young woman shopping at one of the renowned *bouquiniste* stalls along the Seine River in Paris. Here, her defining characteristic is elegance; her clothes, her stylish coiffure, and even her pose suggest good taste and grace. Behind her rises the celebrated Notre-Dame Cathedral, a major tourist attraction in Paris, one that would have been familiar to viewers around the world. The poster itself simply says "PARIS" in block letters above her, equating the famous church, the *bouquinistes*, and the woman in one fell swoop. The French woman is there as an experience to be consumed, just as much as these other well-known symbols of France's capital city.[8]

4.1. Tourism campaigns for the government juxtaposed young, beautiful women with more traditional French attractions – in this case Reims Cathedral, the historic coronation site of French kings (1961). Courtesy of the Archives nationales de France.

4.2. Here, a young, beautiful, fashionable woman browses the booksellers' stalls along the Seine in Paris. Along with the famed stalls and the Notre Dame Cathedral, she is one of the main attractions of the city (1968). Courtesy of the Archives nationales de France.

4.3. Here, French tourism campaigns highlighted the natural beauty of France – the Tarn River in the south of the country, complemented by a young woman. The viewer admires both the natural scenery – and the young woman (1954). Courtesy of the Archives nationales de France.

4.4. French tourism campaigns touted seaside attractions like the beach and sailing – and beautiful women enjoying both (1954). Courtesy of the Archives nationales de France.

Many of the posters displayed a young woman (or two or three) enjoying themselves out in nature. A 1954 image depicts the dramatic Gorges du Tarn, the famed canyon in southwestern France. In the photo, the canyon is again far off in the distance, while in the foreground sits a young woman in a backless garment, gazing out at the impressive scenery.[9]

Another poster from 1954, this time directly aimed at an English-speaking audience, portrays young women at the seaside, about to jump into sailboats, although clearly some of the women seem more interested in the boating tasks than others, who are artfully posed on one boat. At the centre of the image is one particular young woman who smiles and bends a leg gracefully, while stretching the other one out toward the water. She wears a bikini, a garment that was about to become closely identified both with sex and with France itself. Another point about this particular image is that there may in fact be men in it, but they are almost entirely obscured by female bodies. This suggests not that men were unimportant in France in 1954 – far from it. Rather it shows that women's bodies, just as much as fun and frolicking and water, are popular attractions.[10]

The use of femininity juxtaposed with French tourist attractions as a means of drawing interest and, presumably, money, to France is striking in these four posters, which represent only a small sample of the ones published by the Ministry of Tourism in the years covered in this book. However, another aspect of the images is meaningful. In almost none of the posters, not only the ones featured here but also others in the National Archives, did the women appear to be aware that they were objects of scrutiny, indeed of the male gaze.[11] The viewers could thus both place themselves within the image, as either the woman or her presumed male companion, and understand her as an attraction in and of herself, as a typical French woman that one would encounter in France. There is also an everyday aspect to the image, suggesting that no matter where the tourist's glance fell, there would be a woman as part of the landscape, and that woman would be elegant and accessible.

Advertisements enticing tourists to France also touted the country's attraction as a place of romance. Air France, the national airline, often advertised France's romantic possibilities to couples. Depictions of couples in Paris dominated the airline's advertising for years, in a wide variety of forms. A company datebook from 1964 depicted a couple clinging to each other happily as they strolled toward the Eiffel Tower.[12] In 1970, Air France tourism officials put out a promotional puzzle in which a couple frolicked in front of the monument.[13] In 1956, company officials published a tourism booklet that showed couples taking in the famous sights of Paris and embracing along the Seine River; the text (in English) read, "Twenty-four hours is all it takes to fall under Paris's spell."[14] In this case, Paris itself is an enchanting character, promoting love and romance, both Cupid and his target.

Air France hostesses themselves were also implicitly on offer in many of the company's ad campaigns, which used the hostesses' alleged sex appeal as enticements for prospective passengers. Where in the *Vogue* ad cited above the hostess was an enabler of romantic and sexual congress, in this particular type of publicity, the hostess herself was the object of lust. One tourist pamphlet from 1963 literally depicted a hostess on a tray being offered to the pamphlet's reader by an elegant server from the times of French royalty.[15] In 1963, an Air France ad depicted a businessman climbing a stairway onto a plane, with a hostess awaiting him expectantly at the entrance. The ad read, "There is good business in the air …" In French, the word for business is "affaires," clearly a double entendre, especially considering that the next line read, "Seize them in the air!"[16] The association between hostesses, France, and sex became even more explicit when, in 1975, the *New Yorker* published an ad entitled "Have You Ever Done It the French Way?" The ad featured a rendering of a couple on an Air France jet, toasting with champagne, and a caption that read, "A Hedonist's Guide to Air Travel." The ad painted a picture of a hostess, here referred to as "one of our lovely ladies," ready to "pleasure" couples on board "artfully." It went on to assure travellers that exposure to feminine "charms" did not cease at the end of the flight, for welcome hostesses were also widely available to see that all couples' needs were met.[17] Other airlines, advertising in similar magazines, touted pilot experience, or speed, as their main assets for passengers, so it is telling that Air France relied on France's reputation for love and romance, located here in the body of the hostess.[18] Air France was not alone in using sexuality for the purposes of marketing, but it was unique in the way that it nationalized and commodified that sexuality in the bodies of its women.[19]

Air France ads also sold the nation of France as a place where sex was readily available to single travellers, a direct rebuke of government policies in earlier years. Indeed some of the more interesting advertisements are the ones that featured single women. These ads served two purposes simultaneously (albeit heteronormatively in this analysis): they allowed potential women travellers to identify with the women in the ad, and they also allowed potential male travellers to consider the sexual possibilities of such a trip. I would imagine that, given that most travellers in this era were of the male variety, the ads were more targeted at the latter, but it is worth considering both angles. For example, in 1963 Air France marketers published an ad entitled "Your trip just got so much prettier!" The ad showcased a young, smiling woman with slightly windblown hair looking over her shoulder at the camera, wearing a bathing suit or spaghetti-strap dress – only her top half was visible – and possibly out on a boat.[20] In 1970, in a push to increase summer tourism to France, the company published an ad featuring a large photograph of a woman in a white bikini, running out of the ocean toward the viewer, arms outstretched and smiling widely.[21] A similar ad had appeared in 1965, in which another bikini-clad woman lounged in a pool, not looking at the viewer at all, testing the water with her hand and smiling.

Advertising targeting male business travellers, the most common flyers, often relied heavily on sex to sell France and Air France, especially in the latter period covered in this book. One Air France ad, entitled "The Rake's Guide to Paris," appeared in the relatively staid journal *Foreign Affairs* in 1969, accompanied by an image of Edouard Manet's famous painting *Déjeuner sur l'herbe*. In the copy, the ad described a randy man's jaunt through the city. With an unsubtle wink, the subtitle acknowledged the traveller's likely activities: "We Know Where You're Going." First, the advertisement promised to entertain him on the airplane, "to keep your mind off the stewardesses," implying that their charms were nearly irresistible. It implored the "naughty devil" reading the ad to try to wait for Paris. Once in Paris, the ad listed services and shops, restaurants where he could dine *à deux* with a young woman, and the essential items he may want to pick up while in town, like furs, diamonds, and candy, presumably all for his paramours. It instructed him in how to use a public telephone, just in case he did not want to use the one in his residence or hotel room, implying the illicit nature of his call as well as the permissiveness of the French. For entertainment, the ad listed the best places for "le strip-tease," and advised on what to order the morning after a night on the town to cure his hangover. This content is remarkable, given that Air France is a state-run airline, for a state with a history of trying to protect the country and its women from disrepute. And yet, in this ad, the airline acts as a wingman for a roué.[22] In another ad, this time targeted at solo male business travellers, the main copy reads "A beautiful French hostess with a beautiful French accent is a beautiful French hostess with a beautiful French accent." The words were printed over a large picture of a man, seated on an airplane, being served a selection of gourmet French desserts, by a woman whose chest and stomach were her only visible parts. He stares up at her (unseen) face, smiling, clearly pleased with everything – and everyone – on offer. The copy below the picture touted that "beautiful French girls alone do not make Air France Air France," going on to list inside knowledge and information about business in Europe that the airline could provide. Still, the ad insists that everyone knows that Air France has the most beautiful hostesses, and that their accents and their bearing are irresistibly attractive.[23]

Even seemingly innocuous ads contained double entendres and sexual innuendos. One Air France ad, targeted at people who wanted to follow Ben Franklin's trail in Paris, reminded readers that "Ben a aimé les jolies filles …" (Ben loved pretty girls). "And if you like pretty girls too," it advised, this time in English, "stroll down the rue Tronchet at lunchtime, while they dart in and out of the shops. Sit at a table at Le Mabieu 65, blvd St Michel where they cram for exams at the Sorbonne. Watch the models pop in and out of Dorian Leigh's agency, 16, rue Malakoff. Or ask them to dance at Castel's, 15, rue Princesse, still the liveliest of the exclusive discothèques." This advertisement, again operating under the ostensible purpose of tracing Ben Franklin's history in Paris, devotes considerable space to demystifying and locating beautiful French women for these history buffs to consume, one way or another.[24]

Through this kind of advertising, the government of France and closely associated companies like Air France and Air Inter cunningly wielded France's reputation as a sensual place, a ploy to attract tourists to the country. In most of these ads, the women were unknown, anonymous, and hence potentially accessible. However, the most famous sexual lure for Americans, the target of the majority of this kind of publicity, did have a name: Brigitte Bardot. Many historians, including Susan Weiner and Vanessa Schwartz, have demonstrated Bardot's centrality to understandings of postwar France, especially ones that concern themselves with social, cultural, and gender history. However, in Schwartz's case, she positions Bardot as the turning point between France's "long-established reputation as a beacon of traditional culture" and the country's ability "to continue to lead into the future."[25] I do not disagree with Schwartz's analysis of Bardot's centrality to the postwar French cultural narrative, but I would argue that the idea of a break between France's espousal of its traditional reputation and a post-Bardot era is overly simple. The following section will demonstrate how Bardot's image became intertwined both with France itself and with all French women in something of a twisted formula designed to attract Americans to France.

French Celebrity

In 1969, Brigitte Bardot became the face of Marianne, the traditional female symbol of the French nation, indeed the embodiment of the republic. Statues, images, and busts of Marianne had, by tradition, long been displayed in mayors' offices and government buildings across the nation and the world, exposing her not only to local citizens, but also to international dignitaries and visitors. The conflation of Bardot and this widespread French symbol is pregnant with meaning, especially given that Marianne had been an unattributed, anonymous personage prior to Bardot's appointment. The French state actively chose to make Marianne specific to one woman. This raises questions about the specific attributes of Bardot, known commonly as BB (aka "baby") in France, and why her brand of femininity was so attractive, so important, that the state itself held it up as an international icon. While a number of historians have analysed Bardot, French film content of the time, and Hollywood's attraction to Paris, in this section I will analyse how BB came to serve as the standard for all French women in the American mind, not through the plots of her films or those of other contemporary French actresses, but from reviews and reactions to Bardot, and the sexualized, gendered form they took.[26] Emphasizing how unusual

114 Charm Offensive

4.5. Brigitte Bardot as Marianne, the feminine representation of France, as sculpted by the artist Aslan (late 1960s). Courtesy of the Musées de France.

this is, literature scholar Cécile Hanania has noted that France is the only country in the world where government officials work under the watchful eyes of "national stars."[27]

The choice of BB as a stand-in for Marianne was largely the result of a campaign led by Jean-Jacques Servan-Schreiber, the famous intellectual and erstwhile leader of the Radical Socialist Party.[28] Servan-Schreiber was a celebrity in his own right at the time, best known for writing the international bestseller *The American Challenge*, in which he proposed that Europeans' best hope for meeting American intellectual, economic, and cultural domination was with European unity and creativity. Servan-Schreiber, for his part, appears to have been somewhat enthralled (obsessed?) by BB, asking people to call him by his initials as well and even using her likeness as a backdrop for his press conferences, which generally dealt with matters of politics, economics, and literature, rather than film, women, and celebrity. JJSS was wholly committed to Bardot's sexual international power, once commenting that she was "as valuable to French exports as 'Roquefort cheese or Bordeaux wine,'"[29] rhetorically equating Bardot's image to actual inanimate objects that the world associated with France and enjoyed consuming, as well as to objects that literally grow on French soil, hinting that she, as well, was one such object.

In his quest to remodel Marianne and proffer a new vision of France to the world, Servan-Schreiber apparently deployed what he thought was his best weapon: BB's considerable assets. In a press conference, when asked why BB was the right model, he famously gestured to the proposed statue and quipped that "the reasons for the choice ... are evident."[30] He apparently went further; a less cautious article described BB's "well rounded charms" and quoted JJSS as saying, "the reasons for the choice of her bust as symbol of France are evident."[31] One article cited BB's qualifications as the "nation's best known sex symbol," while another described the statue as "republican hagiography – or bust."[32] One newspaper pronounced Bardot "a perfect 38,000," in reference to the number of towns and cities where she would be displayed, all while touting the number – and her – as a "round figure" and "well-rounded."[33] Even further, one article attributed the decision to "two very good reasons," a nauseating description for any modern reader of why a particular woman ought to embody her nation.[34]

The French government was not hard to convince, having already honoured Bardot with a coin in 1966 to commemorate her achievements. Still, one commentator, who called Bardot the "national sex kitten of France," expressed some disappointment that the image on the coin did not adequately represent BB's assets.[35] That the incarnation of France was located in one particular woman is perhaps problematic enough – there are many iterations of French femininity, and to point to one as the ideal delineates the boundaries of French feminine identity in extraordinarily narrow terms, as this project has shown in its exploration of hostessing. And yet the equation of BB's qualifications for the status of national symbol – again, this is the very first time that Marianne was embodied by a real woman – with her voluptuousness and sexuality necessarily points to the fact that women's sexuality was their most important attribute in national – and international – representation. France's national symbol, the way it presented itself both within the borders of the Hexagon and globally was now defined by a woman's seductive fecundity, not her brain or her achievements (cinematic in BB's case). Maurice Agulhon, the foremost scholar of Marianne imagery, called the modelling of Marianne on Brigitte Bardot "radically new" for the republic, in that people would accept a "fully recognizable" image of one woman to represent the whole country.[36] The choice of that woman, then, carried extra symbolic weight.

Interestingly, it appears that Bardot herself never posed or modelled for the Marianne image. Instead, a well-known pin-up artist, Aslan, created the initial statue from several pictures of her. In one article, Aslan attributed the inspiration for BB as Marianne to a dinner he had in the company of a small-town mayor from Normandy. Aslan speculatively asked the mayor what he would do if he had a statue of Bardot in place of the Marianne bust he currently displayed:

"'I'd grab it,' exulted the mayor."[37] A mayor from the Eure-et-Loire region then adopted the statue in his own town hall and, as Agulhon described it, Bardot's Marianne captivated the populace quickly, having "become the new Marianne in an almost enigmatic way."[38] Soon, JJSS found and requested a copy of the statue, as did André Malraux, the former minister of culture, who displayed it above the hearth in his country house.[39] In many ways, the development of the statue itself parallels the overall experience of women serving as *ambassadrices* for France – the state and other stakeholders deployed and possessed women's images at will, while simultaneously not imbuing the women themselves with the power inherent within those kinds of gestures.

Even in her well-documented fall from grace, the result of her extreme and hate-filled racist, xenophobic, and misogynist political views, Bardot's body was the centre of critical language. When he pulled her statue from his town hall in 1996, François-Henri de Virieu, mayor of a small town near Paris, stated "Brigitte Bardot was chosen as the model of Marianne because she had generous curves … Today, she has ideas that we don't find generous."[40] A lede in another newspaper for the same Associated Press story declared "Support Is Sagging," while a third newspaper joked "Bardot's bust is sagging."[41] Another mayor, Bernard Poignant of Quimper, in Brittany, also removed Bardot's bust, stating that "Bardot had sadly gone from embodying freedom, beauty and talent to becoming a symbol of rejection."[42] Bardot's body, the qualification for her identification as Marianne, was deployed by pundits in her downfall.

"The hottest thing since fire" and "screen's most fiery temptress" was how Anthony Noel, reporter for the North American Newspaper Alliance, described Brigitte Bardot in 1958, soon after she debuted across American screens in *And God Created Woman*.[43] In the late 1950s and 1960s, Brigitte Bardot was arguably the most famous woman in the world, a rare designation for a French film actress. Indeed one newspaper deemed her "the most instantly recognizable female face" in the world.[44] Bardot's captivation of the French and the world began early, when she modelled for the cover of *Elle* magazine at the age of 15 and was then discovered by the director Roger Vadim, who ubiquitously credited himself with moulding and creating Bardot. Her early defining role, a "spectacular breakthrough," according to film scholar Ginette Vincendeau, in the 1956 film *And God Created Woman*, shocked viewers with its candid sexuality.[45] The poster for the film, created by noted artist René Péron, depicts Bardot in the foreground, her head thrown back, eyes closed, mouth open, and topless, with the ends of her hair covering the tips of her breasts. In the background of the poster, three clearly perturbed men look either at BB or at the viewer, as if challenging ownership of the star. The poster reflects both the plot of the film, in which Bardot portrays a sexually free woman who tempts three jealous men, but also the way in which Bardot's sexuality is objectified, without her even necessarily recognizing it. As

Selling Postwar French Femininity 117

4.6. Even the poster for *And God Created Woman* emphasized Brigitte Bardot's physical attractiveness – and its allure for men (1956). Courtesy of Everett Collection, Inc./Alamy Stock Photo.

one ad for the film put it, emphasizing her tantalizing image, "'And God Created Woman' ... But the Devil Invented BRIGITTE BARDOT."⁴⁶

Interestingly, the film was not a great success initially in France, but rather first entranced the American film-going public. As one Parisian newspaper crowed in a 1958 front-page headline, "The Americans have discovered Bardolatry!" The coverage went on to note, "[her] face ... has so overwhelmed [*bouleversé*] Americans that they invented the word Bardolatry!"⁴⁷ And in one interesting piece of anecdotal evidence, the very first song the American singer-songwriter Bob Dylan ever wrote was a ballad dedicated to Bardot; doubtless he was not alone in his attraction.⁴⁸ This US-centric enchantment, then, boomeranged back to the Hexagon, informing the French that they had a special commodity on their hands, one that they could mould to serve economic and cultural interests. As film scholar Diana Holmes put it, Bardot's "international success ricocheted back to France: Bardot became a major export, not only an asset to the national economy but also a representation abroad of that sexy, male-oriented femininity on which French culture has long prided itself."⁴⁹ Describing how he had helped discover Bardot, the producer of *And God Created Woman*, Raoul Lévy, told John McCarten of the *New Yorker* in starkly commodified terms, "Brigitte had been in minor roles before, but who could tell what a property she was?"⁵⁰ Similarly, another article depicted the French populace as slowly awakening to Bardot's potential, "as reports of her immense success in America ... filter back in press reports."⁵¹ Ultimately, as Sarah Fishman notes, mass culture in France had become more diffuse in the 1960s, "although," Fishman concedes, despite the diffusion, "every woman's magazine regularly featured Brigitte Bardot."⁵² This section will examine American reviews of the film in order to gain a better understanding of the overall reception of Bardot; it will also analyse her sex appeal vis-à-vis Americans, the main target of French tourism at the time.

American reviews of *And God Created Woman* focused almost entirely on Bardot and her sexuality. Well-known film critic William Zinsser penned a review of the film that typified the genre. He described Bardot as "the newest love queen of France ... that amatory land. Her films send men panting to the boxoffice [*sic*] in huge numbers, and it is safe to assume that her photograph hangs on walls from Picardy to Provence." Zinsser devoted almost every word in his review to Bardot and her body, a fact he readily admitted. "What elusive quality does the girl have?" he pondered. Responding to his own query, he wrote, "Call it sex, for lack of a better word." Zinsser used words like "undulate" and "ripe," and he referred to her body as "a study in rounded surfaces for anyone who likes to study rounded surfaces." Bardot's clothing in the film also inspired fits of sensual wordsmithing from Zinsser, who accused Bardot of "breaking all skirt-raising records" and "unbuttoning her blouse to admit the Mediterranean winds," and "wearing a series of garments notable only for their brevity, including a bikini that looks like a Band-Aid." And, Zinsser noted, "she looks like she enjoys every minute." Reinforcing Bardot's French identity along with her femininity, Zinsser reminded the reader that the film was a "Gallic fable" from a director who "wants to make sure you understand this girl's effect on a man – especially if you are a man."[53] In Zinsser's review, he touches on Bardot's sensuality and her Frenchness, establishing a relationship between the two that would set the tone for other American critics.

Zinsser's rapt review set forth the themes – clothing, bodies, and overall French sensuality – for the other Americans who stretched the limits of their thesauruses to explain Bardot's film. Bardot's clothing – or lack thereof – captivated reviewers. One writer in the *New York Times* expounded: "She is looked at in slacks and sweaters, in shorts and Bikini bathing suits. She wears a bedsheet on two or three occasions, and, once, she shows nude behind a thin screen."[54] The construction of this sentence is interesting, in that it grammatically renders Bardot an object, a focus of the viewer's gaze, through the writer's use of passive voice ("she is looked at"). Marjory Adams, a reviewer for the *Boston Globe*, equated her sartorial scantiness with her sensuality: "she has no inhibitions and she wears almost no clothes." For her, Bardot's bikini was a major focus: "her bathing suit, if such as it can be called, wouldn't cover a 2 year old."[55] Yet another reporter added this titillating detail about Bardot's dress: "the only time she wears undergarments is when there is a stiff wind blowing."[56] In his travel narrative, humour writer David Dodge circled back to the scandalous swimming apparel mentioned by Adams. Dodge argued that Bardot's bikini became synonymous with the French Riviera, writing that "the year Brigitte appeared early on in the season wearing three butterflies of pink-and-white checked gingham, it is said that by August you could not tell where the tablecloths of the Saint-Tropez waterfront cafés ended and the beach began, except that the beach had navels."[57]

If Bardot was the main attraction of the movie, it was because of her body, which became in turn the main attraction for reviewers. "The leading glamour girl of France today is a lithe blonde," announced Hollywood reporter Joe Hyams in a profile of Bardot that appeared on the front page of the *New York Herald Tribune*.[58] Similarly, Bosley Crowther of the *New York Times* called her a "round and voluptuous little French miss" who "is put on spectacular display and is rather brazenly ogled from every allowable point of view."[59] He later described her floridly as "a perambulating peril for all males. She tempts them with her unrestrained gyrations. She joys in having them chase after her."[60] And Marjory Adams, writing for the *Boston Globe*, described Bardot as "a girl with the kind of figure men dream about."[61]

Even small components of BB's physical person resonated deeply on a sensual level. Bardot's mouth elicited particular attention from reviewers. Even in a relatively negative review, Melvin Maddocks of the *Christian Science Monitor* called her pout "formidable."[62] One reviewer described her mouth as one

4.7. Brigitte Bardot became the face of the increasingly popular association between the French Riviera, bikinis, and female sensuality (1953). Used under a CC BY 2.0 license. Photo courtesy of Wikimedia Commons.

"which expresses sullen sensualism and selfish disregard for others."[63] And a reviewer in the *Baltimore Sun* called her "loose-hipped, pouting lipped."[64] Another profiler of Bardot said that her mouth had two poses: "open-mouthed surprise and a pout."[65]

It was clear that Bardot – with her specifically French brand of sensuality – was the bright, shining reason to see the film. Upon its release, one reviewer remarked that BB was about to become "more popular than even Crêpes Suzette."[66] A later profile equated Bardot's sexiness with a French national monument: Bardot "looked sexy, which is like saying the Louvre is a museum."[67] By this trick of writing, Bardot's sexiness was not simply a given, it was a national treasure. According to the reviewers, there was something about Bardot that drew people to watch her. As one writer put it, "even with all the censor board trims, sexy Parisian star Brigitte Bardot's shemoting in 'And God Created Woman' is still plenty, plenty (and biz is big, big)."[68] Melvin Maddocks entitled his review "Brigitte Bardot at the Gary," with no mention of the film's title whatsoever.[69] Marjory Adams in the *Boston Globe* described BB as having "an undoubted and dazzling fascination."[70] Still another review in the *Los Angeles Times* oozed that BB was "the most fabulous wench of the decade," and she was "smoking up the screen."[71] In the *Baltimore Sun*, reviewer R.H. Gardner pondered the appeal of the film, which had broken local box office records, and he came away with the conclusion that Bardot's openness about sex, which he described as a French quality, was absolutely the key ingredient. Further, he argued, the sex on screen was of a sort that appealed greatly to viewers of the film, and he suggested that "French-produced" Bardot and her film "knew exactly how to appeal" to men in the audiences.[72] Film reviewers clearly established that Bardot and France shared a certain sex appeal.

The film itself was secondary for most reviewers, many of whom barely mentioned the plot. One reporter, as though under a spell, wrote that "the most remarkable thing about BB is that after one has seen the film, one comes out trying to remember if she can act."[73] Bosley Crowther praised the visuals of St Tropez in the film, going on to paint Bardot as simply part of that scenery: "The outstanding feature of the scenery is undoubtedly Mlle. Bardot." Crowther continued, ending his review with the complete objectification and muting of Bardot as a person: "She is a thing of mobile contours – a phenomenon you have to see to believe."[74] Perhaps even more disparaging for Bardot, far removed as she was from the era of silent movies, one film reviewer argued that dialogue was unnecessary for Bardot in films. "At best," he wrote, "words are for her merely adjuncts like background music and one can listen or not, for like the Grand Canyon she is essentially a natural feature. The fact that she is also animated [i.e., alive and human] one must regard as something of a stroke of genius."[75]

Brigitte Bardot is thoroughly objectified in the reviews of her American film debut, but early on it became clear that the French state sought to profit off of her and her sensuality, rendering France's reputation itself attractive and sensual precisely because of BB's presence. The French Senate, debating the appropriation of funds for the French film industry, bemoaned the "crisis in French cinema," particularly focusing on how the money previously allotted seemed to have been misallocated. Senators especially decried French film stars' allegedly inflated salaries. The special investigator they appointed, Édouard Bonnefous, echoed the senators' disenchantment, with one major exception: Bardot. She and Roger Vadim, he argued, were France's most valuable stars abroad. "With Brigitte Bardot," Bonnefous continued, "I would pay her anything."[76] Similarly, in a government publication, a budget-minded writer argued that stars usually were not worth their large salaries, but he stipulated that Bardot was an exception, precisely because of her attraction for Americans. Pay her handsomely, the writer argued, because "everyone knows that Brigitte Bardot has high value in the American market."[77] And the minister of finance and economic affairs (and former prime minister) Antoine Pinay informed Bardot that, following her American success in *And God Created Woman*, she was more valuable to France's economy than that erstwhile symbol of French success, the Régie Renault car.[78] Indeed Vanessa Schwartz has argued that Bardot's *And God Created Woman* had a clear economic message: "The Côte d'Azur is ready for tourism."[79] Schwartz argues that the film showcases the weather and beauty of the region, which is true, but I would argue that Bardot herself, in her sensual, almost carnal portrayal, replete with bikini (or occasional lack thereof) was also offered up as an attraction to be consumed, as I go into later in this chapter.

Air France also took advantage of Bardot's potential appeal to American tourists. In its on-board magazine, just at the time of Bardot's film debut in the United States, it printed a giant picture of Brigitte Bardot in bed, nude, clutching a bedsheet to her chest, and pouting and looking off camera. "Yesterday unknown," the caption read, "today Brigitte Bardot has conquered the world."[80] Later in Bardot's career, the airline again devoted a large amount of space in their magazine to a trip Bardot took to New York. The magazine detailed how Bardot often travelled with a large entourage and attracted a multitude of followers – but of course, the airline noted, Air France was fully ready to accommodate BB. Upon her arrival in New York, the magazine described how BB was greeted by a veritable flood of admirers. Moments after disembarking, "the French star, flanked by four G Men, was brought to a press room – amply decorated with Air France 'seahorses' – where 280 journalists, photographers and cameramen from all the American television stations awaited her under the light of the projectors. (It is likely that the Brigitte Bardot press conference in front of a seahorse was seen by 3 to 4 million spectators around the world. Great publicity for Air France!)"[81] In this case, Air France profited from Bardot both in the press conference and in the post-trip recap in the pages of its publication.

While Bardot was clearly the most famous French film star to be embraced by the American press, other French female actresses also had their moments in the limelight, contributing cumulatively to the phenomenon of French feminine sensuality. American writers' descriptions took many forms, but they inevitably portrayed French actresses as sensual creatures. In one paper, the French actress Genevieve, a mainstay on Jack Paar's weekly television talk show, was deemed "a morsel of French femininity who fizzes like champagne," and "a zesty, bubbly gal" who oozes "charm."[82]

One writer declared French female sexuality and attractiveness as one of France's gifts to the world, expounding that "France has given the world any number of great things – Charles de Gaulle, the Statue of Liberty, Maurice Chevalier, cooked snails, Claude Debussy, and vintage champagne, to mention a few. It also has presented us with some movie actresses of unsurpassed beauty and sex appeal." While he went on to mention Bardot, the article was actually about Corinne Calvet, frequently cast as a French temptress in Hollywood films throughout the 1950s. Hollywood reporter Joe Hyams described Calvet as a "sexy French movie actress," in a way making her Frenchness and sexuality her trademark.[83] Hyams wrote about Calvet's career frustrations in the United States, where, because of her French citizenship, she "is considered a French girl and the only parts she is offered are oo-la-la [sic] types."[84] Here, Calvert's career is defined by her Frenchness, which is equated with allure. Calvert bemoaned her Hollywood status in another article: "I must be all the time slinky, sexy, tempting. At first, it is fun. Then, it becomes boring."[85] Still, she felt she had to conform to an image of alluring French woman, for, as she noted in a different article, if you want a career, "it is difficult to change your type."[86] For Americans, Calvert's type was French, and consequently, sexy.

In 1965, the actress Claudine Auger appeared as Domino in the film *Thunderball*, a James Bond movie starring Sean Connery. In an article covering her press tour for the film, *Los Angeles Times* reporter Don Alpert depicted Auger, a former Miss France from 1958, as a natural Bond girl, largely due to her French status. He wrote: "A James Bond movie without a sexy girl is like a tuxedo without satin, a bikini without skin, a French girl without a pout. Fortunately for Bond fans, they won't have to do without the tuxedo, bikini, or pout."[87] In this way, Alpert treated Auger's sexiness as a quality essential to French femininity, as well as a hook for male audiences. Auger went on to state that all of her film roles have served her marriage well, despite the distance, because "it is nice to see each other as lovers instead of married people," to which Alpert responded, "James Bond couldn't have described it better." After an interview spent describing her beauty and allure, Alpert commented "somehow you get the feeling that whatever Claudine wants, Claudine gets."[88] Similarly, in a profile of Jacqueline Beer, star of the TV show *77 Sunset Strip*, writer Charles Witbeck described her as a major draw for American men: "her handsome nose and cheekbones are drawing more male fans. All they see is a couple of scenes with Suzanne, and that seems to satisfy them. The accent goes over big, too." Beer, herself a former Miss France, "charmed" Witbeck immensely, to the point that he dryly advised that "Jacqueline should not lose that accent."[89] Beer's French charm was the key ingredient to winning over both Witbeck and the all-American man.

Mylene Demongeot, a famous French actress in the 1960s, captured the American imagination via her sensuality in a series of profiles. For example, Joe Hyams described Demongeot in languid terms, describing how, at Cannes, she lounged on the beach: "she held interviews while stretched sleepily on the sand in a Bikini." A photographer working with Demongeot, Bob Willoughby, enjoyed their session immensely, saying "she's a combination of innocence and temptation that makes her a photographer's dream – that languid, sexy look."[90] And Demongeot herself promoted French sexuality as something more advanced and different from the more puritan American variety, calling "nude scenes in movies ... old fashioned in her country." The article went on to note that Demongeot herself did not mind a little nudity, explaining that "pictures of Miss Demongeot wearing less than a bikini have been a frequent feature of men's magazines." Here, Demongeot is clearly a male fantasy, a young woman laid out nearly nude on a beach, who posits that the French have liberated views on nudity. Still, Demongeot argued that sexuality and nudity were not necessarily the same thing; rather, she argued for her own ability to be sexy in anything, saying, "You don't have to be naked. You can be sexy in a fur coat."[91]

In 1968, the popular women's magazine *Elle* posed a question to readers of the Bordeaux newspaper *Sud-Ouest*: "Are you a natural woman like Brigitte Bardot? Or a powerful one like Moreau?"[92] The "Moreau" cited here referred to Jeanne Moreau, who was probably the best-known French actress of Bardot's generation – besides Bardot, of course. Tellingly, a major profile of Moreau in the *New York Times* in 1965 ran under the title "The Name Is Moreau (Not Bardot)."[93] Cast as a more artsy, intellectual version of a French film star, Moreau nonetheless found herself equated with sex and French openness. In a discussion about the film *The Lovers*, for example, the interviewer, again Joe Hyams, remarked that it had "featured some remarkably intense love scenes in a story best described as extremely adult." Moreau countered that the reporter's question reflected a national bias. "In America," she parried, "it was considered a sexy picture. I never thought of it as sexy when we made it. What we thought was important was to show the strength and power of love." Still, she acknowledged that the film – and presumably stereotypes of French women – had somewhat pigeonholed her in the United States into more "sexy" roles, because "you don't seem to have parts in American pictures for sexy and thinking women."[94] Hyams made the choice to end the piece with a quote from Moreau, who apparently uttered, "I like to act and make love ... Is there anything more for a woman in life?"[95] No doubt Moreau said that, and potentially meant it wholeheartedly, but the fact that Hyams opted to leave the reader with yet another example of a French actress wholly embracing her sexuality is telling, playing as it does into a specific narrative of French women as sexy and more sexually open than their American counterparts.

Similarly, the *New York Times* article depicted Brigitte Bardot and Jeanne Moreau as two sides of the same coin, of "what the French like to consider a uniquely Gallic art – sexuality. Miss Bardot incarnates the pouty, sulky magnetism of a beautiful animal. Miss Moreau represents the more studied sexuality of the mind."[96] Whether instinctive or cerebral, French women all laid claim to strong sexuality – or rather had claim laid for them. Indeed Moreau, the article's authors went on to say, had "few of the assets commonly thought to be prerequisites for sex appeal."[97] Even without Bardot's more evident allure, the authors posited, there was something about Moreau that appealed on a sexual level. They went on to comment about her prolific love life, citing Moreau's own words: "'There are men one goes through like a country,' she once remarked to an interviewer; and she is a well-traveled woman."[98] Despite Moreau's difference from Bardot, the article seems to suggest, there is an innate sensuality about her that attracted many men.

Bardot was often portrayed as emblematic of all French women, adding a sexualized sense of possibility to a visit to France. One writer, in a front-page profile, called BB a "magic mirror" in which French youth saw themselves.[99] Via this equation, BB and the French youth embodied the same commodity, making all French youth in Bardot's image. Bardot even described herself as a common type in France: "I am the kind of girl every man in France has a chance to meet. I play myself in films." In this way, the fantasy of Bardot could be transferred to all young French women, who, in Bardot's words, were "wild and sexy." She noted their ubiquity, saying, "I can be replaced by someone else with the same set of dimensions."[100] Her allure, then, was a fantasy that men lusted after, but the fantasy was an achievable one: a traveller could simply go to France and meet any number of BBs, a type that was not available widely in the United States. Said one GI who happened to share a return flight with Bardot from Paris, "They don't make them like that in Pottstown."[101]

Sometimes French actresses pushed back against the notion that all French women were sexually available. Clearly the Corinne Calvet interviews cited above exposed that her sexpot persona was simply a role that Americans expected. Similarly, Genevieve, who worked on Jack Paar's show, spoke in one sexual innuendo-laced profile about how younger French girls were in fact highly chaperoned in her home country, a policy of which she wholeheartedly approved. As for French claims on superiority in love and marriage, Genevieve dismissed them as an American idealized vision. "Love, romance," she stated, "It's the same all over the world, I think."[102] Just after Bardot splashed onto the American scene, Liliane Montevecchi, who starred with Elvis Presley in the film *King Creole*, objected to the stereotyping of French women: "we're no more, how you say, sazy, then [sic] women anywhere … We just like English girl, American girl, Swedish girl or Italian girl. But here in America everyone theenks French girl is … deeeferent. That all we theenk about is love. Thees is nonsense. We are normale like everyone else."[103] The *Daily Defender*, to which she gave her interview, had just described her as "brunette sexy."[104]

Still, the fact that these French female stars felt they needed to counter that line of thinking demonstrates just how synonymous notions of feminine sensuality and French identity had become. A French woman, not an actress, was quoted in the *Atlanta Constitution* as saying, "Americans think French girls are all tall and blonde and sexy – like Brigitte Bardot."[105] And the French press crowed about BB's allure for Americans. An article for Agence France Presse bragged that there was "not a single midwestern farmer [who] couldn't recognize her," before smugly noting that Bardot was unable to be seduced by Hollywood, preferring to have a France-based career, in which all of her films would be shot "not far from Paris."[106] Reviewer Joe Hyams typecast French women based on Bardot's mouth, writing "Every movie-goer knows what a French girl is. She's Brigitte Bardot – a baby-faced pout with a beautiful body and very few clothes."[107] The French government echoed these American sentiments in a report, writing "the only actress that everyone knows is Brigitte Bardot … [who] reinforces a well-known image of France with Americans …: the cliché that sees Paris as one big Pigalle and the Côte d'Azur as one big nudist camp."[108] Bardot, who retired from film in 1973, served as a translational figure, a synecdoche for all French women in the eyes of Americans, an image that was also useful for fostering a certain form of French pride.

Commodifying All Women of France

As this project has demonstrated so far, a feminine aesthetic constituted the essential qualities promoted by the French government in its creation of *ambassadrices* for the nation in the postwar period. How, then, did Americans receive and internalize their Gallic counterparts' aesthetic dominance? Guidebooks and mass media acted as interpreters of the French look, advising women on how to go about achieving it, while at the same time stressing how impossible it was to attain.

A French woman's beauty, travel guidebooks instructed readers, was unparalleled. Complicating this assertion of unequalled gorgeousness, one guidebook writer, Temple Fielding, described how a French woman could make herself into a legendary beauty no matter how plain or homely she may be. He argued that France was a nation full of "women who make themselves beautiful, no matter how poorly they are endowed."[109] Likely without realizing it, Fielding here demonstrates the tenuousness of an aesthetically defined relationship to power and national identity. The women of France, in other words, have no choice but to focus on beauty, so great is the pressure on them to model feminine perfection.

A French woman's clothing was an essential component of her presentation to the world, an external advertisement of not just that legendary French feminine taste, but also of Gallic design genius.[110] The French fashion industry, back on solid ground after the tumult of the Second World War, was essential to the French economy both as a producer of wealth and as an aspirational industry that attracted global wealth and attention. Women were a key part of the complicated web of producing the clothing (many were employed in the couture houses, although the head designers were almost always male); they were also wearers of clothing and bearers of the national standard to look put-together at all times. French women were characterized as having an innate sense of fashion know-how. As one newspaper writer reported, "France, as most American women enviously suppose, is a nation where ... models and pert seamstresses exert their subtle influence upon the legendary charm, elegance, and femininity of French women."[111] Here the two pieces of the puzzle, the women themselves and the designers/models who guide them, come together in a way that presupposes their superiority and lends it an air of incontrovertibility.

The American media eagerly reported on the latest in French beauty trends.[112] In 1971, for example, Reuters reporter Peggy Massin announced a new breakthrough ingredient in Parisian beauty products: the oyster. "Parisiennes," whom she described as "always on the lookout for exotic health and beauty products, have discovered that you can do more with an oyster than just eat it." According to Massin, dermatologist Ingrid Millet had begun "making face creams out of extracts from live oysters. Her customers are reported to include France's first lady, Mme. Georges Pompidou, and actresses Jeanne Moreau and Catherine Deneuve."[113] Similarly, an article on the French actress Annie Fargé, most famous for playing the titular character in the CBS sitcom "Angel," trumpeted one of Fargé's insider Parisienne beauty secrets. The reporter, Lydia Lane, asked Fargé with a wink, "Have you brought any beauty secrets with you from France?"[114] Fargé, Lane exclaimed to her readers, actually used raw egg on her face to keep it supple! Interestingly, the headline for the article read simply "Egg Yolk Aids Skin and Hair," accepting Fargé's tip as fact and ignoring her as an individual. And *Vogue*, the bible of all things beauty and fashion, touted Produits Organiques on its editorial page as the most important moisturizer a woman could have, created as it was by the French specialist Nina. In an aside, *Vogue* intimated, "Nina, as you might guess, is a Parisienne."[115]

In the more overtly capitalist United States, where corporations can be seen as cultural drivers, iterations of acceptance of Parisian chicness abounded in the market. A wide range of beauty salons and cosmetics companies regularly adopted French names, including the Chic Parisienne[116] makeup company, headquartered not in France but in Hartsdale, New York. "Heaven Is Here!" announced an ad by the Jantzen undergarment company in *Vogue* in 1960. What was this celestial paradise? Jantzen's new "panty-girdle," called the "Parisienne Panel," which the company deemed "a joy to wear!"[117] There was a "total beauty center" called La Parisienne in Boston's Roxbury neighbourhood, a full-service complex catering to black women and men's beauty needs. La Parisienne salon offered an astonishing array of aesthetically driven services, including, according to an interview with its owner, "boutique, beauty salon, makeup counselling, male grooming, exercise room, sauna, wig shop and hair styling."[118] And fashion house head Jerry Silverman and designer Shannon Rodgers more blatantly borrowed from French aesthetics, according to their ad, by successfully translating the "smart, easy-to-wear" look of a French woman into American ready-to-wear in a collection they modelled on French designs and then called "La Petite Parisienne."[119] The idea of French women's aesthetic superiority had legs, not only in France, but also in the United States, the image's intended target.

French aesthetic authority was not limited to cosmetic products in the eyes of US consumers. For an American, to be called fashionable by a French woman felt like a real achievement. In 1963, the *Los Angeles Times* splashed a large "MERCI!" across its headlines, paying thanks to the wife of the French ambassador, Mme Hervé Alphand, who deemed California's women more fashionable than their East Coast counterparts. The paper exalted over the judgment, crowing, "when a Parisienne refers to Southern California women as 'elegant' and better dressed than easterners, that's news."[120] Here, the paper clearly lends aesthetic authority to one Parisian woman, deeming her opinion the end-all when it came to American women's appearance.

Woman on the Riviera – Sex and Bikinis

If the elegant, chic Parisienne was one side of the French feminine coin, then the earthy Riviera seductress was the other in cultural manifestations of French women in the postwar era. While the qualities of both were present in the other, when writers described these two versions of French women, they tended to stick to those tropes. It was in the latter where Brigitte Bardot's influence was more directly seen, so identified was she with the Riviera region and specifically with Saint-Tropez, her adopted hometown.[121] BB's beauty, her clothing – or lack thereof – and her overall sensuality translated directly to the women of the region in the minds of writers, who described them in erotic tones.

Humour writer David Dodge recalled an early trip to Europe with a college friend, George, in which they drove along La Croisette, a beachside boulevard in Cannes. Fresh from Boston, their puritanical expectations quickly clashed with the Riviera's sensual attractions, at least in Dodge's recounting. "The pedestrians [along La Croisette]," Dodge recalled, "are often French girls on their way to or from the beach, and French girls are not only justly proud of their lovely figures but uninhibited about exposing them to the healthful rays of the sun." Dodge went on to detail some of the attractions of this Riviera femocracy: "That particular summer a favorite bathing costume for young women at Cannes consisted of a small *cache-sexe*, or basic triangle, plus two round patches at a higher level which were attached to the wearer by suction or glue or will power, I'm not sure which." Dodge's friend George promptly nearly crashed their car at the sight of all of the beautiful, scantily clad young women. Dodge, alarmed at his friend's lack of ability to watch the road and ignore the many French beauties, screamed, "'Watch where you're going!' 'How can I? Holy mackerel! Look at *that* one!'" In Dodge's account, George's reaction challenged earthly laws: "His hat jumped three feet straight up in the air, the way startled hats jump in the funny papers, although I suppose it was only a trick of the breeze. I said, 'She's got nothing you can't gawp at on the beach any time you're interested. Keep your eyes on the *road*.' 'I'm – My *God!* Where are the police? This is incred – *Look* at that! And *that!* They're all stark, staring naked! Do you mean to sit there and tell me – .'"[122] At that moment, overwhelmed by the allure of the female scenery, George crashed the car into a palm tree.

While the story Dodge tells is comical and fanciful (and likely dubious), Americans' reactions to the Riviera included many of the themes Dodge touched upon in his farce. Much like Brigitte Bardot's bikini came to define her as an object of lust, the bathing suits along the Riviera became symbolic of the sexual lasciviousness of the region as a whole, and the women who wore them were often painted with the same brush. Tourists would be remiss, guidebook author Harvey Olson advised in 1967, if they did not stop in Antibes, a town he paints as "noted for its chic shops and flower-fringed promenades decorated with fetching females." Olson particularly recommended patronizing the Hotel du Cap at Eden Roc in Antibes, where "scantily-clad swimmers and sun bathers perched on the rocks high above the shimmering sea."[123] Here, the swimmers and sunbathers are attractions in and of themselves, calling up complicated questions about the gaze and power. If the selling of French women's charms to the world was supposed to bring power and prestige to France, then the people of France ought to be more than objects in the equation. Olson went on to deem Nice another unmissable destination, largely because of its "round-heeled girls (and girls and girls)."[124]

If the Dior dress was the sartorial embodiment of the Air France hostess, herself an *ambassadrice* of French femininity and style, the bikini was the uniform of the French Riviera woman, symbolizing her sultry, wanton approach to life, another facet of the perfect French woman. The bikini had in fact been born in France in 1946; two designers, Louis Réard and Jacques Heim, were both apparently inspired by the Bikini Atoll. (Heim initially referred to his design as the "Atome," in reference to the nuclear testing at the site.) At the time, the scanty two-piece swimsuit was considered so scandalous that it was worn only by dancers at the risqué nightclub Folies-Bergère. Americans in particular displayed a sense of shock at the lack of coverage, but that shock was, as this section will show, tinged with voyeurism, making the bikini a major draw for travellers.[125]

The government, in travel posters and advertisements, officially promoted bikini-clad women as part of the scenery of a standard French vacation, and travel writers responded enthusiastically. "The bikini," one writer intoned in 1961, "always reigns supreme on the Côte d'Azur, the French Riviera."[126] Writers lavished attention on the swimsuit, deeming the garment – and presumably the woman wearing it – emblematic of the many treasures the French Riviera could offer. The bikini, according to travel writer John Handley, was one of the main reasons to visit the Riviera at all. In a column attempting to persuade readers to patronize the region, he cited "People-Watching" as the top activity, the rationale for going. Handley advised his readers to "Clean your sunglasses," going on to appeal especially to "girl-watchers," who "should know that the bikini was born on the Riviera but fortunately has never grown up; that is, it has never gotten any larger."[127] Handley later repeated his recommendation, writing "the spectacle on the beach is all a girl-watcher ever thought the Rivera could be." Here, Handley, in 1971, writes under the assumption that by that year, most readers had an idea of the Riviera entrenched in their minds, and in his article he confirms that assumption. This assumption speaks to the success of years of French tourism campaigns, and in the case of the Riviera, French tourism could be summed up in its association with scantily clad women. In 1957, many years earlier, travel writer Horace Sutton also characterized bikini-watching along the Riviera as "one of the prime industries of the Côte d'Azur," along with activities like "perfume mixing" and "bet-making."[128] Here, Sutton implies that the women of the Riviera are, like perfume, emblems of the region, produced to attract tourists. Herb Daniels, a well-known travel writer for the *Chicago Tribune*, waggishly chastised himself at the end of an article for the number of mentions he afforded the bikini in an article that was meant to cover the many tourist attractions of the Riviera: "And did I mention those international beauties in bikinis? I guess I did."[129] Bikinis were a sign that you had arrived at the Riviera, according to one writer. "When you wake up in the morning, on the night train from Florence to Nice," women's columnist Eugenia Sheppard recounted, "the first thing you see, besides the cerise and purple bougainvillea vines on the stone walls are girls, hundreds of girls, in bikini bathing suits."[130] In Sheppard's telling, the girls in bikinis are like native fauna, counterpart to the famous flora of the Riviera.

Of course the body underneath the bikini needed to be worthy of the garment: either be thin or do not dare to wear that bathing suit. And writers planted the seed that if you were not wearing a bikini, then you might not belong on the Riviera – or perhaps in France. As one writer stated in 1970, "In St Tropez ... there is no doubt what kind of bikini you should wear. All the sleekest, brownest girls are showing off their tans through the Bikini With The Holes." But the garment was not for everyone, the writer cautioned, even writing "WARNING: Bikini '70 is not ideal for the woman with even an ounce of surplus."[131] Even much earlier, in 1952, regulating bikini bodies was already part and parcel of life, and reports, on the Riviera. Paul Friedlander, writing in the *New York Times*, associated the suit with the Riviera and exclusivity: "The bikini bathing suit, properly worn, which means mostly by a younger, slimmer generation, adds immeasurably to the gala atmosphere on the beach." Putting aside how women's scanty bathing suits in any form would affect the mood on a beach, Friedlander's article again reinforces the worthiness or unworthiness of certain female bodies. In this way, the restrictiveness associated with French women from the air hostess era transcended time and place but had a similar message. Either control your body, or you are unworthy of a public presence, and even a claim on French nationality. One newspaper writer, translating the bikini swimsuit for American wearers, cautioned that even bikinis' "most enthusiastic supporters … are firm that they belong on the young or those with young figures. We doubt if many will be sold in size 16 and up."[132] For Americans, the prevailing model of French feminine superiority meant that they needed to be thin if they wanted to even approach that level of perfection.

The pursuit of Riviera women was often described in guidebooks as a main tourist attraction. In Lyle Engel's 1973 book, one in which he heartily thanks the French government tourist office for its help, he listed the activities a traveller could enjoy along the Riviera. "Southern France is a vacationer's paradise," he declared, "whether you incline toward skiing, skin diving, gambling, sightseeing, or girl-watching. It offers pleasures at all prices."[133] In Engel's telling, the Riviera's reality goes beyond men's wildest dreams, in part because it is full of women, the pursuit of whom had morphed into tourist activities not to be missed.

There was a gender differential in how travel writers approached France, which perhaps reflected biases Americans already held, or perhaps biases that French officials had created. According to Christopher Endy, "in 1951, the Gallup Poll asked Americans for their 'first thoughts' on hearing the word 'Paris.' For men, the most popular responses were such travel icons as the Eiffel Tower, 'dancing girls,' and 'leg shows.' Among women, the list began with fashion, perfume, landmarks, and nightlife."[134] Sections aimed specifically at women travellers in guidebooks inevitably focused on what to buy in France, portraying shopping as a way to attempt to capture a little bit of that elusive French feminine magic.[135]

This kind of consumerism redounded to the French economy. American spending was, as noted earlier in the book, pivotal to the recovery of Europe after the Second World War. As Endy reported, "the average American traveler in 1950 spent $742 in Europe and the Mediterranean, a figure that did not include the ocean crossing, whose costs often went to European carriers." And in 1949, Endy continues, American spending "provided approximately one-fourth of all dollars earned by Western Europe."[136] French political figures knew those figures well. In 1950, Senator Jules Pouget spoke about the association of the tourism industry and the luxury industries that gained France global fame. "The stimulating role of tourism on the French economy is particularly important in the luxury industries," he intoned, "which are directly affiliated with the tourism industry and so specifically associated with France." Pouget went on to point out how Americans benefited from duty-free shopping and advocated for freer "movement of capital" to capitalize on existing interest in French luxury shopping.[137] One branch of these luxury industries, the fashion industry, welcomed American dollars – while maintaining the mystique of the French couture system. In the later years of the period covered in this book, however, couture spending among French women plummeted, leading fashion houses to both diversify their products and attempt to attract foreign consumers. In one startling statistic, the Dior house had more than 25,000 couture customers in 1955; in 1989, Dior and Yves Saint-Laurent (who once worked at Dior) had a combined total of 200, "mostly Americans and Arabs," according to fashion historian Diana Crane.[138] The government's push on tourism aided French couturiers, who now relied on American women to shop their brands; it is no accident that, in American *Vogue*, the number of fashion advertisements doubled between 1947 and 1977, a period that also saw *Vogue's* subscriptions nearly triple.[139]

Even as early as 1945, the members of the Women's Auxiliary Corps stationed in Paris were, according to the media, "the envy of girls all over the world" because of their access to France's luxury consumer goods, and male GIs who came home empty-handed from a posting in France faced approbation from their wives.[140] Here, French women were again objects of consumption, but in a more sartorial and less sexual manner, one that emphasized French women's supreme elegance – and reinforced American women's difficulty in matching it. Writer Alice Martin, who contributed a chapter on shopping to the early edition of *Fodor's Guide*, noted the pressure to conform in terms of fashion. She described a feeling of frustration and inadequacy: "After one hour on the Faubourg Saint-Honoré you'll suspect your skirt's too long, your hat's too practical, your perfume doesn't do a thing for you. *Voilà!* You've got Parisian shopping fever, and you've got it bad!"[141] Shopping for assimilation was a futile exercise, according to writer David Dodge, who penned several tongue-in-cheek guidebooks in the 1950s and 1960s. In his *Poor Man's Guide to Europe*, he described shopping in France as especially geared toward women:

> Where France is involved the list [of good buys] is often unusually long, particularly in regard to items which are designed for ornamentation of the female frame and fixtures. France produces some of the loveliest luxury goods in the world to hang on a dame – perfume, *haute couture*, jewelry, gloves, handbags, hats, lingerie. These things and others like them on the French market are world famous, justifiably so. The sight of a good-looking French doll tripping along the Champs Élysées done up in her Sunday best will knock most normal American males for a row of *prises d'eau*, or French fireplugs. Some wives I know, naming no names, are inclined to say, "Humph! *I* could look like that myself if you weren't so tight-fisted,"

but husbands should never fall for this argument. In the first place most wives couldn't match a Frenchwoman's natural-born *chic* in a million years, given an unlimited amount of money to spend on themselves.[142]

With that breathtaking insult both to his wife as well as to all non-French women, Dodge also reveals how profoundly French women's aesthetic superiority had penetrated the consciousness of Americans, regardless of gender.

Cross-cultural translations provide an interesting insight into French feminine supremacy in action. One of the most important translators was Célia Bertin, a major postwar popular literary figure, having won the Prix Renaudot, an award for literary excellence second only to the Prix Goncourt in France, in 1953. Bertin was later presented with both the Legion of Honour and the Order of Arts and Letters, two of France's most prestigious accolades. Célia Bertin's book, *Paris à la Mode*, was first published in French, then English in 1957, and in it she positioned herself as a sort of investigator and then translator of the fashion industry to aficionados on both sides of the Atlantic. Bertin subscribed to the notion that there was something eternal and perhaps even mystical to the relationship between France, femininity, and fashion. Visitors to the city of Paris, well-heeled or not, Bertin wrote, feel intimidated by its chicness:

> One breathes with the very air of Paris this extraordinary sense of "not too little, not too much," and women, whether they be Parisians, South Americans or Hindus, know very well that what they buy here is not acquired simply by virtue of the money they may be able to spend … From no other source [besides Paris fashion] have I ever seen the same harmony of easy grace. All this is known by instinct, but never put into words. Those who work in *couture* are impregnated with it, as they are with the beauty of our city.[143]

Later in the book, Bertin reiterated the secret ingredient that attracted so many people around the globe to French clothes, stating simply, "it is Paris which makes fashion."[144] By this statement she meant not only that Paris was a physical city where people constructed fine clothing and dictated trends to the world, a stunning assertion of economic and cultural power, but also that Paris was the key ingredient, along with femininity and skill, that provided that mystical allure. But if Paris was indeed the necessary element, then fashion was exclusive to those who knew Paris, who lived there, or even only people who were born there. Bertin seemed to confirm the closed circle of fashion know-how when she connected the role that fashion played in popular culture, particularly song, where writers "know that by honoring this industry, which is both art and unquestionably a spontaneous expression of the grace and delicacy, at once grave and gay, that we Parisians love, they will go straight to the heart of every man and woman in this city."¹⁴⁵ Perhaps American money could open doors, but Paris fashion would remain an enigma forever.

Despite the futility of accessing real French style, guidebooks pushed American women travellers to at least attempt to emulate their more "correct" French counterparts. Most writers published sections on hairstyling, for example, citing how gifted French women were in the beauty department. In her popular novel for young adults, *Fashion for Cinderella*, Laura Vitray, herself an American who moved to France, describes how Cynthia, a young Wisconsinite, desperately wanted to blend with the Parisian beauties. Her friend, Yvette, promised Cynthia she would do her best to teach her the essentials, and hair was high on the list. Yvette promises to take Cynthia to her hairdresser: "He will make a Parisian out of you," Yvette says. Then, reconsidering, Yvette qualifies her statement with "a little bit, anyhow. And then we will go shopping."¹⁴⁶ Temple Fielding counselled women to visit Alexandre, "where the world's most famous beauties now migrate, including our own Jacqueline Kennedy. The immediate predecessor, Guillaume ... is still fine, too ... ask for Mme Labbe. Both [salons] very social, both filled with capable light-footed gents, and both expensive as all get-out ... this nation has long been a leader in the art of hairdressing."¹⁴⁷ Homophobia aside for now, Fielding concurs with Vitray that the French are innately stylish, not solely with clothing, but also with the arts of grooming, hairstyling not least among them. However, should you be unable to score an appointment with a worthy hairstylist, Alice Martin advocated shopping again: "You can fool all of the people all of the time with a Paris hat."¹⁴⁸

For American women travelling to the Riviera in the post-Bardot era, the bikini was a required item to pack – given, of course that their bodies merited such a choice. Indeed, one cultural historian, Patrik Alak, argued that the moment Bardot slinked her way across the screen in a bikini in *And God Created Woman* was a watershed translational moment for American women. Her walk along the beach, Alak wrote, "was followed not only by the camera but also by the attentive eyes of thousands of female moviegoers who intended the following summer to be wearing an identical costume."¹⁴⁹ Popular as the film was in the United States, the pressure on women to not only own a bikini, but display a body worthy of it, was intense. In 1960, women's columnist Eugenia Sheppard suggested that someone should pen a guide for women about what to wear to the Riviera – and then proceeded to write a short version herself. In addition to Pucci scarves and cropped pants, she ordered readers to remember the bikini if they wanted to blend in with the French. "No girl with a passable figure," Sheppard counselled, "is wearing more than a couple of cotton handkerchiefs' worth of fabric to take the sun or salt water anywhere along the Riviera these days."¹⁵⁰ If you want to fit in with French women, fashion columnist Estella Atwell advised, "be prepared – it takes many spiffy resort fashions to keep up with the Riviera pace." Atwell elaborated that a woman traveller ought to bring a bikini swimsuit, adding a sardonic "of course," as though that statement was so obvious as to be beneath Atwell's standing as an expert on French Riviera fashion.[151]

When French women were so clearly superior to their American counterparts aesthetically, the process of packing for a trip to France and trying desperately to fit in and look chic was one fraught with anxiety. Guidebooks fostered this anxiety and advised women on what to wear. In Lyle Engel's 1973 entry into the genre for Simon and Schuster, he clearly straddled the line between advice and criticism, writing, "Other guidebooks may caution women to take their 'most comfortable shoes.' Yes, take something you can walk in for hours – but don't limit your shoe wardrobe to flats. You'll want heels too, to compete with the well-shod Parisiennes ... If you're heading for a Mediterranean resort, and are proud of your figure, take a bikini or buy one there. Otherwise, you'll be overdressed. On a Riviera beach, the one-piece bathing suit looks like grandma's bathing costume."[152] In heading to France, clearly no woman wanted to look like Grandma; rather Engel's expectation was that she would want to "compete with the ... Parisiennes." Engel, who thanked the French tourism board for all of their help in his introduction,[153] here reveals an interesting undercurrent to all of this talk about femininity and fitting in: the sense of competition it fostered between women, here women of different nationalities.

Perhaps most disturbing was the analysis by *Fodor's* about the underpinnings of this construction of femininity. "But for whose delight are women so extravagantly adorned? For whose delight do the women of France make themselves delectable?" Fodor's then answered these questions in definitive fashion: "The ultimate consumer is the male. All down the line, from the society beauty at the top to the factory girl at the bottom, the French woman adorns herself for the pleasure of the French male. It is for the delight of the male that Paris, a man's town, has produced that triumph among her creations, the *Parisienne*, the brightest spot in the crowds that stream by you as you sit indolently on your café terrace, drinking in the spectacle of the streets."[154] The quote here comes from a 1973 edition of *Fodor's* guide to Paris, which included a new, expanded section of content on the *parisienne*; the earlier editions simply mentioned her as a popular figure. Fodor's focus, presumably market- and research-driven, suggests that in the years between the 1950s and the 1970s, Americans' ideas about Parisian women had crystallized and needed to be exploited to sell more books. Also, the book casually reveals a central thesis of this project – that the entire project of crafting the *parisienne* is for men's benefit. Here, *Fodor's* suggests that it is the women who are in control in some way, interpreting and performing in a show controlled by men. But *Fodor's* also explicitly asks and answers the *cui bono* question, stating that it is Paris that has somehow created the *parisienne*, as though a city could manufacture women, in order to please men. In fact, individuals did undoubtedly take pleasure in a variety of ways from women's aesthetic ministrations, but in reality, the larger state apparatus both promoted and capitalized on the primacy of French femininity.

Conclusion

This touristic profiteering off of women, particularly French women in France, is not dissimilar to the French state's deployment of air hostesses as *ambassadrices*. It exhibits a concerted pattern in how stakeholders in the postwar era successfully identified France's attractions for external observers – in this case charming, elegant, and alluring women – and weaponized them in order to bring prestige and power to the state of France. The fact that the model of feminine perfection actually crossed the Atlantic, and that Americans tapped into assertions of French feminine sensuality so profoundly, stand as proof of the project's success. It also attests to the importance of translational figures, those travel writers, actresses, models, and cultural thinkers and authors who served as cultural explainers for Americans, the targets of French advertising campaigns. These translational figures simultaneously helped to hone a vision of heteronormative French female excellence while explaining it to both men and women, albeit for different purposes. For men, the image of French femininity was one of sensuality and accessibility; it represented a visual product they could consume, and perhaps a more tactile experience they could aspire to, as the following chapter will show, by visiting the Hexagon. For women, French femininity represented the opposite – complete *inaccessibility*, but also a responsibility to at least attempt to live up to French feminine perfection. Within that inaccessibility, the aspirational exigencies still remained, as the discussion of bikini bodies makes clear. The power of such efforts is undeniable. Even today, French femininity remains the standard to which so many women worldwide look. If judging success on the basis of duration and financial gains, the model of French femininity is undoubtedly triumphant. If, however, judging on the basis of the millions of small cuts and large wounds women feel for not reaching that aesthetic pinnacle, for not looking and feeling alluring and thin and elegant at all times, then the model is problematic, if not outright dangerous.

Chapter Five

The Gendering and Selling of France

In 1971, Cynthia Proulx and Ian Keown, an Anglo-American couple, the male half of which was a famous and prolific travel writer, published a book entitled *A Guide to France for Loving Couples*. The stated purpose of the book was to show amorous travellers the places in France where they could best explore their romantic, sexual sides. They suggestively contextualized the book, writing, "As Diane de Poitiers [herself the infamous mistress of Henri IV] was heard to murmur, it isn't *what* you do that counts. It's with whom you do it. And how well. Whatever it is you love doing together, we've found the perfect setting for it. In 31 different places from Paris to the Mediterranean. *Bon voyage*." In a footnote to the introduction, they added, "Trios, quartets, and other combinations are free to take the test, too."[1]

By the early 1970s, the identification of France as a place of romance and even libertinism was fairly common. As this chapter will demonstrate, Americans could come to the Hexagon, as Proulx and Keown suggested, to goggle at – and sometimes participate in – scenes of beauty, sex, and romance beyond their wildest dreams. What is also interesting is how France itself became a character in the tableau of sensual pleasures, often depicted as an inviting and alluring woman. Taken together, these images of sensuality present a striking contrast with the image of proper morality French officials embraced at the end of the Second World War in response to sexual aggression by American GIs. This chapter will focus on these two themes: France as a place where romance and sex were prevalent and France as a female character in the Gallic sensual tableau.

France as a Place of Romance

While individual French women represented notions of carnality in the eyes of their state and the world, as shown in the previous chapter, the actual country of France also became synonymous with sex, romance, and eroticism. Some of these notions are not new – Anglo-American travellers in particular had been associating France with sensuality since the time of the Grand Tour.[2] By the middle of the twentieth century, mass media and availability of air travel rendered French sensuality a far more accessible and potent phenomenon. As Christopher Endy has shown in his study of US-France tourism, tourist-class flights launched in early 1950s, allowing more middle-class Americans entrée into the world of European travel; economy class launched in 1958, offering even lower fares. Ultimately, Endy reports, "Americans in 1953 made 376,000 trips across the Atlantic, surpassing the previous record set in 1930. Volume doubled between 1953 and 1959 and doubled again to 1.4 million by 1965. In 1970, Americans made 2.9 million trips to Europe and the Mediterranean."[3] Attesting to the importance the French government ascribed to tourism, the Ministry of Tourism came under the direct supervision of the prime minister in 1962.[4] Americans were coming to France, and among the main lures, along with history and culture, were women, romance, and sex.

Most travellers from the United States during this postwar era did not choose package tours, but instead travelled independently. This development, Endy notes, led to a boom in travel guides.[5] As elucidated in the previous chapter, travel writers at the time acted as translators of culture to a brand-new audience, people who may have had little familiarity with European history and society, but who sought what had previously been an upper-class experience. Even in the years immediately following the Second World War, travel was largely still the bastion of the upper and upper-middle classes, given its high cost and the length of time it took to venture to Europe.[6] During the 1950s, though, travel became somewhat less expensive with the advent of tourist and then economy fares, and therefore more democratic as well, much to the consternation of more cosmopolitan Americans, who feared how Europeans would associate them with these new-money rubes, whom one chronicler referred to dismissively as "Perry Como fans."[7]

Still, for travellers of all kinds, France was *de rigueur* as a stop on a European tour; decidedly foreign and exotic, it felt like an adventure and escape from the pressures of home and the familiar. As Endy argues, France was not a place that had a history of immigration to the United States, making its customs incomprehensible at times.[8] For the less seasoned travellers, guidebooks could provide an object of comfort, an aid to navigating what seemed like a bewildering place, with its own rules and mores.

When postwar travel writers introduced the exotic country of France, it was in gendered ways. Interestingly, during the decades following the Second World War, the guidebooks gradually shifted from describing France and French landmarks in feminine, somewhat sensual, terms to describing France itself as a woman, one to be obtained and intimately known through personal encounter. Likely this progression has to do with two factors. First, the cultural mores with regard to sexuality loosened over the course of the period described in this book. As Sarah Fishman has demonstrated, sexual morality underwent gradual shifts throughout the 1950s and 1960s, culminating in far looser cultural norms, especially following the events of May 1968.[9] Second, the French campaign to promote the country as a beautiful woman had been successful, attracting people to the country, but also inculcating Americans with the idea that France was a place for sensual pleasure and French women were looser than their Anglo-American counterparts. Writers did not expound on the sensual charms of places like England, Norway, Germany, or Scotland. Writers' habits of attributing sensual, romantic, and/or more generally feminine characteristics to France attests to the success of earlier tourism campaigns on the part of the French state.

Travel writers in the early Cold War era were not the first authors to portray France as a woman. Historians such as Lynn Hunt, Robert Gildea, and Maurice Agulhon have demonstrated how depictions of France in feminine terms span the entire history of the country.[10] As recently as the Second World War, both Vichy officials and Resistance groups engaged in a full symbolic battle over whether France was Joan of Arc or Marianne or, in some cases, both. However, rather than using femininity to gain moral or political sympathy, postwar travel writers gender the nation of France as feminine in order to sell it to tourists.

In 1948, well-known travel writer Horace Sutton, the travel editor for the popular American magazine *Saturday Review*, wrote *Footloose in France*. If it was not the earliest postwar travel guide, it was definitely the most popular of its time. In the book, Sutton described his very first encounter with Paris, as a young, exhausted soldier who had traveled in discomfort to see the city, writing: "Paris won me over. A perfume seemed to fill the air – it was pulsating, exciting. This was what was different from London or Sioux City, from Chicago or Madrid. This … is the city for whom men cry when she is captive. Paris has a personality … Whatever else Paris may be, certainly it is a handsome lady with a past that an awful lot of people would travel a long way to see."[11] Those fond reminiscences, Sutton wrote, could now be found again, despite the wartime hardships and deprivations. In Sutton's account, Paris itself is a woman, for whom many men – but not, apparently, women – feel some sort of emotional attachment. Sutton relives his initial, palpable attraction to Paris; its aura and beauty drew him to the city. He describes the attraction, like that between potential lovers, in almost lurid terms, as "pulsating, exciting." Sutton asserts that he and others worried for this beautiful woman when she was captured. Describing Paris in current times, Sutton wrote, "the air is sweet, the crowds walk slowly, and – just like that! – a pretty French girl impulsively turns her head and kisses the cheek of her man. Paris is nearly Paris again. It's very plain to see."[12] In this florid telling, the kiss, especially coming from a "pretty French girl" is the emblem that tells Sutton that Paris is back. Sutton does not mention the Marshall Plan, responsible for the massive physical reconstruction of the country and its infrastructure, or even the ongoing trials of war criminals. Rather, it is the promise of romance, as embodied by a young French woman, which symbolizes Paris's recovery from war.

Horace Sutton deploys the two main tactics utilized by the many travel writers who wrote about France and "her" charms. First, he writes of the country (or city, or landmark, in some cases) as though it were a woman, rendering France a sexual object, an object to care for, or an object to cajole and please. Second, Sutton describes France as a place where romance, sex, and love are the paramount preoccupation, as well as a place where there are women to satisfy every whim.

Reaction to Sutton's travel guide was positive.[13] The book was glowingly reviewed in major publications across the United States, and it kick-started Sutton's popular *Footloose* series, which ultimately inspired other travel writers to adopt Sutton's more casual, literary style. A headline for the book's review in the *Washington Post* gushed that the guide "lilts like Gershwin"; the article goes on to say, "This is my idea of what a guidebook should be. It is gay, informative, up to date and excellently written. It is never blase [*sic*], patronizing or parochial. It is the product of a young American who gets a terrific kick out of life and currently is very much in love with Paris. It should start a new wave of tourists headed for the timeless capital of France."[14] Other reviewers echoed the *Post*'s lavish praise, alerting readers to its "witty" prose, calling it "indispensable" for travellers.[15] Indeed, a writer for the *Los Angeles Times* described the book itself as alluring, much like its subject, stating that it "will tempt any hesitant traveler into rushing down to Air France and booking passage" with its descriptions of winemaking, cathedrals, cycling, and "the shows at the Folies Bergere, the night clubs at the Place Pigalle and bathing suits on the French Riviera."[16] Tellingly, it was a *New York Times* reviewer, Samuel Putnam, who advised readers that "if you can't visit or revisit France, reading [Sutton] is about the next best thing."[17] Through books like Putnam's, it was not only transoceanic travellers who could take in ideas about France's charms; devoid of practical applications, these books could be read far and wide as literature, thus giving flight to fantasies about France. The impact of Sutton's 1948 book was intensified when it was reissued in 1954, attesting to its popularity and resonance with travellers to France.[18]

Guidebooks emphasized how the inimitable women of France, like their Air France *ambassadrice* counterparts, offered a warm welcome to tourists. Writers communicated how tourists could expect to encounter beautiful French women as part of the scenery alongside the Louvre and the Riviera beaches. "The Parisian woman," guidebook author Claire Segal intoned, "dresses to be attractive to men even on the tiniest budget. When she wears a shirt it fits as though custom-made, even if it cost less than 20F (and, more than likely, she'll wear it unbuttoned enough to make it provocative). She has flair and style, even in jeans. And the way she carries herself shows she knows it."[19] Expatriate writer and lawyer James E. Thomas commented on the diversity of the Parisian woman, as well as her defining quality – her self-conscious aesthetic superiority:

> The Parisienne will pass by, in her hundreds and in her thousands. Midinettes and matrons, office girls, shop assistants, fashion models, elegantly aristocratic ladies with haughty, unfriendly stares, other ladies, not so aristocratic, and with a pleasant look for anyone who seeks congenial company to share an afternoon's leisure, all differing vastly, yet having one common denominator, the Parisian woman's "chic," both in the choosing of her clothes and in her manner of wearing them. The midinette may have a cheap print dress which she has confected herself, the aristocratic-looking lady walking behind her may have spent extravagantly in the salons of a great French "couturier," yet you will find that each has that same indefinable quality that seems to stamp every Parisienne, the faculty of choosing just the right clothes, and of wearing them superbly.[20]

Thomas expanded upon his description with a sort of ode to the woman of Paris: "The Parisienne! Authors, psychologists, ordinary men and extraordinary men have squandered their resources in an unceasing attempt to pin down this magnificent specimen on their collector's board. But she has eluded them all. Apparently light-hearted, gay, always ready to sip at the cup of pleasure which the moment may offer her."[21] And Horace Sutton, advising readers on the French climate, even linked such banal information as advice about the weather to the women of France. Paris is quite temperate, he noted, which "is also an incentive for chic ladies to stroll along the boulevards during most of the year, a fact which has helped to make Paris the fashion capital of the world, according to a minority opinion."[22] Humour writer David Dodge laid out the must-view sights of Paris explicitly in his guidebook in a long list, which included the Louvre and the Eiffel Tower "and the Tuileries and the Luxembourg Gardens, and the restaurants and the food and the wine *and the absolutely stunning women you see in the street* and the smell of roasting chestnuts on a nippy fall evening and the taste of onion soup and freshly baked bread at Les Halles at five o'clock of a summer morning ... and several thousand other aspects of Paris which make it the queen of all cities"[23] [emphasis mine]. If physical landmarks like buildings and parks and neighbourhoods could form unexpectedly romantic components of a trip, the French woman, and particularly the *parisienne*, was, like the Eiffel Tower or the Louvre, a definite must-see.

5.1. Air France capitalized on the popularity of its hostesses to sell the company – and France. Here, a hostess features prominently in one of Air France's campaigns, which depicts her as one of the many famous attractions awaiting visitors to France (1971). Courtesy of the Air France Museum.

France Is a Place Where Romance Happens

In their 1963 guidebook *Paris!*, Sylvia and Lawrence Martin devoted an entire section to the tourist attraction of … "LOVE-MAKING," which they called "by far the Parisian's most popular sport." Like seeing art in a museum, they went on, "hugging, kissing, snuggling, cuddling, cooing, nuzzling couples are all over the place. You see them even in the crowded Métro coaches, the loving couple hemmed in, and loving it … From the old Academician who has nothing left but his memories, to the young teen-ager who has nothing but hopes, the Parisian loves love." They then made the argument that Americans and French people had very distinct attitudes toward the national sport. "The American loves it too," they wrote, "but indirectly, through ads, the movies, and jazz ballads. It's different over there. The male loves women. The female loves men. As a result, the two sexes make contact with less difficulty than their opposite numbers in the Anglo-Saxon world. This is something you feel, as well as see, in Paris. It's in the air, it's catching." The Martins suggest that there is a mystical quality associated with Paris that can affect even the most jaded traveller. They continued to explain that even "the middle-aged or elderly tourist couple begins to feel he-ish and she-ish. But, not being French, they content themselves in public with holding hands." Again, expressing a sense that couples are a part of the French landscape, they made a suggestion for a new national monument, writing, "There should be an Arc de Triomphe in Paris put up to Venus and Cupid where foreigners could lay a wreath before an eternal flame in recognition of the French championship of the world."[24]

Guidebook authors emphasized the ubiquity of physical love in France, depicting it as a necessary experience for tourists to check off on their to-do lists, much like visiting Versailles Palace or eating a croissant. It was also inimical to the French, writers emphasized, distinguishing Gallic sensuality from Anglo-American prudery. As the Hollywood star – and Parisian transplant – Olivia de Havilland opined in her own story about falling in love in the Hexagon, France is clearly "the country most sympathetic to lovers."[25] Portrayals of the French as at ease with expressions of love proliferated in the postwar era. Two real-life lovers, one American and one British, taking their leave after a nighttime rendezvous in London during the Second World War, were the inspiration for Marcel Wallenstein's popular postwar pulp novel *Red Canvas*. Wallenstein, himself married to a French woman, contrasted American awkwardness with Gallic suaveness. He remembered, "I had seen many lovers' partings in Paris, usually before one of the little hotels at the end of the lunch hour. There the two always had something left to share, always a last clinging kiss. Love was a painful transaction for the Anglo-Saxons."[26] In the realm of *amour*, at least, the French triumphed.

Ads from the French state airline also promoted France as a place where couples could explore their own romantic predilections. In 1965, the company

5.2. The idea of Paris as a place of romance found support in advertisements like this one, depicting a happy tourist couple visiting one of the most popular sites in Paris, circa 1962. Courtesy of the Air France Museum.

used a poster that depicted a man and a woman near the Louvre, sitting with their heads together, looking at the Tuileries Garden, with the Eiffel Tower in the background.[27] A 1962 Air France advertisement used four separate images of couples enjoying themselves in Paris, whether walking a dog down the Champs-Élysées or strolling through Montmartre and smiling, eyes only for each other. The archival notes for that particular ad betray the company's aims, describing it as a "publicity document boasting about the joys of romantic visits [*visites en amoureux*] to Paris. Young couples seen near the Arc de Triomphe or Montmartre …"[28] In 1963, an ad for Air France, which was ultimately used in four different venues, featured a photograph of a couple in evening attire, sitting in a horse-drawn carriage in front of the Eiffel Tower.[29] In these images, the major landmarks of France play a central role, reminding potential tourists that France has this impressive history and culture, but also, and perhaps more importantly, given the foregrounding of the couples, that France is a place where couples – and romance – thrive.

Instead of emphasizing history and culture, some advertisements focused on sex and romance. Air Inter, another of France's public airlines, which focused more on domestic and continental flights, held a major promotional giveaway in 1970, in which it promised the winner a free weekend in a hotel in France. In order to promote the contest, Air Inter released a very suggestive ad, in which three couples were depicted in various locales, one cavorting on the tarmac and the two others within the hotel itself, one couple in a semi-dressed state just having enjoyed breakfast in bed.[30] Another Air Inter ad from the same year promoted the airline as the best way to enjoy a carefree weekend with a significant other. The headline read: "A getaway, a weekend, your first flight with Air Inter." One of the striking aspects of this ad is the acknowledgment that the couple in question is likely unmarried, and yet still taking a weekend getaway. While the sexual revolution was in full bloom, this suggestion still would have been shocking, especially in its blatancy, even in 1970.[31] In this case the dominant picture in the ad consisted of a couple sitting close to one another, having a drink at a café, and staring into each other's eyes (the man's hand on the woman's cheek), all while looking out over a placid harbour scene.[32] Perhaps because Air Inter was identified more with domestic travel in France, the landmarks were taken for granted, and the sexual component of the ad could be more explicit.

Air France's embrace of heterosexual couples and their romantic love was nowhere more blatant than in an ad that ran in high-end magazines like *Vogue* in the late 1960s, which depicted a couple, hand-in-hand, taking in the sights of Paris. The extensive copy listed several sites in Paris dedicated to love [*Monuments d'amour*], and "Deserted Museums," where couples could celebrate romance both historical and contemporary. The ad also reinforced France's familiar association with romance: "You're young, you're in love, and you're coming to Paris. Welcome aboard the world's wisest airline, we know exactly how you feel. Our stewardesses are discreetly French. The service is unobtrusive. The meal will make you glow. Pull down the shade, watch the movie and hold hands. We won't mind. We're taking you to a city dedicated to the pursuit of happiness. We know where you're going."[33] Here, the sexual undertones – and overtones – are clear. Paris is a place for sex and love, and Air France hostesses' responsibility is to enable it in whatever way possible.

For authors promoting France, physical locations participated in the dance of romance. In her popular novel for young adults, *Fashion for Cinderella*, Laura Vitray, who had herself married a French man, sang Paris's praises, describing it as a place that simply oozed romance. Vitray wrote: "Spring, more enchanting in Paris than anywhere else in the world, had spread a veil of golden tulle over the city. The river cut through it like a belt of shining silver. The Tuileries Gardens were embroidered with gorgeous flowers; the Champs Elysées, from the Place de la Concorde to the Rond Point, wore sleeves of variegated green that no designer could hope to imitate. Even the business sections like the grand boulevards, or the ancient, narrow streets on the left bank, breathed the aroma of romance."[34] In Vitray's words, Paris is a romantic, beautiful woman, clothed in the voluptuous haute couture that only the French could create.

Other writers were far more direct in equating France with sex and romance. As renowned travel writer Horace Sutton wrote in 1957, "It is widely rumored that in many parts of France French people are acutely interested in the birds and the bees."[35] Sutton was writing about exploring the wine region of Burgundy, which should presumably have nothing to do with sex. In this, Sutton was not alone in making these associative leaps. In a book review, columnist Ruth Wagner described the French language as one of pleasure: "The French have words for it. Fascinating words, when 'it' concerns romance, beauty, good living and the like."[36] A 1950 newswire story about an infamous crime in France, a daring robbery of the Aga Khan, referenced the nation's purported predilection for the art of love, beginning with the line, "France, as everyone knows, is a land of friendship, philosophy, and romance."[37] The assumption that "everyone knows" about France's essential characteristics proves just how deeply the conflation of France and romance had penetrated the global consciousness. This is but a small sample of similar articles and statements about the pleasure-seeking nature of the people of France.

One guidebook explicitly catered to couples seeking romance and sex in the Hexagon. In the aforementioned *Guide to France for Loving Couples*, Cynthia Proulx and Ian Keown deliberately suggested hotels and experiences that would fulfil couples' sensual expectations of France. They wrote, "maybe Paris isn't the most romantic city on earth. But a hundred movies, a thousand love songs, and about 50 million lovers say it is. They can't all be wrong ... trust your instincts to lead you to your own little finds, where $8.50 can buy an excellent dinner for two with enough candlelight, quiet, and good wine to make holding hands and sighing sighs a natural reflex again."[38] Here, Paris was a restorative agent, able to help couples spark the romance that their presumably sad Anglo lives lacked. Proulx and Keown had far more concrete suggestions for this amorous reclamation as well. For example, they recommended that Parisian travellers stay in the Ritz Hotel if at all possible. The Ritz was expensive, they acknowledged, but worthwhile, for "how many times do you have a chance to make love in a national monument? Sometime after midnight, have the sommerlier [sic] bring you a bottle of Dom Pérignon, have the chambermaid throw back the draperies, clap your hands in a kingly manner, and voilà – the floodlights on the Place Vendôme pop on ... Just for your love. A courtesan at the peak of her profession could ask for no more."[39]

When it came time to dining, another of the sensual pleasures at which the French excelled, the book recommended two kinds of restaurants. The first type was one where the food was secondary to the beautiful people around the table, like Moustache in Paris's 7th arrondissement, which they described as "more for admiring clusters of great-looking girls and their cinema-vérité playmates than for grand cuisine. But go anyway – the view is ravishing." The second type was quiet and intimate, a place for reconnecting, like La Taverne du Sergent Recruteur in the 4th arrondissement: "Small, hushed, and candlelit, this is a place for whispering secrets, holding hands, and letting the *vin rouge* go to your head."[40] No matter what, the food would be very good, the book assured readers, for "it is one of the great achievements of the French that they have acquired a reputation both for cuisine *and* amour."[41] It is interesting that here the great French achievements are not historical, economic, military, or artistic, as in the French promotional literature and tourist information of the past; rather they are ones associated with sensual pleasure. Jean Sainteny's earlier demand (cited in the previous chapter) that the French government look beyond traditional attractions to drive tourism to the Hexagon, had clearly resonated.

Paris was not the only place in France where couples could heighten their experiences of love. For example, Proulx and Keown recommended a particularly discreet hotel in Burgundy, where the owner eschewed guest books, deeming them "too dangerous." Why the danger? The hotelier, René Hure, went on to explain: "Perhaps a husband arrives this week with a lady friend and next month her husband arrives with his ..." The authors, Proulx and Keown, deemed Hure's policy "probably a wise precaution because La Poste is as cozy a trysting place today as it has been for two and a half centuries."[42] The sexual morality associated with Americans, the main tourist targets of France, could be tossed aside in favour of sensual experiences and experimentation in France. Proulx and Keown told readers to pay particular attention to the pool at the pleasure-filled Hotel Byblos in Saint-Tropez, popular with Brigitte Bardot, where "you'll see a sexy sculpture of the mythological Leda rapturously enfolded by her loving swan. Probably more than any other one thing, this little piece of granite characterizes the out-and-out hedonism of this remarkable hotel."[43] At the Cap Estel in Èze, they described how a traveller could request anything at all: "Whatever you want you get. Fast." They suggested spending those requests on "a vibrating massager – either man or machine (the hotel provides both, in your room or at the sauna baths)."[44] Discretion was the word in the Chateau de Mercuès, near Cahors, where couples could stay in an isolated old tower. There, "only the larks can see you, and they won't tattle."[45]

Nightclubs formed another major component of guidebooks' recommendations in France, acting as they did as spaces where tourists could have uniquely Gallic experiences of erotic floor shows, described in one guidebook as something "like you never saw in Peoria!"[46] Nightclubs, writers advised, were ubiquitous, catering to all manner of tastes. In his section devoted to Paris nightlife, doyen travel writer Temple Fielding noted the clubs' ubiquity: "practically on every corner ... Take your pick, because Paris has them all."[47] Fielding then recommended several clubs in his book, including Le-Sexy, a club in Paris "stuffed with slack-jawed, bug-eyed gents" there to see "scintillating – if not tit-tillating poses by luscious bonbons ... Provocative." Or perhaps, he continued, your tastes ran more toward Lucky Strip, which he described as "the type of place where you could take your children – *if* they happened to be junior delinquents." Maybe you would be more interested in La Dolce Vita, where "Lauren-Bacall-voiced Manageress Catherine Zago is a charming hostess who casts a mystic spell of her own."[48] The Paris clubs, Martin Fleer advised in *Fodor's Guide*, were indeed "noted for the amount of clothes female entertainers do not wear." Given that, one of his highest recommendations was Club Paradise near Pigalle, where the performance consisted of a high-stakes wrestling match. "The main event," as Fleer described it, "is when a big sort of boxing ring is set up and the Jarretelle Catch is announced. *Jarretelle* means garter. One gets the idea immediately when two female wrestlers appear in the ring wearing one-piece bathing suits and a garter on each thigh."[49]

The two most famous clubs in Paris during this time were the Folies-Bergère and the Lido, which, by Temple Fielding's description, were "about as popular with Americans as the World's Series" [*sic*]."[50] Guidebook writers both fostered and responded to nightclubs' popularity. Virginia Creed and Henry Milo reported that "some visitors come to Paris chiefly on account of its night life, which is varied and can be brilliant, sordid, or merely fun ... Everyone wants to see the Folies Bergère once."[51] Harvey Olson wrote, "It is not unusual for a visiting American to enjoy the worldly pleasures of the Folies Bergère, Lido, Casino de Paris, Le Jockey, and Nouvelle Ève, in five days' time."[52] Olson especially raved about the Lido, calling it "the quintessence of international entertainment at its best." What was this cultural phenomenon? In Olson's further description, it was where "the girls, who appear nude from the waist up, are usually bosomy, hippy French demoiselles who reveal their charms and hide their defects." He compared the French dancers favourably to their English counterparts, remarking in some astonishment that "one wouldn't believe that the narrow English Channel separates such diverse female forms."[53] Paris was synonymous with beautiful, nude women, and for Olson, the Lido was unsurpassed in that regard.

The Riviera also offered night clubs with beautiful, near-nude women. In 1948, Stuart Murray colourfully described the typical reaction to a famed Nice *boîte*, "the hat-check girl of the *Copacabana* won't mind if you are hatless when you arrive and breathless when you depart."[54] In his guide, Temple Fielding listed the "girlie cabarets" of Nice, which he labelled "tailor-made for butter-and-egg men with fistfuls of francs and a fine lack of interest in who grabs them."[55] Horace Sutton, who had been in France in the Second World War, described a different kind of club that had operated along the Riviera. It was, as Sutton noted, *the* place to mix and mingle with Riviera women. During the times the club was open, according to Sutton, "that's when the corps of French hostesses really rang the bell. The mademoiselles were paid assistants, hired by the Red Cross. If the army never had it so good, neither had they. They were danced, dated, wined, dined, and adored. One of the girls … said 'no' to no less than one thousand Yankee officers."[56] Flashing forward to 1948, the time of his book's publication, Sutton talks about how now the American fleet docks at Villefranche, where "it is said to be the ambition of every local maid to ensnare an American sailor when the fleet is in, and many maidens have turned the trick."[57] Here, the conflation of women lusting after American husbands with women helping GIs is interesting, painting as it does the potential for Americans to view all Riviera women as sexually available. It is also problematic, considering the high incidence of sexual violence and unwanted attention inflicted on French women during the war by American soldiers.

Some of the most controversial – and hence sought-after – shows flirted (or romanced openly) with homosexuality, still a major taboo in France and elsewhere in the 1950s and 1960s. Despite France's reputation as a place for all manner of sexual experiences, gay tourism was rarely mentioned by tourism experts. Julian Jackson has shown how, despite the reality of gay people visiting places in France and beyond, there were almost no guidebooks for gay tourists until the late 1960s. He argues it was only in the early 1970s, when police began ignoring anti-homosexual laws and a new generation of young gay people sought spaces to gather more openly that gay tourism became more public.[58] The research for this book turned up very few references to homosexuality in France, likely a reflection of archival and institutional silence rather than a lack of gay people visiting France.[59]

For the purposes of this project, when references to homosexuality did appear in print, they were certainly not offered as resources for gay travellers, but rather as a spectacle for heterosexual travellers to take in as part of their

Gallic experience. Keown and Proulx, for example, pointed to the Café Flore as a must-visit, along with its equally famous counterpart Les Deux Magots. They referred to the cafés as "the two most spellbinding entertainments in Paris," recommending them not because of the official floor shows but as places to observe the sexual peccadilloes of the patrons. "At Flore," they intoned, "what you'll see is a lot of fast and furious sexual shopping – most of it men-and-men and girls-and-girls." After that, they recommended a stop at Magots, "where things are a lot more hetero and a lot less tense. Either way, it's a great bargain – all for a 15-cent cup of coffee."[60] Proulx and Keown mentioned lesbianism as a small part of the show at the Crazy Horse Club: "The lights go off, the light show goes on, and there you have eight of the tastiest bodies ... you'll ever catch swinging a pelvis. The show ... is a combination sex parody and put-on with enough eroticism to keep your hormones humming for a week. The girls hand out a little something for everyone. Voyeurism. Lesbianism. Auto-eroticism (apparently, it doesn't make you blind after all) ... the essentials remain unchanged: great bodies going through all the motions with great style."[61] Proulx and Keown did recommend one club geared specifically toward lesbians, called Elle et Lui (She and Him) in the 6th arrondissement. They described the club's official show in desultory terms, saying it "consists of lesbian chanteuses, lesbian comediennes, and lesbian strippers. By and large, it's about as sexy as last year's dildo – and almost as awkward." For them, the real reason to patronize Elle et Lui was for "the *un*official show (meaning the customers)," which, they snickered, "is something else again. For instance, a tall, blond knockout about 23 walks in with a handsome boy (the real thing), demurely sips her drink until another boy (the unreal thing this time) asks her to dance. Our heroine spends the next half hour on the dance floor being kissed, caressed, and all but devoured by her dancing partner, who isn't, of course, doing much dancing."[62] These descriptions are clearly intended for curious heterosexuals, not as a resource for gay travellers.

What if the traveller was single? The previous chapter has already shown how the state airline sold licentious experiences as part of the overall allure of visiting France, while the state itself, at least early in the chronology covered by this book, insisted on the moral rectitude of its female population. Guidebooks and novels also offered seriously mixed messages about the sexual morality of French women. In his pulp novel *Red Canvas*, Marcel Wallenstein depicted the common narrative of French women's willingness to service GIs, portraying it as a reward for their liberation. When the Americans rolled into Paris, he described the scene as one of sexual chaos: "Girls were kissing the jeep driver ... 'He's mine,' one of the girls laughed. 'I shall marry him and go to America.' The others took turns kissing him. 'The little fat one,' the driver said. 'Tell her I'll bring the jeep here at eight tonight.' I made the assignation. The girl agreed with vigorous nods of her head. She was envied by them all. She kissed the driver again with moist ardor and said, 'Poor boy! I will kill you with love!'"[63] Later in the day, the narrator, standing in front of a hotel, surveyed a scene where "thousands of civilians crowded into the street ... An American was a novel and tremendously interesting species, worthy of all attention. Women of a type who do not loiter ogling strangers were there, ready for anything. A man had only to reach out his hand to find a delightful and willing companion."[64]

Particularly in the years closer to the war, when relations with the United States became fraught over allegations of sexual assault by GIs, many writers took pains to emphasize the good breeding of French women. No less than the US Department of Defense, in their 1951 guidebook to France for GIs, pointedly told soldiers to view France as more than a place to "cut loose ... France is *not* a frivolous nation where sly winks and coy pats are accepted forms of address ... you're going to be disappointed if you have the idea that you'll find a nation of pretty girls with you on their mind."[65] In a head-spinning twist, this stern assertion was, however, accompanied by a cartoon in which an officer is propositioned by two buxom women sitting in a café and drinking wine, with the caption "As always ... there are some fast gals in the business!"[66] George Mikes, a British satirist with a large American following, echoed this ambiguity in his own musings on French women. "I have heard it said," he wrote, "that it is easier to enter a Frenchwoman's bedroom than her dining room. This is basically true, in the sense that it is almost impossible for a foreigner to enter French family life." And not all French women are looking for sex, he conceded. When they did welcome sexual congress, though, it was a moment worthy of great celebration. According to Mikes, French women "love because they have warmth in their hearts and red blood in their veins. They love because they cannot help it. And – God! – how they love!"[67] Here, Mikes reinforces this double stereotype about French women – that they are somehow prudish and sexually reserved and simultaneously sexually insatiable. I speculate that this stereotype derives a constellation of forces in the postwar era, some having to do with the renegotiation of norms about sexuality more broadly in France and West, and some related to Americans' shifting assumptions about the French, influenced by France's own marketing.

Most guidebooks, in a nod to France's sexual reputation, included sections on prostitution and solicitation, despite its illegality at the time (the *loi Marthe Richard* had led to the closing of houses of prostitution in 1946). Temple Fielding reassured readers that "there are still plenty of streetwalkers, despite the current 'ban' on prostitution; there are still plenty of 'exhibitions,' orgies, gigolos, feelthy pictures [*sic*], if those are what you're looking for."[68] He reiterated the constancy of prostitution again later in the book; the best efforts of de Gaulle and the current regime, he observed, had failed to put a damper on the practice. Having spoken to prostitutes, he reassured readers that "business [was] never better."[69] Harvey Olson commented similarly on the situation of prostitutes, acknowledging legal shifts but asserting the quick availability and pervasiveness of prostitution in France's cities and towns: "Girls may not now walk the streets for soliciting purposes, but there is no law against walking their dogs ... On the Promenade des Anglais in Nice, the Champs-Élysées in Paris, and principal thoroughfares in other resorts and cities, one will always see swarms of dogs being aired by sexy looking dames. Not *every* girl who walks a dog is soliciting business, but many are. French girls brag that they instituted curb-side pickup service, and sleek cars scoot around the cities and resorts with gorgeous babes on the make ... France has changed but is still exuberant."[70] Indeed Olson spoke of the prostitutes as a wonderful benefit of activities like casino gambling along the Riviera. The women, he wrote, known as the "poules du casino," "are unofficial, and perhaps their presence would be denied by the managements, but each casino of France ... has a few unobtrusively attractive girls on hand to help winners celebrate and losers assuage their sorrows – and offer other feminine solace. Some wander from table to table making small wagers, others adorn the bar or terrace. They bleed beautifully into the scenery, and until you have been a regular in the casino for a few nights, they will not be readily apparent. But they're there – and eager. (For the uninitiated: *poule* – hen – is the standard and slightly improper slang for a girl of limited virtue.)"[71]

In Paris the Pigalle neighbourhood was the original centre of sex tourism for Americans, a distinction it had held for several generations. Once the home of artists and intellectuals in the nineteenth century, by the 1920s the Montmartre/Pigalle neighbourhood had become popular with tourists, who flocked to the clubs and cafés and engaged in what historian Roy Levenstein deemed the popular sport of "prostitute-watching," as well as partaking of the numerous shows and entertainments in the area.[72] In the 1930s, "Paris by Night" tours took travellers searching to gaze upon – if not touch – risqué attractions to nightclubs in Pigalle, and these same travellers, perhaps attracted by films like *Minuit, Place Pigalle*, which painted the location as the centre of Jazz Age Paris, also looked there for the salacious films, live shows, and photographs for which Paris had become famous.[73] During the war, Pigalle was a popular place for GIs, who famously dubbed it "Pig Alley," looking to blow off steam. Mary Louise Roberts has gone so far as to describe how the city of Paris "transformed itself into a lean, mean sex machine" to serve American soldiers, a machine in which Pigalle was a, if not the, main engine.[74]

After the Second World War, however, respectable American travel writers were divided on whether or not their readers ought to visit the neighbourhood. Horace Sutton's *Footloose in France* called "Paris after dark ... gay, exciting, and uninhibited." In places like Pigalle, he continued, "petite demoiselles will take you by the arm, and offer to show you things you never saw before."[75] Here, Sutton expresses a kind of exuberance for the carnal pleasures Pigalle could offer. Similarly, in his 1967 guidebook, Harvey Olson referred to Pigalle as "sometimes naughty, always exciting."[76] Columnist Joey Adams enthusiastically detailed his exploits on the rue Pigalle with his wife, Cindy, as they sampled some of the delights in the clubs on the first night of their honeymoon. Adams compared the street to Times Square in New York, but stated that Pigalle was on a whole other level in terms of lasciviousness, saying it made the New York fleshpots "look like an old maid show." Travel writer Gwen Morgan identified Pigalle in 1950 as one of the quintessential sights of Paris, along with Dior's atelier and Maxim's restaurant. "Up the shabby streets to Montmartre," she wrote in the *Chicago Tribune*, "night clubs served any drink with a fixed price of $5 a glass with views of female anatomy thrown in free. The Rue Pigalle, better known as Pig Alley, glowed with neon lights. Right on top of Montmartre, two giggling girls tried to lift their drunken escort from the gutter." It was, according to Morgan, all part of the atmosphere of Paris in the spring.[77]

Pigalle as a location to look for women had acquired a reputation as being somewhat washed up or disreputable. In her 1970 guidebook, Claire Segal acknowledged the American visitor's tendency to seek out women in Paris, but she advised against looking for them in Pigalle, with what she called its "rather beaten women." Instead, she counselled, look for women near the Arc de Triomphe, even offering specific instructions for how to go about soliciting available women: "Mini-Coopers are the little cars they favor, and they will probably drive, in pairs, with the interior light on so they can be spotted more easily."[78] In the words of William Buchanan, a *Boston Globe* reporter, Pigalle was "shoddy" and "ominous," and just because a traveller could buy "everything for a price" there in the year 1965, it did not mean he should.[79] Reporter Georges Menant, writing about crime in Paris in 1966, described Pigalle as a place where "the color has faded," and its attractions had become "old hat."[80] And H.P. Koenig of the *Chicago Tribune*, in an article narrating a full walking tour through the most glamorous places in France's capital city, warned that "American tourists would be well-advised to avoid this particular after-dark trap."[81]

In the event one wanted to import a bit of Paris to the United States, however, it seemed that Pigalle was considered essential to any representation. When the Georgia chapter of the sorority Epsilon Sigma Alpha planned a weekend with a "Gay Paree" theme in Macon, they devoted the first day entirely to Pigalle, even featuring the famous Apache dance associated with the neighbourhood (but likely without the understanding that it depicts a fight between a prostitute and a pimp). The sorority sisters also included a café scene with French poodles and a dance meant to look like it was at the Paris Opera.[82] In New York, delighted at the proposal to create a Paris-style café in Central Park, the famed writer Joseph Wechsberg suggested other ways to "Parisianize" the city: in addition to the flower gardens and *garçons* carrying trays of Dubonnet, New York needed to import far more "*Parisiennes*, or the whole project could be a dismal failure." If New York wanted the "Paris tradition," as it claimed, Wechsberg advocated for bringing in many of these "pretty women in chic dresses who don't mind your looking at them and might even look back," juxtaposing the inviting *parisiennes* with the women of New York, who "never, *nevair* look back even if they feel like it." Here Wechsberg argues that the quality that cements Parisian women's superiority was their alleged openness to the opposite sex. Setting aside how Wechsberg would know if the New York women welcomed comments from passersby, he also called for bringing in some of the Pigalle atmosphere, specifically to Rockefeller Plaza. The Plaza, he continued, "lacks a characteristic smell. Pigalle is full of wonderful aromas: the trees, the flowers, the *pommes frites* and the inimitable perfume of the Paris Métro, that mixture of asphalt and dust, oil and stale Houbigant [a famous French perfume brand] that makes little men reckless and cures virtuous women of inhibitions."[83]

Another indicator of just how profoundly Americans associated sex and Pigalle was the number of clubs and restaurants named after the neighbourhood, likely dating back to associations from the interwar and wartime eras. Every single major American city of the timeframe covered in this book contained a Pigalle. One of Atlanta's most famous cabaret clubs was called Leb's Pigalle,[84] while in Miami people flocked to Club Pigalle for over 20 years to see Pearl Williams, whom one commentator referred to as "the sauciest old broad in town, who called her jokes venereal material."[85] Modelled on the Pigalle Club in London, long one of the city's mainstay *boîtes*,[86] the identically named Los Angeles version had to be expanded to three times its size to accommodate major draws like the musician Earl Grant.[87] Place Pigalle restaurants have featured (and continue to thrive, in some cases) in the dining scenes of cities from Seattle to San Francisco to New York City. Pigalle the neighbourhood may have garnered mixed reviews from travel writers, but as a concept, the name resonated with Americans looking for loose, fun times.

One notable aspect of all of the Pigalle commentary is how all over the place it is in terms of dates, recommendations, and condemnations. This situation may reflect shifting attitudes about sexuality and openness, but it also demonstrates just how intrinsic notions of sex were tied in with Paris, and specifically with Pigalle.

All of this sex and romance, travel writers insisted, was simply natural for the French citizenry, and an expected, nay happy, part of visiting France. For the Anglo-American tourist, they urged them to relax and enjoy a lifestyle looser than what they presumably were used to at home. Temple Fielding stressed aspects of cultural difference: "The French are mature about sex. You'll find the maturity expressed in the Paris shows, which are bare and bawdy, in the bold approach of prostitutes who might just as well be asking for the time … The maturity is also expressed in the frank approach of women in all social spheres which is quite unlike the characteristic well-should-I or well-shouldn't-I vacillations of the ladies here at home, the Kinsey report be damned. A French lad and a French girl in love have eyes only for each other. You may think it's a disgusting display, a fortunate exhibition, or ain't France romantic! Locally they think it's lovely. After a while you may too."[88] Losing sexual inhibitions was, in the eyes of many writers, a pleasant side effect of French travel, a far cry from the uptight morality of France during the Liberation.

France/Paris Is a Woman

In 1964, famed fashion journalist Lucien François put pen to paper to describe exactly what made Paris so special. François connected that mystical quality to Paris's ability to create beautiful things for beautiful women: "It is no doubt from this specialization [in feminine perfection] that, on certain evenings when the light is fading in the rose-hued sky, Paris derives that chic feminine perfume, that jewel-like superiority, that muslin-like delicacy, that downy softness, that slight flippancy and that seeming futility. There are dresses for cities as well as for women, and Paris is the best-dressed city in the world. Elegant, fateful and free, with her river as haughty as a captive prince, the gilt of her façades, the gracefulness of her gardens, the elaboration of her historic stones."[89] François traversed the distance between describing France's beautiful women, who as seen above were viewed as part of the beautiful scenery of Paris, to seeing the city – and the country – itself as a beautiful lady. The majority of the travel writers from the period covered in this book referred to France, either in parts (like cities) or as a whole, as a woman. Often the correlation of France with a woman was direct, with the use of female pronouns or in descriptions of the country in feminine terms.

Travel writers typically felt no need to refer to other countries and their citizens in such gendered or sensualized terms. In his pan-European travel guide, Harold Newman described the pleasures of France, writing that in France, "the tourist … will have opportunities to gratify every taste, mood, and desire." French people, according to Newman, "excel in satisfying the superficial wants," an attitude which "attracts" and lures tourists.[90] In contrast, London is "an active, efficient, yet dignified metropolis," and Danes possesses "peacefulness, orderliness, and progress."[91] Similarly, in 1967, the well-known writer Harvey Olson published a guide to road trips throughout France, Switzerland, and Italy, an accompaniment to other, similar guides for other parts of Europe and the world. Olson devoted 511 pages to describing France, allocating only a relatively paltry 130 pages to Switzerland and Liechtenstein and a slightly more robust 294 to Italy. Olson consistently referred to France as "her" or "she," describing, for example, France's food as "her classical cuisine,"[92] and Paris as "retaining her *joie de vivre*"[93]; Switzerland and Italy were referred to with feminine pronouns only once. And Temple Fielding, dean of postwar travel writers, portrayed the people of France versus those of other nations in radically different terms. Of the French, he wrote: "For 13 centuries the French have offered the world a puzzling, provocative personality, as multiple and unpredictable as a psychiatric patient … Many foreign travelers like the French people on first sight and become hair-tearingly exasperated with them on second sight. Some, such as my Nancy and I, finally fall in love with them, never to waver."[94] Fielding's description is passionate, particularly when compared with his depiction of other countries' characteristics. Of the English, he stated that "they have all the warm, human values of your next-door neighbor in your own home town."[95] West Germans, Fielding offered, were incredibly hard-working, displaying the "traditional Teutonic" values of "tenacity, organizational ability, and attention to detail."[96] Clearly France was a place apart in Europe, much like a mercurial lover whose attraction – unlike that of the comfortable English and the enterprising Germans – held you in its thrall.

France, unlike its European counterparts, seemed to embody the stereotypical characteristics of femininity in all its stripes. The hugely popular travel magazine *Holiday*, headquartered in France, published annually (but rarely updated) its guide to France starting in the 1950s. The 1973 version described France in decidedly feminine terms: "The reasons for her popularity are many, and they are reasons of the spirit, as well as of the flesh. But if there is any single overriding attraction of France, it is probably this matter of individuality: the French just don't mind what you do so long as you don't intrude on their pleasures. The French also seem to understand better than most peoples the values of pleasure and are not a bit ashamed of the joy they derive from it."[97] Here, France itself is a woman whose life is devoted to sensual experiences. The book goes on to describe how even the French terrain, the body of the symbolic woman that is France, is "sensuous," with "Frenchmen taking pleasure in his landscape."[98] In this quote, French men view their own country as a female body in which they can satisfy their desires. The book then cites both the natural and built environments of France as part and parcel of this sexual topography, noting in phallic imagery that "You see the lines of yearning poplars and spires seeking heaven."[99] The "You" here is symbolic, implying agreement on all fronts – reader, French man, and writer – with the assertion of France's sexually charged horizon. The universal enjoyment of France's offerings is on display a few pages later: "Unless every one of your senses has been numbed, a trip to France is bound to be a joy."[100] If a traveller cannot take pleasure in France, the book implies, the problem lies with the interloper, not the bountiful buffet supplied by the Hexagon, described on the next page as "this nation that is quite shamelessly committed to enjoyment."[101]

Where in some depictions France was a feminized site of carnality, others portrayed France as a place for love and romance. Famed guidebook author Eugene Fodor, in 1952, described France as "the country with which the rest of the civilized world will perhaps never fall out of love." Temple Fielding described France as a mercurial woman, but one not to be missed. He concluded his lengthy section on France by writing, "Finally, there's France: … a reinvigorated nation, stirred into pride and fire, again approaching the threshold of her traditional greatness. If the ominously rising discontent doesn't cause her to stumble on the way, she's now ready to give you a holiday that is Fit for the Gods."[102]

Paris also received the sensually evocative linguistic treatment at the hands of guidebook authors. For example, to writer José A. Dos Santos, a contributor to the *Fodor's* guides, Paris was like a woman he was trying to conquer, the terminus of a long, passionate courtship. "To discover Paris," he wrote, "enter into the intimate secret of this capricious city, as disconcerting as a woman who provokes and eludes, who sometimes gives herself utterly and without reticence and yet will reveal a thousand subtleties to him who has the patience to seek to know her further." He called upon travellers to take the major natural and physical landmarks and transform them "into a living synthesis" to be explored in wanton fashion.[103] Similarly, Welsh lawyer and writer James E. Thomas, writing in the same guide, depicted Paris as a powerfully attractive woman. "From countless lands," he began, "come those who have heard the call of this imperious siren. And Paris welcomes them, sometimes gravely, sometimes gaily, sometimes cynically. For she has in abundance that which they seek, but there are treasures which she reserves for those whom she deems worthy of her rarest gifts. Cynical she can be, for she has a profusion of gay, tinseled toys to toss to those who have not the understanding nor the desire to possess her intimate secrets." Tourists, he continues, can visit Paris's attractions, but never understand the real character of this "breath-taking beauty." Thomas describes Paris as entrancing; the main tourist sites, in his words, are but "an infinite particle of that fascination which has endowed this city with the witchery of Lorelei – so many having heard its subtle music as they wandered perhaps one clear June night under the shadow of Notre-Dame, and, enchanted as the mariners in the legend, have abandoned friends, kin and country to stay for ever [*sic*] in its magic emprise. Even those who have had the courage to leave, can never quite forget." Here the correlation of Paris with a mysterious, sensual woman is overt; she is a "siren," luring travellers to her "magic emprise."[104] Paris, for Thomas, is like a difficult – but worthy – female conquest: On him who approaches her with sincerity and humility she will bestow moments of rare beauty when all her history will lie naked and radiant for his delectation."[105] Paris, for Thomas, is a delectable woman, ready to satisfy "his" deepest desires.

French travel writers also employed the city-as-seductress metaphor when describing their country's capacity to entice tourists. In the satirical magazine *Le Crapouillot*'s extensive Paris guide, for example, the introduction, written in 1951 by the popular writer and Goncourt Academy member Alexandre Arnoux, depicted Paris as an object of desire for the recently arrived tourist. Some people, Arnoux acknowledged, already love Paris well before they meet her for the first time. Such travellers "have a total love, that sensually [*voluptueusement*] blinds [them] to the cold and the mist, that dangerously exalts the spring sun." The language Arnoux uses is passionate, describing an all-consuming love, really an obsession. Paris, Arnoux went on, would be anything the traveller wanted her to be, like an adventurous lover. "This city," he wrote, "has the ability to transform herself according to the fantasies and dreams of the one who visits her, to become exactly, by way of mirage, the scene that he wishes for." Here, Paris is like an experienced lover, who instinctively understands what the visitor needs and shape-shifts to give it to him. Arnoux extends the metaphor to the whole country of France, which he refers to as "a nation that exists according to [the traveller's] inclinations and his dreams."[106] The corporeality of Paris – and France – in Arnoux's description reinforces the notion that Paris is a willing participant in a sexual encounter between city and tourist.

Individual features of the city of Paris also offered sensual delights, either in the form of a gendered portrayal or in the sense that such places were conducive to love-making. Many postwar writers wrote of the Seine, for example, using it as a form of shorthand for all the charms and attractions of the city, while celebrating the river as a landmark itself. Claire Segal, writing for the popular Nash Travel Guide series, straightforwardly called it "a major part of the beauty of the city,"[107] while Harvey Olson described it as "esthetic, historic, romantic, and commercial ... as imposing as any man-made Paris landmark."[108] Others portrayed the Seine as a voluptuous woman. James E. Thomas, cited above, wrote about the river as though describing a woman's relationship with several suitors: "The Seine, as if loathe [sic] to leave the town which she does so much to enrich, winds slowly in long languorous curves before she reluctantly pursues her journey northwards to the sea, and, accompanying the river with jealous insistence, the embankments perpetually caress her, whilst the bridges ... span her dark waters as if to retard her departure from the City of which she is Queen."[109] Here, the embankments and the bridges form romantic entanglements for the languid lady river. Similarly, the Seine was for José A. Dos Santos a welcoming woman, ready to greet the traveller. "But the Seine," he wrote, "seems to summon us, the Seine, which, with a tender gesture, seems to enclose its precious islands ... within its arms."[110] The *Holiday* travel guide also extolled the virtues of the Seine by way of celebrating the Île-St-Louis as though it were a child in the Seine's womb: "This lovely island, protected by the two arms of the river, was the small nucleus from which Paris grew ... the heart of the city."[111] The Seine was also celebrated by non-travel writers, who again used the metaphor of feminine corporeality to describe the river. In a review of a French film, the *New York Times*'s Bosley Crowther depicted the city of Paris as a character in Duvivier's *Under the Paris Sky*. "Ah, Paris!," he wrote, "City of rich and mellow beauties! City of romance and mystery! City of wisdom, indulgence, echoing footsteps – where lives mingle and flow in a restless, endless stream!" Crowther finished his elegy by calling Paris "the great city that lies wrapped in the arms of the Seine."[112] And journalist William Millinship portrayed the Seine as a muse, one "which supplies song writers with their romantic ideas."[113]

Parisian parks attracted particular notice from travel writers, who celebrated them for their hidden nooks and crannies, perfect for engaging in or observing lovers' dalliances. While it was less common for writers to depict the parks as actual women, romance and sexuality abounded in their descriptions. No less than Air France itself, in its 1968 English-language travel guide, advised that the Luxembourg Gardens was one of the great "pleasures of Paris," describing the park as "a favourite place for students and young people in love … a delightful spot at the upper end of the Boulevard St. Michel."[114] Similarly, in their 1967 *Paris! And Its Environs*, travel writers Lawrence and Sylvia Martin urged American travellers to go on a sort of safari to the same park in order to spot French students in their native habitat. "The Luxembourg Gardens are gardens of youth, the park of Sorbonne students," they wrote. "Here they sit studying, or reading (perhaps Verlaine) to the golden girl of the moment."[115] Air France reinforced the notion that lovers were part of the touristic landscape of Paris in its own guide: "The gardens and parks of Paris are justly celebrated. There are dozens of them, bright with flowers, children, birds and lovers, each with a charm and a personality of its own."[116]

The famed Bois de Boulogne, the large park located on Paris's northwestern border, also sparked similar romantic descriptions. Travel writer Horace Sutton used Paris's reputation for romance as a way to show how the Bois was a microcosm of the French predilection for all things amatory. In May 1958, Sutton wrote that "in Spring a young Parisian's thoughts turn to the Bois de Boulogne. (Nobody's thoughts turn to love since they think about that in Paris all year around.)"[117] In describing the Bois de Boulogne in 1955, guidebook writers Virginia Creed and Henry Milo termed it "the chief outdoor pleasure resort of fashionable Paris." They contrasted it with its counterpart across the city, the Bois de Vincennes, which, in their words was the "pleasure ground of the working people of Paris, [and] lacks the elegance of the Bois de Boulogne."[118] In both cases, the parks were sites of "pleasure," of either the high- or low-brow varieties. José A. Dos Santos lamented the nineteenth-century transformation of the Bois by Baron von Haussmann, whose "numerous roads and avenues … destroyed the privacy so necessary for intimate tenderness." Still, those in search of romance need not despair entirely, according to Dos Santos, who implored readers to walk toward the Porte Dauphine at the end of Avenue Foch: "there you will see the Etoile bathed in the light of the setting sun. This is the most romantic and most unforgettable of all rendez-vous, the rendez-vous with Paris."[119] Dos Santos's statement is remarkable for its encapsulation of the role played by Paris in the minds of writers and influencers in the postwar era. Here, the Bois is both a place for sexual encounters between individuals – although not with the impunity enjoyed by nineteenth-century thrill seekers – and also a place to fall in love with Paris, in a very literal and sensual sense. The parks of Paris and France are lovely places to walk around or rest aching feet, but the choice to portray them – and their occupants – as potential sites of romance, to experience actively or passively, reflects a broader set of assumptions about France and its people.

Paris may have been, in the words of *Los Angeles Times* reporter Henry Miele, "the city of radiance and romance," but writers also lavished floridly romantic language on many other parts of the Hexagon.[120] Miele himself later wrote about Touraine, a region in the Loire River Valley, calling it the "romantic heart of France."[121] Well-known travel reporter Leonard Panaggio traced Petrarch's life along the "romantic" Sorgue River in southeastern France, describing how the poet settled there, in a state of unrequited love for Laura de Noves. Panaggio emphasized how Petrarch's love for the river was another major "romance" in his life, one that tourists could understand if they visited.[122] For tourists who wanted to visit less-frequented destinations in France, H.P. Koenig recommended the Alsace wine region in 1972, employing romantic language: "To follow the wine route that runs parallel to the Rhine along the foothills of the Vosges from west of Strasbourg to south of Colmar is to experience Alsace at its most romantic, traversing some of the gentlest countryside in France, passing through a chain of wine-producing villages, one more attractive than the other."[123]

Other writers again equated places in France with romantic and sensual women. Arthur Meeker of the *Chicago Tribune* urged his readers to visit Beaucaire, a town that "lies dreaming of her romantic past on the Rhone below Avignon."[124] Temple Fielding labelled the Atlantic resorts of Deauville and Trouville twin sisters, writing "*Deauville* and *Trouville* are *tête-à-tête* resorts linked by bridge over the Touques River. The former is a head taller than her less glamorous twin – a patrician lady with a flair for *la vie joyeuse*. Her amorous perfume draws tryst-minded, off-the-record week-enders, because she offers all the accouterments of High-Life leisure."[125]

Probably no place offered more sensual enjoyment in France than the French Riviera, which, as the previous chapter pointed out, had long enjoyed a reputation as a romantic destination. However, those seeking to boost tourism were nervous about the region's ability to rebound following the war; the Allies had literally landed on the beach in Saint-Tropez. Many of the old guard never returned to the Riviera, and those who stayed lived in what one historian described as "penury" during the war, a condition not uncommon throughout the Hexagon.[126] When it came to recovery, though, apparently tourism professionals need not have worried so. As early as 1948, Stuart Murray observed in his travel guide, "Romance seems to be in the very air of this always delightful, semi-sophisticated land of terraced *villas*, resort hotels, tiled roofs, casinos, palm-lined boulevards and flowers."[127] A couple of years later, Harold Newman echoed Murray's thoughts, describing the Riviera as a "semitropical playland … where daytime life centers on the beaches and at the pools, where sunbathing is the principal sport and infinitesimal bathing suits are the popular costume."[128]

Like France as a whole, the French Riviera was personified as a sensual woman. Of the Riviera town Antibes, expatriate James E. Thomas wrote, "She remains aloof from the ultra-smart casinos of Juan-les-Pins and Nice, and observes with generous and sympathetic amusement the frenzied and impatient gaiety of the modern generation. For Antibes can live with her memories. Over two thousand years of history give her a rich heritage. Above all she is picturesque." Similarly, of Nice, he called the city "*Nizza la Bella*, Nice the beautiful, Nice the Queen of the Riviera!"[129] Horace Sutton distilled the feminine comparison down to its smallest parts, writing in 1948 that "like a long, lacquered eyelash, the Riviera is still fluttering gaily on the tired face of Europe."[130] Sometimes the comparison was not in the (French) woman's favour. "*Nice* is the capital," Temple Fielding wrote. "Once a lady of breeding and refinement, she is now attracting more and more of the visibly unwashed, the aging, the infirm, and the unattractive cheapjack excursionists. She is a metropolitan city, with the same dress size as Dayton or El Paso; her contrast with smaller, more sophisticated Cannes seems sharper every year."[131]

Sometimes, travel writers acknowledged, a trip to France was not possible, but, they stipulated, there were other places in the world reminiscent of France, particularly in terms of *amour*. In a pinch, Arthur Meeker wrote, Switzerland could be a worthy substitute, saying that in terms of "romance" Switzerland is "much like France." He continued, "If we feel, as sometimes we do, a thirst for France, and haven't quite time to go there, we do the next best thing – head the car west and keep driving until the mountains flatten out and the neat chalets give way to the rather untidy stone villages of Canton Fribourg."[132] Here, France was clearly the standard for travel, and particularly romantic travel, but there were a few also-ran substitutes. Places with French influence received the romantic treatment from writers as well. Louisiana, perhaps the most culturally French place in the United States, was described by travel writer David Laird Watt: "Romantic places breed romantic people – and legends. Nowhere is that more evident than in Cajun country, rich in the lore of the Acadians, those displaced persons from France who migrated and later were expelled from Canada."[133] Here, France is like a sire of romance, first breeding the Acadians, who then bred the Cajuns. The South Pacific also received the romantic treatment. H.P. Koenig of the *Chicago Tribune* described Noumea, capital of France's overseas territory New Caledonia in the South Pacific, as a romantic treasure. He called Noumea "an extremely small-scale Paris indeed, closer to a provincial Mediterranean port, only infinitely more romantic. But French it is."[134] And no less than Air France itself depicted Tahiti, part of French Polynesia, as full of "handsome people" and "charm."[135] Go to Guadeloupe in the Caribbean, urged a writer for the *Baltimore Sun*, to taste a "romantic 'corner of France,'" for Guadeloupe is a place that is "pulsating with the spontaneous gaiety of both France and native *joie de vivre*. Everyone's dream can be anyone's discovery."[136] Martinique, another of France's Caribbean territories, served as a fantastical place in the words of a *Chicago Tribune* writer, who described it as, "this romantic island" full of "tall, handsome, uninhibited people" and a "delightful paradox – France in the Caribbean."[137] H.P. Koenig of the *Chicago Tribune* described Martinique as "unmistakably French." What was his evidence for this characterization? "The people ... manifest typically French qualities of pride, dignity, *joie de vivre*. Women are reputed to be the most beautiful in the Caribbean. They carry themselves with style, dressed to the nines." He also stated that Martinique was "lush, lovely, and exotic," calling the island and Guadeloupe "the most romantic islands in the Caribbean."[138] When looking for a piece of France outside of the metropole, writers advised people to seek out romance and sensuality, which had become synonymous with the essential characteristics of France and the French.

Even articles not devoted to French or francophone travel used the motif of romance. Describing clean-up efforts along the heavily polluted Rhine, the *Boston Globe* called it that old "river of fable and romance," before going on to deem it a modern-day "sewer" in 1972, hardly an image to inspire feelings of love.[139] When addressing the housing crisis of the 1960s in France, *Christian Science Monitor* journalist Carlyle Morgan wrote that "'Under the Roofs of Paris' made a romantic-sounding title for a French movie decades ago. The decades-old problem of where to live in France, however, is romantic for relatively few people."[140] Ardour and its association with France had so permeated the American mindset that writers deployed it as a common subtext or motif.

Not only landmarks received the romance treatment from writers; any and all interactions with French people or their government were subject to floridly romantic language. Reporting on a new accord signed by Charles de Gaulle and Konrad Adenauer of West Germany, *Wall Street Journal* reporter (and later editor of *Fortune* magazine) Edmund K. Faltermeyer called the agreement and the talks a "Rhine Romance."[141] In 1961, famed political reporter Robert Hartmann portrayed John F. Kennedy's visit to Paris as though he were a suitor "wooing" a potential date. In 1963, when it appeared that de Gaulle would officially recognize China, Marcelle Fouquet deemed the move a "Chinese Romance," and speculated that "from Hong Kong and Paris hints are whispered."[142] Hartmann labelled the trip a "romance with a nation," and he essentially depicted France as an irrational woman whom JFK, here symbolizing strong American masculinity, would calm and tame with his words and deeds of romance. On his trip, Hartmann wrote, "Mr. Kennedy did not reason with France but rather wooed the French people and their formidable president as one would woo a desirable but difficult woman." This American-French courtship had its stops and starts, Hartmann continued: "In making unashamed love to France, right out in public, the way Parisiens [sic] do, President Kennedy was sometimes carried away. As lovers often do, he said some things which were painful, some which were exaggerations and some which were downright untrue." Ultimately, JFK turned to a tried-and-true tactic, according to Hartmann, who described how "finally, as suitors must, Mr. Kennedy relied heavily on flattery, comparing his host with all the great men of history." The end result of this breathless pursuit? "It is impossible to say at the end of the first day's courtship to say with any assurance how this courtship will end," Hartmann concluded, "but when President Kennedy talks to the NATO ambassadors today he may give some hint as to whether it is true love or just another young man's fancy."[143] In 1968 the *Christian Science Monitor*'s columnist David R. Francis wrote about France's global economic negotiations as if they were a dating ritual. "In romance," he explained, "it is said that a good strategy for a woman is to keep her suitors guessing. France – generally portrayed as a woman by cartoonists – appears to be following this strategy in international financial affairs."[144] The widespread use of romantic language for meetings, events, and people that had nothing to do with love at all demonstrates just how deeply the association of France with notions of love had penetrated the American mindset.

It came to the point that France and romance were used as synonyms by American writers: anything at all that had to do with France was described as romantic, and anything that was called romantic was described as French. Air France was "a romantic airline,"[145] for one writer, words that today feel exceedingly incongruous. Even more implausible was another reporter's description of the road signs in France as "sexy," a descriptor for which he cites absolutely no evidence in the body of his article.[146] Perfume, long a luxury product associated with the French, became a representation of the nation and its devotion to sensuality. Shopping adviser Alice Martin remarked on how "Everybody takes perfume seriously in Paris. Even men who've known nothing more seductive than mother's rose-water-and-glycerine suddenly become conscious of such provocative names as 'Fleur du feu' [Flower of Fire] and 'Le baiser du faune' [Animal's Kiss]."[147]

Fashion, that bastion of French identity, often received the romantic treatment by American writers. The fashion editor of an Atlanta newspaper wrote, "[With] French design to weave the spell of fashion romance and American precision of workmanship to complete the finished product what results can you expect? ... These suits seek only to suit you in taste with the flair that is the spirit of Paris couture."[148] About the 1946 Paris fashion Jean Baird of the *Christian Science Monitor* wrote, "Nothing is more romantic, more musical than the rustle of skirts, full and sweeping. They recapture the spirit of days of gracious ballrooms and graceful dances."[149] In yet another fashion review, romance was the defining quality of French fashion: "Despite the growing importance of other fashion capitals, Paris still speaks with authority through its couturier collections. While no revolutionary silhouette made its bow at the January showings, the mood was romantic and feminine, with an appealing softness which is both flattering and wearable."[150]

Conclusion

The fact that an entire nation was consistently described in gendered, feminine terms ultimately has much to do with the postwar exigencies that led French government actors to deploy the nation's women as to promote tourism and economic growth. But in the final reckoning, aesthetic power is something quite different from political power. French women, despite their much-vaunted beauty and the state's interventions, saw limited gains and influence during this period. Likewise the nation itself, in being cast as feminine both by its own design and in the eyes of other nationals and nations, found itself a secondary power. This is a chicken/egg situation – it is difficult to know what comes first: that women use beauty as a weapon in order to access power, or that they are locked out of power and thus use one of the few tools that society affords them – their appearance. On the scale of the individual, when women have limited power, are they wrong to turn to their femininity to survive and even thrive? That is a judgment I am unwilling to make, but I see little to no evidence that French women, from Brigitte Bardot to the *midinette*, benefited hugely from the way that the state capitalized on their beauty.

On the scale of the nation, it is ironic that French femininity became such a lure for tourists. Ultimately, the feminization of France itself occurred, largely driven by this image of femininity, a narrative that the state eventually lost control over and which was co-opted by writers from other countries. And in the end France lost power on the international stage, perhaps based on this feminine, secondary status. Writer Alexandre Arnoux portrayed the interaction between feminized state and tourist as a sexual one, in which France, like a sensuous woman, knows what her prospective lover needs and gives it to him, thereby cementing the relationship. A traveller is never a stranger in Paris, Arnoux writes; it is a city that has "seduced him and has him eating out of the palm of her hand."[151] For Arnoux, it is France that holds the power, using her sexuality to get the man – the traditional power – to do what she wants. France is like a doomed Marie Antoinette, dissimulating to get her subjects to do what she wants. However, that episode in history of course ended poorly for Marie Antoinette, whose power, as many scholars have noted, trended aesthetic rather than political. It would be hard to argue that France's seductive powers have proven more successful than those of the ill-fated queen in measures of hard power.

In a telling comment, satirist George Mikes both lauded and lampooned the French and their tourism efforts, writing in a *Fodor's Guide* in 1952: "Remember that France has long been the standard-bearer of Western civilization, that without her neither English liberalism nor the American Constitution would exist today. Remember all this and then proceed to the Folies-Bergère. I always do the same."[152]

Conclusion

In 2015, Air France released a new safety video for its passengers. The video features a female flight attendant who walks the viewer through the standard rules of safe air travel. While she speaks and gestures, her instructions are acted out theatrically by a quintet of beautiful, thin, elegant women, wearing Breton stripes and full skirts. They move in unison, performing a series of what I can best describe as choreographed dance moves in the background, as the flight attendant host reminds us to fasten our seatbelts, both for safety and because "it will elegantly highlight your waistline." Smoking is prohibited, she tells us, reminding us that "a no smoking flight is simply chic." When seeking out the closest exit, each elegant woman in stripes performs a series of model poses, ending by spinning around to look directly at the camera, a hand posed on her hip, like a photo shoot. "Because it is trendy here [in France, presumably]," the flight attendant reminds us to "set your electronic devices on airplane mode." The video concludes with an ethereal voice singing "love is in the air," and then the video fades out, and the Air France logo appears, with the motto "France is in the air" underneath.[1] Played before each flight, the video is a stunning testament to the staying power of the images of femininity detailed in this book. It reifies the notion that women in France are "chic," thin, and beautiful, and it equates a trip to France with love and, potentially, sex. More than 70 years since the beginning of the time period covered in this book, the messages, like those of any proven marketing strategy, are still amazingly consistent. Today France remains the most visited nation on Earth.[2]

The hostessing journey in this book is a remarkable story for many reasons, not least of which is its exponential expansion. At its inception as a profession in 1946, a few air hostesses existed to comfort passengers and show a pretty face on behalf of the national company and France. Then, the government expanded the project in two major ways. First, acting as aesthetic diplomats for France at all manner of events, air hostesses were deployed as *ambassadrices*, devoid of political power but weaponized for their superior "French" charm and beauty.

Second, the government, buoyed by the success – both in reputation and tourist spending – of the air hostess program, decided to expand the hostesses far beyond the realm of air travel, placing young, beautiful women in train stations, information booths, and other locales frequented by tourists. Ultimately, that expansion project was successful enough that certain people in government hoped to use hostesses as a model for all French women. Finally, actors in the state, culture, and tourism industries metaphorically turned the nation into a welcoming and alluring woman, casting France itself, as well as specific places like the Riviera and Paris, as a space where romance and hedonism existed in varying degrees, coexisting with more traditional draws like history and culture, all for the satisfaction of the – preferably American – traveller.

While the history of postwar hostessing is astounding in and of itself, the implications of endeavouring to turn all French women into proxy hostesses are controversial on a number of different levels, especially when considering the demands placed on hostesses themselves. The women faced significant pressure to look perfect, from top to bottom, at all times, imposing a personal financial burden at a moment when women earned far less than men. The emotional labour that women were called to perform as hostesses was also onerous, and it required them to mask their true emotions in order to be constantly pleasing. In their roles as *ambassadrices*, the women lacked political power – there is an argument to be made among scholars for hostesses' politicized status, but no one intended hostesses to use their aesthetic power as a stepping stone to greater individual or collective voice, although occasionally – as in the case of the Air France hostesses' age discrimination suits and other battles for workers' rights – they did just that.

As all of the state-mandated qualities of hostessing amalgamated into one perfect, unattainable paradigm, it is difficult not to speculate about the impact hostesses had on the role of women in society more broadly. More women entered the public sphere over the course of the 1950s and 1960s, making forays into the realms of work, politics, and culture; it is therefore important for us to interrogate the notions of progress that dominate the narratives of women's lives.[3] Rather than some sort of linear story, I would attest that the experience of hostesses reveals a far more complicated negotiation of roles and boundaries, in which these *ambassadrices* owed the performance of beauty and friendliness to the state, which then commodified and sold it as a way to lure in dollars and interest. While the women were not at all automatons – see again hostesses' union organizing – on balance I would argue that the women's dividends were minimal compared to the amount of labour – aesthetic, emotional, and otherwise – that the women performed. The aesthetic power that such roles afforded hostesses was not designed to translate into equality.

The model of air hostesses that the French offered the postwar world shifted in the 1970s with the rise of jumbo jets and the oil embargo late in that decade, which necessitated a far more intense focus on increasingly thinning profits rather than luxury or even basic comfort. With passengers packed into ever-bigger planes that hurtled across the globe, there was far less time for the kind of service and elegance on which Air France had built its reputation. As hostesses faced serving more passengers in reduced time, many of them again protested their expanded workload, to little or no avail.[4] Air France, mirroring other major airlines around the world, also limited women's ability to transition from hostess to pilot. The French did not allow women to train as pilots in official schools until 1973, and as of 1984, Air France counted three female pilots across the whole company.[5]

At the outset of this book, I noted three interventions in the prevailing scholarship that the book makes; I want to revisit these now and address their interconnected legacies. The first intervention has to do with the study of the innovative use of femininity as soft power, the second with decolonization as the backdrop of the project, and the third with gender and universalism. Despite the dearth of tangible benefits for the women weaponized in pursuit of French hegemony, assumptions about the superiority of French femininity have remained stubbornly persistent, as the contemporary Air France safety video suggests. A perusal of the feminine and self-help presses reveals French women's apparent authority on any number of subjects: they "don't get fat";[6] they have "Parisian chic";[7] they know better beauty secrets;[8] they have better marriages and sex;[9] they are ageless;[10] they raise their children better;[11] and they just generally live better than *you*.[12] This authority's adaptability across different platforms is also noteworthy; social media teems with "French Girl" style and beauty accounts, and even a basic internet search reveals how style and beauty websites seek out and curate French influencers and then advertise them to an apparently insatiable audience.[13]

Clearly this celebration of French femininity is not a cottage industry, but rather a powerhouse built on the combination of femininity and soft power, a national identity/beauty-industrial complex that sells the world on an aspirational image of French female superiority. The perfection of the French woman is astoundingly diverse in these idealized manifestations, and the pressure on both sides of that equation – on the French women, to uphold that standard, and on other women around the world, who are taught to aspire to it and yet are always found wanting – is considerable. That the image is largely dominated by whiteness is both a throwback to its development in the era of decolonization and a testament to the resounding power of racism and the centralization of power in white hands. It suggests more continuation than rupture in the era of decolonization, and it also represents yet another barrier to actually achieving that dominant image of perfect femininity for people of colour today.[14] The image of femininity has proved to be remarkably resilient overall, with women spending massive amounts of money and time to attain this ideal of French feminine beauty.[15]

When I was in the early stages of this project, I went for coffee with a good friend in the field of history, and we talked about my tentative ideas. He was intrigued by the premise, but he cautioned me as well, saying that my project was about a time when France no longer mattered much in the context of the world. While conceding the larger point, I countered that my book would be about how the French government was using femininity to make itself matter, to dig itself out of irrelevancy. Now, many moons later, I realize that we were, in part at least, having the wrong conversation. The question of "what matters" is a politicized one in the historical field, and it has shifted over the years to include questions of race, class, and gender. Clearly, though, it has not shifted enough. This book does not primarily deal with traditional economic or military history, nor is it a history of high politics or law, although all of those subjects inform major parts of the narrative. Instead, it is a history of women, power, and influence, or the lack thereof, told primarily through subjects like beauty, fashion, and the body, in France, a place that packaged – and continues to package – femininity and offer it to the world as a coveted commodity. That story matters for reasons empirical (the massive industries that the image supports, like tourism, beauty, and fashion) and emotional (the serious human toll of maintaining and resisting gender and beauty norms), and yet stories like it continue to be dismissed, even at the highest levels of the academy. It especially saddens me that I, as a historian of women and gender, someone who thinks about these issues every day, failed to recognize the dismissal of female experience inherent in that particular conversation.

These traditionally female subjects deeply affect how all people live their lives, as well as how the world itself is ordered. We know that the beauty and fashion industries are multibillion dollar ones, and these industries continue to profit handsomely off of the gendered standards outlined in this book. We also know, and actual studies show, that if women do not apply their makeup just right, or do not don the appropriate clothing for every situation, they face profound disadvantages, not only in the workplace but also in simply walking through life.[16] The pervasive issues about bodies and perfection, specifically regarding the demands that society places on women's shoulders to achieve an arbitrary ideal, have deeply touched millions of people's lives both directly and indirectly, including my own. These are not unimportant issues even though their significance for politics, the economy, or the military is not always evident. They are not unimportant even though they wear the "soft power" label, or because they are painted with the brush of the feminine. They matter, and they affect the most intimate ways people live their lives, both in the past and today. The intersection of femininity, beauty, race, and power plays on a loop throughout our society, whether we are talking about female leaders' fashion choices or reading about a celebrity's pregnancy weight at the supermarket checkout line. The drive for female perfection, that narrowly constructed ideal that runs right through the Hexagon, and the impact that this image has on women, is something that pierces our consciousness on a daily, if not hourly, basis. To steer historical inquiry away from issues of femininity and female power and their origins, to say that they do not "matter," to suggest that they are somehow frivolous, is both to ignore their importance today as well as to block paths to understanding how such standards developed in the past and how we as a society can perhaps ease their continuing impact. Instead, it is up to the academy to foreground such stories, to create more space for them in scholarly circles and beyond, and, in so doing, ensure that underrepresented voices of all kinds can be heard.

Notes

Introduction

1 While the book will go into specific ideals of beauty and femininity, it is important to note that the ideas and conclusions presented here are indebted to the vast scholarship on the subject of historical ideal femininity that exists globally. I found several of these works particularly noteworthy for the purposes of this book. In the global context, Geoffrey Jones's *Beauty Imagined* does an excellent job of laying out beauty standards and their relationship to the various industries that support, promote, and/or undermine them. I also found Peter Stearns's *Fat History* to be quite useful. In the French context, historians like Morag Martin (*Selling Beauty*) and Holly Grout (*Force of Beauty*) discuss how beauty norms are both established and transmitted through vastly different modes and processes, depending on the specific historical context. I would also be remiss not to mention Kathy Peiss's *Hope in a Jar*, a landmark work in this field.
2 France Senate Archives, Séance of 9 December 1969, 1539.
3 Fred Tupper, "60,000 See De Gaulle Declare Winter Games Open in Grandiose Setting," *NYT*, 7 February 1968, 53.
4 I think that the term bunny also likely references the figure of the Playboy bunny, whose presence in American life was widely known, not least because of Gloria Steinem's undercover article about the Playboy Club. See Gloria Steinem, "A Bunny's Tale," *Show Magazine*, 1 May 1963, 90, 92, 94, 114. The *Playboy* reference adds an even more overt element of sex and commodification to this tale.
5 Will Grimsley, "French Hostesses Dress Up Games," *Washington Post*, 31 January 1968, D2.
6 See Enloe, *Bananas, Beaches, and Bases*, 1. Enloe acknowledges how women in the formal world of state diplomacy have often been overshadowed or ignored, despite their massive contributions. She also asks scholars to consider informal ways in which women have shaped international politics, through activities like booking vacations, showing films of foreigners to classes of students, or engaging

in sex work for American soldiers. Enloe, 6–7. Historian Dana Cooper took up Enloe's call, arguing that the upper-class American women who married into the British nobility in the late nineteenth and early twentieth centuries were in fact privy to high-level diplomatic talks, and indeed may have influenced them greatly. See Cooper, *Informal Ambassadors*. While Cooper attempts to show how private sphere activities impacted public decisions, this book demonstrates how women's physical appearance became a tool of the state of France to promote its national and economic interests.

7 Endy, *Cold War Holidays*, 2. Other historians have also argued that gender deserves a far more robust place in these historiographical discussions. Scholars Carolyn James and Glenda Sluga assert that a "focus on women raises critical historical questions about the changing and consistent ways in which political power was wielded over the centuries ... and opens the field to a broader interpretation of diplomatic work and the nature of modern international politics." James and Sluga, *Women, Diplomacy and International Politics*, 1.

8 See "Les essais de la première aviatrice," *L'Aérophile*, 15 November 1909, 515; "Savez-vous?" *L'Air*, December 1943, 13; "Chute grave de Mme de Laroche," *L'Aérophile*, 15 July 1910, 315. France had many other female pioneers in flight, including Thérèse Peltier, who may have been the very first woman to pilot a heavyweight aircraft; Marie Marvingt, the first female combat pilot (she flew for France in the First World War); the infamous Violette Morris, the sportswoman who later became a Gestapo spy; and Jacqueline Auriol, a test pilot who was the daughter-in-law of Vincent Auriol, president of France from 1947 to 1954. See Bernard Marck's *Elles ont conquis le ciel* and *Les aviatrices*, Eileen Lebow's *Before Amelia*, and Stéphane Nicolaou and Élisabeth Misme-Thomas's *Aviatrices: Un siècle d'aviation féminine française*.

9 "La femme et l'avion," *Échos de l'air* 1, no. 1: 11.

10 What follows is a brief discussion about the pre-air hostess history of women as poster children for major national and corporate interests. I make no pretence that this discussion is in any way exhaustive, as the subject deserves its own consideration. There has been some scholarly work on related subjects, such as Tamar Garb's *Bodies of Modernity* and Jennifer Scanlon's *Inarticulate Longings*. Still, I very much hope that more historians take up that call.

11 "Discours prononcé par M. Chassaigne Goyon, président du Conseil municipal de Paris, au banquet du Syndicat général de l'industrie hôtelière et des grands hôtels de Paris, le 8 décembre 1913," *Bulletin municipal officiel de la ville de Paris*, 31 December 1913, 1–2.

12 "La bonne hôtesse," *La Tribune de Marseille et La Provence hôtelière, touristique et sportive*, June 1928 (A8).

13 The first documented auto show model was Hazel Jewell, who worked the International Automobile Show in New York in 1909. Auto shows around the world have continued to use models well into the twenty-first century. Even today, these

women, known as "booth babes," wear couture, pose on or around the vehicles, and, in some cases, are not permitted to speak. See Krevsky, *Sirens of Chrome*, 5–6, 16.

14 Affiche de l'Exposition Internationale d'Automobiles au jardin des Tuileries du 15 juin au 3 juillet 1898, organisée à Paris par l'Automobile Club de France (Poster for the International Exposition of Automobiles in the Tuileries Graden from 15 June to 3 July 1898). A photo from the event depicts women attending, but not at all modelling or posing in front of cars. See "Exposition de l'Automobile Club de France, Tuileries, 15 juin 1898," Collection Jules Beau, *Photographie sportive* 7, no. 14 (1898). The auto *Exposition* was not the only arena to use mythological and surreal women in advertising. Private car companies, like A. Teste Moret & Cie, did so as well, with a 1900 poster featuring a winged goddess in an auto chariot, being propelled, oddly enough, by flies. See Krevsky, *Sirens of Chrome*, 8–9.

15 Poster: "Automobile Club/De France/2ème. Exposition Internationale/ D'automobiles/au jardin des Tuileries/du 15 Juin/au 9 Juillet/1899," Musée Carnavalet, Paris. The poster for the fourth auto show, in 1901, depicts a similar goddess-like figure surrounded by auto equipment. See poster: Georges Antoine Rochegrasse, "Automobile Club de France. 4ème exposition internationale. Salon de l'automobile, du cycle et des sports, 10 au 25 décembre 1901," Bibliothèque Forney, Paris. While I could not find every single *affiche*, most later posters either do not display women or show them in a more passive role in the background, for example as passengers in vehicles. This reflects the work of historian Adam C. Stanley, who has analysed women drivers in interwar French advertisements, concluding that their depictions essentially "consign[ed] women's use of [cars'] potentially transgressive technology within acceptable limits." Stanley, "Hearth, Home, and Steering Wheel," 249. Such fears of women's independence have been amply catalogued by historians, including Mary Louise Roberts, Sian Reynolds, and Carolyn Dean.

16 See Hunt, *Politics*, 93.

17 Stephen L Harp's study of Michelin's advertisements hews closely to my conclusion that women are objects, not actors, in early twentieth-century ads.

18 Paul Sentenac, "Le thème artistique et poétique de l'automobile," *La Renaissance* 17, no. 1 (January 1934): 36–8, 36.

19 The first air hostess, Ellen Church, worked for United Airlines in the United States in the 1930s, and her role was primarily to act as a nurse and assuage some of the many discomforts of early commercial flying. Vantoch, *Jet Sex*, 15, 18. These early white, middle-class air hostesses also served to reassure passengers that flying was safe. Barry, *Femininity in Flight*, 18–19.

20 In regard to the United States, see Vantoch, *Jet Sex*, and Barry, *Femininity in Flight*. For Australia, see Prudence Black, *Smile, Particularly in Bad Weather*. The Irish author and feminist Mary Kenny described the profession as "carry[ing] an almost impossible level of prestige" in her country. Kenny, "Forty Years On," 8. In places like India, entry into the profession was limited to middle-class, fair-skinned

women. See, for example, Aneel Karnani's "Doing Well by Doing Good," 1353. See also Picton's "The Complexities of Complexion," 87. For Papua New Guinea air hostesses, see Zimmer-Tamakoshi's "What Is Holding Them Back?," 410–11.

21 See Levenstein, *Seductive Journeys*. Expectations for French women differed across class lines; the French *jeune fille*, for example, was destined for marriage, her virginity protected and her behaviour restricted, despite France's reputation for permissiveness. Whitney Walton's work demonstrates how young American women who travelled to France for study often felt constrained by the regulations associated with this *jeune fille*. See Walton, *Internationalism*, 88.
22 Levenstein, *We'll Always Have Paris*, 75.
23 Roberts, *What Soldiers Do*, 63; see also Endy, *Cold War Holidays*, 22.
24 Roberts, *What Soldiers Do*, 74.
25 See Roberts, *What Soldiers Do*, 131–2. See also Walton, *Internationalism*, 88–9.
26 Chapter 1's section on air hostesses and labour disputes complicates those ideals, although the cultural norms remain quite pervasive even today.
27 Walton, *Internationalism*, 114.
28 Quoted in Levenstein, *We'll Always Have Paris*, 88.
29 Communists, as Christopher Endy shows, and some others in the French left were ambivalent about American dollars and their corresponding influence. Endy, *Cold War Holidays*, 57.
30 Gildea, *France since 1945*, 10.
31 Cynthia Enloe points out the gendered implications of dismissing tourism from serious studies of international relations: "That conventional political commentators do not discuss tourism as seriously as oil or weaponry may tell us more about those commentators' own ideological constructions of 'seriousness' than it does about the politics of tourism." Enloe, *Bananas, Beaches, and Bases*, 69.
32 Endy, *Cold War Holidays*, 57.
33 The love was not one-sided. American interests also called for increased aid and leisure spending in the context of the Cold War and for preventing Communism from gaining a hold in France. Endy, *Cold War Holidays*, 204.
34 Endy, *Cold War Holidays*, 101–4.
35 See Endy, 6; see also McKenzie, who calls tourism "the largest dollar-earning industry in France until it was surpassed by military aid during the rearmament years of the Korean War. In addition, American tourists spent more in France than did any other group of international tourists." McKenzie, "Creating a Tourist's Paradise," 36.
36 See, for example, the work of Lizabeth Cohen (*Consumers' Republic*) and Elaine Tyler May (*Homeward Bound*).
37 Endy, *Cold War Holidays*, 6–7.
38 Notes from the French Senate, Séance du 19 août 1948, 2531–2.
39 Notes from the French Senate, Séance du 12 avril 1949, 966.

40 The World Bank historical data on passenger travel shows that in the United States there were around 164 million passengers on airplanes in 1970 (many of them repeat flyers). By 1979, that number had almost doubled, to nearly 314 million. France showed a similar trajectory, going from 9 million passengers in 1970 to just about 18 million in 1979. See https://data.worldbank.org/indicator/IS.AIR.PSGR?locations=US-FR.
41 Endy, *Cold War Holidays*, 125.
42 Notes from the French Senate, Séance du 14 avril 1964, 123.
43 Notes from the French Senate, Séance du 14 avril 1964, 123.
44 Notes from the French Senate, Séance du 9 décembre 1973, 2632.
45 Notes from the French Senate, Séance du 9 décembre 1973, 2648.
46 Notes from the French Senate, Séance du 9 décembre 1973, 2643.
47 Endy, *Cold War Holidays*, 54.
48 *Journal officiel de la République française: Avis et rapports du Conseil économique*, 3 February 3, 1959 (Année 1959, N4), 329. Emphasis in original.
49 Sampson, *Empires of the Sky*, 119.
50 Sampson, *Empires of the Sky*, 31.
51 Vielle, *Air France, 1933–1944*, 159.
52 Quoted in Espérou, *Histoire du transport aérien français*, 89.
53 Neiertz, "Air France: An Elephant in an Evening Suit?," 19.
54 Neiertz, "Air France: An Elephant in an Evening Suit?," 20.
55 "Des jeunes filles volantes sont cultivées dans une serre nommé 'Jonas,'" *Le Monde*, 26 May 1955, 4.
56 See, for example, Virgili's *Shorn Women*, Capdevila's "Quest for Masculinity in a Defeated France," and Shepard's *Sex, France, and Arab Men*.
57 Beauvoir, *Second Sex*, 104.
58 Foucault, *Discipline and Punish*, 138.
59 Bartky, "Foucault, Femininity and the Modernization of Patriarchal Power," 142.
60 As Bartky puts it more concretely, "no one is marched off for electrolysis at the end of a rifle." Bartky, 143.
61 Bartky, 132. Any woman, as Bartky notes, who does not start out with the inherent advantage of being white and relatively wealthy is destined to fail at the project of claiming ideal beauty, adding an intersectional angle to the analysis of bodily discipline as well. See also Susan Bordo, *Unbearable Weight*.
62 I would particularly note the work of Joan Scott, Lynn Hunt, Mary Louise Roberts, Todd Reeser, Joshua Cole, Carolyn Dean, Judith Surkis, Andrew Israel Ross, Mary Lewis, and Elizabeth Everton. In addition, recent work by a number of scholars has demonstrated how an intersectional lens, using race and gender, further puts the lie to the universalist claim of blindness in the face of the law. See, for example, work by Naomi Davidson, Joan Scott, Nalini Mayanthi, Bronwyn Winter, Todd Shepard, Nimisha Barton, and Anna Kemp, among many others.
63 Scott, *Politics of the Veil*, 96.

64 In my view it is no accident that two of the oldest, strongest democracies – France and the United States – have never elected female leaders. If democracy was defined as masculine at its very origins, beauty is something apart from masculinity, and women's only access to power is through aesthetics, it stands to reason that it is not despite democratic ideologies that women have had so little access to power, but because of them.

65 Hunt points to Marianne's non-threatening femininity as one of the reasons for her selection as the new symbol of France at the time. Women like Marie Antoinette or Mme de Roland represented challenges to the desired masculine authority of the revolutionaries. However, "the French Republic could find in the feminine allegory [of Marianne] a figure suitably distant from the real-life-heroes-turned-villains of the revolutionary process." Hunt argues that Marianne's "abstraction and impersonality" are the very reason she survives as a symbol even today. See Hunt, *Politics*, 93. This use of female symbols to represent a nation – while denying the agency afforded to male citizens – is not unique to France. As Cynthia Enloe writes, women "often have been treated by male nationalist leaders and intellectuals chiefly as symbols – patriarchally sculpted symbols – of the nation." Enloe, *Bananas, Beaches, and Bases*, 76.

66 Neiertz, "Air France: An Elephant in an Evening Suit?," 36.

67 Sontag, "A Woman's Beauty," 805.

68 Many gender historians, theorists, and other scholars have engaged with that concept of gender and power, including notable names like Judith Butler, Judith Lorber, and Anne Fausto-Sterling.

69 See Virgili, *Shorn Women*; Capdevila, 'The Quest for Masculinity in a Defeated France"; Shepard, *Sex, France, and Arab Men*, 2018.

70 See Henry Rousso's famous work on *résistancialisme*, especially his *Vichy Syndrome*.

71 Here I should make the distinction between attracting and taking American tourist dollars, something quite different from and far less fraught than allowing American interests to influence France and the French economy, something which major figures like Charles de Gaulle adamantly opposed, perceiving it as a "challenge" to the French way of life. Even people in the business community in France, who might be counted as some of the friendliest toward American investment, "accepted the need for vigilance" against American domination, according to Richard Kuisel. Kuisel, *Seducing the French*, 160, 167. Kuisel does not consider women or gender in his analysis. There is also a distinction to be made with regard to American military influence and prowess. France famously, under de Gaulle, partially withdrew from the NATO alliance in protest against what de Gaulle saw as "American predominance in the alliance"; France's withdrawal was also an attempt to assert French "security and grandeur." See Kaplan, *NATO and the US*, 90. See also Bozo, *Two Strategies for Europe*, 163–78.

72 Brogi, *A Question of Self-Esteem*, 233–4; Vaïsse, *La Grandeur*, 35. Vaïsse describes the word "grandeur" as "constant" under de Gaulle's leadership.

73 Hecht, *The Radiance of France*, 37. I would also note that the concept of "men of action" was present during the Third Republic, especially with respect to figures like Joseph Gallieni and Hubert Lyautey. In this case, we are seeing "men of action" constructing France's technological empire. For more, see Edward Berenson's *Heroes of Empire: Five Charismatic Men and the Conquest of Africa* and Geoff Read's *The Republic of Men*. In his guise as the titular head of France's aeronautics industry, Henri Desbruères could be described as one such "man of action" in the postwar era. Desbruères delivered a speech at the Brussels World Exposition in 1958 in which he lauded the major advances the French had achieved in aviation since the time of the Liberation, calling it a triumph for all people in the nation. The statistics he cited were striking: 80 per cent of the country's aviation-related factories had been destroyed during the Second World War, but, he argued, "thanks to the will of all those who participated in this national effort," the French industry could be counted in the top ranks of global aviation. Desbruères, "Réalisations aéronautiques françaises," 341.
74 Sampson, *Empires of the Sky*, 119.
75 Gibson, *The Flag*, 158.
76 Sampson, *Empires of the Sky*, 145.
77 I think the massive efforts to control air traffic to the francophone world necessarily complicates the (porous) line between colonial and postcolonial. In the context of the American empire, see Daniel Immerwahr's *How to Hide an Empire*, which details how the United States used innovative methods – including military airbases on far-flung outposts – to control vast swaths of the world. See also Jenifer Van Vleck's *Empire of the Air*.
78 Gibson, *The Flag*, 193.
79 Sampson, *Empires of the Sky*, 146. Perhaps unsurprisingly, though, one of the most successful and collaborative African airlines, Air Afrique, was essentially controlled by a French company, UAT (which later became UTA).
80 Desbruères, "Réalisations aéronautiques françaises," 345.
81 Sampson, *Empires of the Sky*, 118.
82 Schwartz, "Dimanche à Orly," 29.
83 "À Maligny avec nos futures hôtesses," *Terre et ciel* 1, no. 4 (May–June 1946): 10.
84 France was not necessarily alone in tacitly promoting whiteness as a criteria for becoming a flight attendant. It was not until 1958 that the United States saw the first Black flight attendant, Ruth Carol Taylor of Mohawk Airlines, who was selected from 800 applicants to break the colour barrier – and had recently been rejected from TWA based on her race. See Barry, *Femininity in Flight*, 114–22. See also Vantoch's story of Patricia Banks, who fought racial discrimination to become a flight attendant with Capital Airlines. Vantoch, *Jet Sex*, 63–86.
85 The time period covered in this book coincides with a massive increase in immigration to France. From 1946 to 1975, the number of immigrants living in France doubled. See Gildea, *France since 1945*, 94. Additionally, there is a long

history of race, sex, and empire in France, with white women often standing as symbols of civilization, hygiene, and superiority, in contrast with women (and men) of colour. See, for example, Marie-Paule Ha's *French Women and the Empire*, in which she describes how white women's presence in Indochina became essential to the process of colonization. See also Patricia Lorcin's *Historicizing Colonial Nostalgia* and Sarah Curtis's *Civilizing Habits*.

86 For more context on race and postwar France, see Maud Mandel's *Muslims and Jews in France*; Joan Scott's *Politics of the Veil*; Mayanthi Fernando's *The Republic Unsettled*, and Todd Shepard's *The Invention of Decolonization*. Shepard, in particular, discusses how the French effectively "othered" Muslims during the process of decolonization, both in denying them rights and in perpetuating and promulgating racism on the ground in France. See Shepard, *The Invention of Decolonization*, 229–47. Where Shepard's concern is largely political and formal, the racism I refer to above is more cultural. American historians of the aviation industry have been more intersectional in their analyses. See, for example, Arlie Hochschild's *Managed Heart*, in which she makes the case that the American flight attendant, while heavily influenced by her French counterpart, also has origins in the white, genteel, Southern hostess model, dating back to antebellum plantations. Hochschild, 93.

87 Sampson, *Empires of the Sky*, 119.

88 Van Vleck, *Empire of the Air*, 185. Aviation was not the only arena in which France impeded former colonies' efforts to carve out their own identities in the era of decolonization. Jessica Pearson has argued that the French government actively stifled WHO efforts to improve health services in places like sub-Saharan Africa, as French officials were fearful that such measures would inspire anti-colonialism and rebellion. See Pearson, *Colonial Politics of Global Health*, 89–112. Pearson also lays out this claim forcefully in her article on French officials' negotiations about the future of its empire during the founding of the UN. In an article, she quotes a memo from the Ministry of Foreign Affairs which stated: "A global France of more than one hundred million people can survive and try to play a decisive role in world politics. A France reduced to its metropolitan territory so comparatively inconsequential and to a population so weak that it ceases to count, ceases to exist. At San Francisco, France is gambling its definitive fate. To play and win, what can be done?" Clearly, the stakes of such transitional institutions as health organizations and airlines were quite high at the time. Pearson, "The French Empire Goes to San Francisco," 35–6.

89 K. Ross, *Fast Cars, Clean Bodies*, 7.

90 Nye, *Soft Power*, x.

91 Nye, 13. Nye also notes that France is by far the world's largest spender on soft power even at the time of his writing in 2004, allotting $17 per capita, four times as much as second-place Canada, and dwarfing the United States' comparatively paltry 65 cents. Nye, 85.

92 Nye, 76. There are some historians of France who have employed Nye's theory within the context of the Hexagon. Perhaps most notably, François Chaubet has delved into France's linguistic outreaches, starting with the Alliance Française in the nineteenth century and extending into France's campaign to ensure that France remains a dominant language in developing regions.

93 Endy mentions the French anti-rudeness campaign. Walton discusses the resumption of study abroad after the Second World War, and Kuisel explores France's protectionist measures in the face of American cultural invasion.

94 Whitney Walton points to the distance between models of behaviour and lived experience in her work on study abroad, stating that "information from hearsay or from the media still could not replace or reproduce the kind of understanding often achieved through study abroad." Walton, *Internationalism*, 192. However, the number of students studying abroad – indeed attending college at all – was still quite low (fewer than 40,000 total in the dozen years between 1959 and 1971), meaning that few people on either side of the Atlantic had access to such direct confrontations of their stereotypes. Walton, 144–5.

1 Creating the Model Hostess

1 Philippe Roland, "Une révolution dans le ciel," *Le Figaro*, 3 March 1946, 1. The very first air hostesses were actually recruited directly from the French Red Cross, based on their experience in health and safety protection. It was later, in 1946, under the authority of Bernard d'Astorg, that they became cultural icons, recruited from the ranks of French laypeople. Air France editor and writer Philippe-Michel Thibault has described their 1946 mission as "the sensual woman who inspires dreams and brings comfort, halfway between the femme fatale and the mother at home." See Thibault, *Mythologies à bord*, 26.

2 Catry, *Sur les ailes de l'hippocampe*, 17. Another hostess, Madeleine Thiplouse, referred to passengers as "pilgrims" because they were constantly praying on flights. See "Madeleine raconte," *France-aviation*, April 1978, 1–2.

3 Autier, *Air France, Des années héroïques à la refondation*, 27. See also Ugalde, *Histoire de l'hôtesse de l'air*, 38–40.

4 "Le Ruban rouge à Solange Catry," *France-aviation*, no. 292 (October 1979): 10.

5 "Air France Annales: Le Bilan 1946," *Terre et ciel*, December 1946, 17.

6 Effectif du personnel d'Air France, 31 December 1948. Air France Archives (hereafter AF Archives).

7 "Les effectifs," AF Archives & "Personnel," AF Archives.

8 Still, this statistic does not take into account the massive growth of hostessing beyond airplanes, which is covered in chapters 2 and 3. Also, it should be noted that within Air France, women were relegated to either hostessing or secretarial positions; for all their publicity as the face of Air France, they constituted less than one-quarter of the company's employees in 1979.

9 Roland, "Une révolution dans le ciel."
10 Duchen, *Women's Rights and Women's Lives*, 51.
11 Duchen, *Women's Rights and Women's Lives*, 161. Scholars, especially in the field of sociology, have recently used the term aesthetic labour to denote the kinds of requirements placed upon women (and, to a lesser extent, men) in public work settings. Retail and service industries, which burgeoned in the postwar period and to which category air hostesses belong(ed), were the main target for such requirements. Scholars' recent focus on aesthetic labour tends to concentrate on stores and events, with little emphasis on the historical antecedents of how demands on workers play out in today's markets. These historical subjects merit much more attention in particular, with regard to women in positions working with the public. For more on aesthetic labour, see the work of Lynne Pettinger, Anne Witz, Chris Warhurst, Dennis Nickson, Deborah Dean, and Kjersten Elmen-Gruys. One exception to the historical treatment of women in such careers is Donna Halper's *Invisible Stars*, a popular history which delves into the aesthetic requirements for female broadcasters.
12 Although certainly subjective and (sometimes) less overt than those associated with air hostesses, women's beauty requirements remain all around us today in workplaces where people interact with the public. See Nancy Etcoff, *Survival of the Prettiest*, Deborah Rhode, *Beauty Bias*, and Daniel Hamermesh, *Beauty Pays*, for more on how perceptions of beauty continue to impact financial and career success for all people, regardless of gender identification.
13 Catry, *Sur les ailes*, 25.
14 Roland, "Une révolution dans le ciel," 1.
15 Roland, "Une révolution dans le ciel," 1.
16 "À Maligny avec nos futures hôtesses," 10.
17 "Jeunes filles devant la porte du ciel," *Le Monde*, 17 April 1948, 8.
18 T.V., "Jeunes filles volantes," *Aviation française*, 17 April 1946.
19 Catry, *Sur les ailes*, 25–6.
20 Roland, "Une révolution dans le ciel," 1.
21 Quoted in Ugalde, *Histoire de l'hôtesse de l'air*, 44.
22 Hymans, "L'Hôtesse de l'air," 261–2.
23 Hymans, "L'Hôtesse de l'air," 262.
24 Hymans, "L'Hôtesse de l'air," 264.
25 J-C G, "Charme: Examen de passage pour l'air: Quand passent les hôtesses," *Sud-Ouest*, 17 December 1967, 3.
26 Catry, *Sur les ailes*, 49–50.
27 Catry, *Sur les ailes*, 50.
28 Duchen, *Women's Rights and Women's Lives*, 144.
29 Catry, *Sur les ailes*, 15.
30 D'Unienville, *En vol*, 112. D'Unienville later became quite disillusioned with the company, as is evident in her memoir. In 1950, she won the Prix

Albert Londres, sort of an equivalent of the Pulitzer Prize for young French journalists, for *En vol*.
31 "Notre dernière gagnante nous écrit," *France-aviation*, no. 19 (June 1950).
32 Robert Belleret, "La passion Air France," *Le Monde*, 8 October 2003, 14.
33 Catry, *Sur les ailes*, 49.
34 Catry, *Sur les ailes*, 50.
35 Cadet, Jean-Roger, Denise Fabre, and Claude Mennessier, "Marie-Josée: hôtesse de l'air," *Magazine de la jeune fille*, 1967, Office de la radiodiffusion et de la télévision, INA.
36 "Une dacquoise représente la France à New York," *Sud-Ouest*, 22 April 22, 1957, 2.
37 "Huit charmantes girondines seront hôtesses au service Air France," *Sud-Ouest*, 10 December 1968, 7.
38 For purposes of comparison, today's requirements for flight attendant training generally include safety course of several weeks' duration at company headquarters; they do not include body, age, or marital criteria, which is in part due to anti-discrimination cases brought against major companies – including Air France – by flight attendants themselves.
39 "Répondez Monsieur X., L'aviation, hôtesse de l'air," 30 January 1958, INA, #CPF86635762, Collection RTF/ORTF.
40 Catry, *Sur les ailes*, 27.
41 Catry, 27. Still another hostess, Madeleine Thiplouse, recalled listening in rapt attention to a lesson from the famous poet Bertrand d'Astorg. See "Madeleine raconte," *France aviation*, April 1978, 1–2.
42 PNC Manual, 1/1/1954, Air France Museum, Part Two, Chapter Two, p. 4.
43 Catry, *Sur les ailes*, 27.
44 PNC Manual, 1/1/1954, Air France Museum, Part Two, Chapter Two, p. 6.
45 Untitled photograph, *France-aviation*, December 1961 (A8 N38), C.
46 PNC Manual, 1/1/1954, Air France Museum, Part Two, Chapter Two, p. 5.
47 "Des jeunes filles volantes sont cultivées dans une serre nommé 'Jonas,'" *Le Monde*, 26 May 1955, 4.
48 Untitled article, *Air-France Revue*, no. 32 (November 1962–May 1963): 21.
49 "Des jeunes filles volantes," 4.
50 PNC Manual, 1/1/1954, Air France Museum, Part Two, Chapter Two, p. 3.
51 Manuel du commissaire et de l'hôtesse, 1948, Air France Museum, Part Two, Chapter 1, p. 1.
52 Cadet, Fabre, and Mennessier, "Marie-Josée: hôtesse de l'air."
53 T.V., "Jeunes filles volantes."
54 Roche, *Culture of Clothing*, 229.
55 Woolf, *Three Guineas*, 21.
56 Indeed the women had to pay for half of their uniforms until 1953, when the company took over the full cost. Thibault, *Mythologies à bord*, 27.

182 Notes to pages 31–5

57 Catry, *Sur les ailes*, 188. Georgette de Trèze, another designer, created an updated look in 1951.
58 "Le siècle de la casquette," *Air-France Revue*, no. 29 (March–August 1961): 68.
59 Air France Manuel du commissaire et de l'hôtesse, 1948, Air France Museum, Part 1, Chapter 5, p. 2.
60 Air France Manuel du commissaire et de l'hôtesse, 1948, Air France Museum, Part 1, Chapter 5, pp. 2, 8, 10.
61 Thibault, *Air France*, 44. There had been another version, designed by Georgette de Trèze, that appeared in 1951, but it was similar to the Renal version. Thibault, *Mythologies à bord*, 30.
62 http://www.airfrancelasaga.com/en/content/uniforms
63 Hélène Kernel, "La mode des vacances," *Air-France Revue*, no. 31 (June–August 1962): 10. See also "Nouvelle tenue pour les hôtesses d'Air France," *France-aviation*, no. 90 (May 1962): 4.
64 Kernel, "La mode des vacances," 10.
65 "NEW-LOOK pour les hôtesses d'Air France," *Le Monde*, 5 April 1962, 13.
66 Kernel, "La mode des vacances," 10.
67 Philippe, *Sylvie, hôtesse de l'air*, 21.
68 Puget, *The Long Haul*, 38.
69 Cadet, Fabre, and Mennessier, "Marie-Josée: hôtesse de l'air."
70 Roe, *La Vie d'une hôtesse d'Air France*, 32.
71 PNC Manual, 1/1/1954, Air France Museum, Part Two, Chapter Three, p. 2.
72 T.V., "Jeunes filles volantes." Interestingly, sociologists Melissa Tyler and Scott Taylor have described flight attendants' contemporary cabin performance as a gift exchange in the spirit of Marcel Mauss. In their work, flight attendants essentially commodify their femininity, or what Tyler and Taylor refer to as their "Otherness" as women, and use it to serve, coddle, and please passengers. Tyler and Taylor point out that nowhere in their job description does it state that flight attendants *must* commodify femininity, which renders that quality an unpaid, unrecognized "gift" to passengers. See Tyler and Taylor, "The Exchange of Aesthetics," 165–7.
73 Air France Manuel du commissaire et de l'hôtesse, 1948, Air France Museum, Part 2, Chapter 2, p. 1.
74 Air France Manuel du commissaire et de l'hôtesse, 1948, Air France Museum, Part 2, Chapter 3, p. 1.
75 Air France Manuel du commissaire et de l'hôtesse, 1948, Air France Museum, Part 2, Chapter 3, p. 4.
76 Hervé Lauwick, "Les femmes voyagent en avion," *France-aviation* 2, no. 25 (December 1956): 1, 4, 5.
77 PNC Manual, 1/1/1954, Air France Museum, Part Two, Chapter Two, p. 1.
78 ASSEMBLEE NATIONALE – 2e SEANCE DU 20 AVRIL 1948, p. 2380. http://4e.republique.jo-an.fr/page2/1948_p2380.pdf

79 Catry, *Sur les ailes*, 18.
80 D'Unienville, *En vol*, 11.
81 D'Unienville, 56.
82 Robert Savreux, "Le produit vendu: Du souvenir. Le client s'attache à la marque," *France-aviation* 4, no. 37 (December 1957): 3.
83 Hochschild, *The Managed Heart*, 36–7.
84 Hochschild, *The Managed Heart*, 49.
85 Air France Manuel du commissaire et de l'hôtesse, 1948, Air France Museum, Part 2, Chapter 3, p. 2.
86 Other airlines also mandated smiles, but Air France made it a hallmark of both the hostess training program and of company advertising for decades. See Black, *Smile, Particularly in Bad Weather*, regarding Australian hostesses.
87 1959 Air France ad, Air France Museum. Kammerling (photographer).
88 Air France ad, "Comment voyager sans devises," *Sud-Ouest*, 25 January 1969, 7.
89 1956 Air France ad, Air France Museum, unattributed.
90 1969 Air France ad, Air France Museum, Pietrini Bastard Fouqueray (printer).
91 "Entretien avec M. Joseph ROOS, Président d'Air France," *France-aviation*, no. 85 (December 1961): A, F.
92 B.R., "Les voix qui sourient: Les téléphonistes à l'avant-garde des ventes," *France-aviation*, no. 19 (June 1956): 4–5.
93 Jacques Vulaines, "Cinq cent millions de kilomètres dans le ciel," *Sud-Ouest*, 1 March 1959, 10.
94 "Mademoiselle, voulez-vous devenir … hôtesse de l'air," *Sud-Ouest*, 11 May 1952, 9.
95 Delahaye, *Martine en avion*, 7. Although the author of the series was Belgian, it was hugely popular in France.
96 Probst, *Caroline en avion*, 8.
97 Beaumont, *La journée de l'hôtesse et du stewart*, 6.
98 Vulaines, "Cinq cent millions de kilomètres dans le ciel," 10.
99 J-C G, "Charme," 3.
100 Supplement, "Un frais bouquet de sourires," *France-aviation* 5, no. 38 (September 1958): B.
101 Solange Catry, "Sourires nouveaux," *Air-France Revue*, December 1961–February 1962, 57–8.
102 Puget, *Long Haul*, 38.
103 Puget, *Long Haul*, 59.
104 Puget, *Long Haul*, 110.
105 Puget, *Long Haul*, 169.
106 Puget, *Long Haul*, 219.
107 Philippe, *Sylvie, hôtesse de l'air*, 9.
108 Roe, *La Vie d'une hôtesse d'Air France*, 26.
109 Roe, *La Vie d'une hôtesse d'Air France*, 27.

110 D'Unienville, *En vol*, 12.
111 D'Unienville, *En vol*, 11.
112 Patricia Pullan, "Forced Gaiety," *The Sun*, 7 October 1969, B1.
113 Hochschild, *The Managed Heart*, 21.
114 Philippe, *Sylvie, hôtesse de l'air*, 74.
115 Philippe, *Sylvie, hôtesse de l'air*, 148.
116 Philippe, *Sylvie, hôtesse de l'air*, 151.
117 "Annick, hôtesse de l'air," *Les Cahiers du GRIF*, no. 11 (special issue, *Le travail c'est la santé*, 1976): 15.
118 "Solange Catry: Sa vie en l'air," *Versailles Magazine*, September 2009, 10.
119 "Eléments du confort à bord," *Aviation française* 3, no.19: 10–12. Fathers are not mentioned as child providers, in keeping with the gender expectations of the time.
120 "Le voyage commence … la perfection du confort," *Air-France Revue* 15 (June–August 1948): n.p.
121 Bookmark, Air France Museum, undated. The bookmark is unattributed, but Air France phased out the Constellation over the course of the 1950s and 1960s.
122 D'Almeras, Roger, "Les enfants préfèrent l'avion," *Air-France Revue* 15 (September–November 1950): 39–42.
123 Roe, *La Vie d'une hôtesse de l'air*, 29.
124 Pierre Probst, "Cahier coloriage de Caravelle," colouring book, Air France Museum, 1959.
125 Pamphlet, "Your children travel …," Air France Museum, 1960.
126 Air France Manuel du commissaire et de l'hôtesse, 1948, Air France Museum, Part 2, Chapter 3, p. 4.
127 Delahaye, *Martine en avion*, 14.
128 Delahaye, *Martine en avion*, 15.
129 Probst, *Caroline en avion*, 19.
130 Philippe, *Sylvie, hôtesse de l'air*, 147.
131 Roe, *La Vie d'une hôtesse d'Air France*, 28.
132 B.R., "Ce que femme veut," *France-aviation* 6, no. 60: 1.
133 D'Unienville, *En vol*, 24.
134 Catry, *On the Wings*, 59.
135 Catry, *On the Wings*, 62.
136 Hervé Lauwick, "Quand les hommes iront aussi vite que le soleil," *France-aviation* 3, no. 29 (April 1957): 4–5.
137 Puget, *Long Haul*, 59.
138 Puget, *Long Haul*, 67.
139 Cadet, Fabre, and Mennessier, "Marie-Josée: hôtesse de l'air."
140 Puget, *Long Haul*, 51.
141 Puget, *Long Haul*, 94.
142 Puget, *Long Haul*, 96.

143 Air France Manuel du commissaire et de l'hôtesse, 1948, Air France Museum, Part 2, Chapter 3, p. 1.
144 Air France Manuel du commissaire et de l'hôtesse, 1948, Air France Museum, Part 2, Chapter 3, p. 2.
145 PNC Manual, 1/1/1954, Air France Museum, Part Two, Chapter Three, p. 2.
146 Puget, *Long Haul*, 85.
147 Puget, *Long Haul*, 183.
148 Hymans, "L'Hôtesse de l'air," 264.
149 Philippe, *Sylvie, hôtesse de l'air*, 151.
150 Catry, *Sur les ailes*, 48.
151 Duchen, *Women's Rights and Women's Lives*, 168.
152 Catry, *Sur les ailes*, 171.
153 Puget, *Long Haul*, 42.
154 "L'hôtesse de l'air désire se marier … elle deviendra, hôtesse d'accueil!" *Aviation française*, 1 January 1947, 3.
155 R.J., "Deuxième conférence internationale sur les problèmes sociaux de l'aviation civile," *France-aviation* 7, no. 73 (December 1960): 2–3, 7.
156 "Les hôtesses de bord d'Air France doivent rester célibataires," *Sud-Ouest*, 16 June 1961, 3. (UPI article.)
157 Paulette Carret, "Cette maman qui a fait peur aux compagnies aériennes," *Sud-Ouest*, 12 May 1963, 9.
158 "Les hôtesses de bord d'Air France doivent rester célibataires," 3.
159 Stanton Delaplane, "Postcard from Salt Lake," *San Francisco Chronicle*, 21 February 2010, Q16 (reprint). See also "The Right to Marry," *Asian and Indian Skyways*, July 1963; "£1000 Award to Air Hostess," *The Guardian*, 1 May 1963, 10; "Right to Wed," *Florence [SC] Morning News*, 1 May 1963, 8 (API article); "Fired for Marriage, Hostess Wins Suit," *Washington Post*, 1 May 1963, A11; and "Stewardess, a Mrs., Wins Suit against Air France," *NYT*, 1 May 1963, 78; "Seat Belts, Please," *NYT*, 5 May 1963, 192.
160 Carret, "Cette maman qui a fait peur aux compagnies aériennes," 9.
161 *Barbier vs. Air France*, Appeal Decision, *Recueil Dalloz*, 1963, 24th Fascicle, 428.
162 *Barbier vs. Air France*, Appeal Decision, *Recueil Dalloz*, 1963, 24th Fascicle, 428. The couple, Anne-Marie and Pierre Barbier, would go on to help found the SNPNC, the labour union of Air France's in-cabin workers.
163 "Air France battu en appel: Les hôtesses pourront se marier," *Sud-Ouest*, 2 May 1963, 1, 14.
164 "£1000 Award to Air Hostess," 10.
165 A similar phenomenon developed in other countries, where hostesses also often came to the fore of women's postwar labour actions. See Vantoch, *Jet Sex*, and Barry, *Femininity in Flight*.
166 Catry, *Sur les ailes*, 176.

167 "Mademoiselle, voulez-vous devenir ... hôtesse de l'air," *Sud-Ouest*, 11 May 1952, 9.
168 "Annick, hôtesse de l'air."
169 Catry, *Sur les ailes*, 176.
170 Catry, *Sur les ailes*, 169.
171 Roe, *La Vie d'une hôtesse d'Air France*, 35.
172 J-C G, "Charme," 3.
173 Duchen, *Women's Rights and Women's Lives*, 164.
174 The following chapter will demonstrate many of the informal requirements, like beauty and body shape, that women faced, as opposed to formal opposition, like court cases and company rules.
175 1958 Air France ad, *New York Herald Tribune*, September 14, 1958, D13.
176 1967 Air France ad, Air France Museum, Joe Hamman (Photographer).
177 1971 Air France ad, Air France Museum, Kremer (Photographer).
178 "L'hôtesse de l'air," music by Jacques Dutronc, words by Jacques Lanzmann. Cited in *Un siècle de chansons françaises: Vol. 1969-1979, 301 chansons françaises de 1969 à 1979* (Paris: Chambre syndicale de l'édition musicale, 2006), 191.
179 Fishman, *From Vichy to the Sexual Revolution*.
180 "La femme et l'avion," *Échos de l'air* 1, no. 1: 11.
181 Ravon, "Les voyageurs imaginaires," *Air-France Revue*, September–November 1950, 96-9.
182 Daley, *A Priest and A Girl*, 90.
183 Nadine B., *32 Escales* (Paris: Éditions du Trèfle d'or, 1966), n.p.
184 Catry, *Sur les ailes*, 142.
185 Catry, *Sur les ailes*, 45.
186 Catry, *Sur les ailes*, 79.
187 "Madeleine raconte," *France-aviation*, April 1978, 1-2.
188 Daley, *A Priest and a Girl*, 92.
189 Daley, *A Priest and a Girl*, 95.
190 Catry, *Sur les ailes*, 33.
191 Catry, *Sur les ailes*, 33.
192 Puget, *Long Haul*, 140-3.
193 Catry, *Sur les ailes*, 74.
194 Catry, *Sur les ailes*, 176.
195 Catry, *Sur les ailes*, 173-4.
196 Catry, *Sur les ailes*, 175.
197 Aude Carasco, "La vie comme elle va," *La Croix*, 7 October 2003, 28.

2 Hostessing beyond the Airplane

1 Endy, *Cold War Holidays*, 54.
2 *Journal officiel de la République française: Avis et rapports du Conseil économique*, 3 February 1959, 326-7.

3 Catry, *Sur les ailes*, 96.
4 Air France ad, Yves Alexandre, créateur, Air France Museum, 1949.
5 L.-C., Z., "C'est ça la France !" *Le Monde*, 3 April 1957, 13. The article noted that the television broadcast would not be live, unlike the radio one.
6 Jean Couvreur, "La reine d'Angleterre et le prince Philip ont traversé les rues pavoisées de Paris au milieu des acclamations De l'aéroport d'Orly au palais de l'Élysée," *Le Monde*, 9 April 1957, 1.
7 "Orchidée mauve à leur corsage: Les débutantes américaines arrivent à Orly," *Sud-Ouest*, 11 July 1958, 14.
8 "Une dacquoise représente la France à New York," *Sud-Ouest*, 22 April 1957, 2.
9 "Cette jolie dacquoise est la dauphine de l'hôtesse de l'air idéale," *Sud-Ouest*, 25 April 1957, 3.
10 "Air France Plane Here from Paris; Flowers Arrive for First Lady," *NYT*, 26 June 1946, 12; see also "French Air Line Celebrates," *New York Herald Tribune*, 27 June 1946, 27.
11 Photograph, *Terre et ciel* 1, no. 10 (December 1946): 21.
12 "Air France Celebrates with 20 Candles Tuesday," *WWD*, 23 March, 10.
13 "Mardi soir, au Couroucou, un cocktail a fêté la liaison directe par Air France Bordeaux-Genève," *Sud-Ouest*, 14 April 1967, 10.
14 Jacques Forlacroix, "'Versailles' de Verre: La nouvelle aérogare d'Orly a reçu hier ses premiers passagers," *Sud-Ouest*, 9 March 1961, 1, 14.
15 "Pour moderniser son aviation civile le roi Hussein de Jordanie envisage l'achat de 'Caravelle' et de 'Mystère-20,'" *Sud-Ouest*, 17 September 1963, 14.
16 Jerry Hulse, "French Jet Transport Arrives at 395 MPH," *LA Times*, 6 June 1957, 5.
17 "People and Places," *Chicago Tribune*, 29 August 1965, H4.
18 Frances Cawthon, "Glamour? They're Way Up There," *Atlanta Journal and Atlanta Constitution*, 18 February 1962, 6E.
19 Vantoch, *Jet Sex*, 108.
20 "14 French Stewardesses Arrive," *New York Herald Tribune*, 28 May 1956, A1.
21 "Hostesses with a French Accent," *Washington Post*, 1 June 1956, 2.
22 "Airline Goes French: Allegheny Will Use Air France Stewardesses as 'Envoys,'" *NYT*, 27 May 1956, 185.
23 "14 French Stewardesses Arrive."
24 Wendell P. Bradley, "Barnes Guides Fast Rise of Allegheny Airlines: Firm Has Doubled Passenger Traffic in Past Four Years," *Washington Post*, 24 March 1957, C11.
25 Volney D. Hurd, "World-Wide Shopping Habits Offset Stiff Working Hours," *Christian Science Monitor*, 24 May 1949, 10.
26 "Air France Hostesses, Guests of Northeast," *Boston Globe*, 6 May 1962, B5.
27 Kathleen Neumayer, "French Stewardesses Give America a Try," *Atlanta Constitution*, 30 August 1969, 18T.
28 "Photo Standalone 35," *Boston Globe*, 27 May 1962, 78.

29 "Riviera Wardrobes Shown aboard Plane," *NYT*, 8 December 1948, 40.
30 Agnes Ash, "Customs Men and Store Brokers Get to See Imported French Styles First," *NYT*, 4 March 1958, 24. See also "The Flight of the Pelican," *Vogue*, 15 April 1966, 150.
31 Advertisement: Christian Dior, *Vogue*, 15 September 1962, 67, 68, 69.
32 Neiman Marcus ad, *Vogue*, 1 October 1957, 101–35.
33 "Airline Will Offer Cards to Showings," *NYT*, 13 August 1960, 9.
34 "Doors Opened to Fashions of Paris," *LA Times*, 2 May 1965, J5.
35 Air France ad, *WWD*, 28 June 1961, 22.
36 Ad for Davison's, *Atlanta Constitution*, 28 November 1960, 3.
37 "Lane Bryant Will Show Air France Flight Fashions," *Boston Globe*, 10 March 1959, 3; Abraham & Strauss ad, *NYT*, 22 June 1952, 16; "John W. Miller's Storewide Semi-Annual Sale," *Washington Post*, 13 August 1960, A6; May Co. ad, *LA Times*, 6 November 1946, 28.
38 "Dior Designs Will Fly," *Christian Science Monitor*, 23 April 1962, 4.
39 "Paris Nurses Get Uniforms in High Style," *NYT*, 19 July 1963, 10; "L'Air de France," *WWD*, 3 April 1962, 16.
40 Caroline McColl, "Minding the Store," *WWD*, 1 February 1963, 6.
41 "Doors Opened to Fashions of Paris," *LA Times*, 2 May 1965, J5. See also Marylin Bender, "Some Women in Uniform Wear Designer Fashions," *NYT*, 29 November 1963, 45; Eugenia Sheppard, "Farthest in for Spring," *New York Herald Tribune*, 30 March 1962, 17.
42 Rosalind Massow, "The Fashion Race in the Sky," *Boston Globe*, 28 May 1967, C12.
43 Eugenia Sheppard, "Before Lunch," *LA Times*, 26 November 1968, D7.
44 "Top Parisian Hair Stylist Visits Filene's," *Boston Globe*, 24 October 1954, 2.
45 Rebecca Blake, "FASHIONS: French Hair Stylist Visits Filene's New Beauty Salon," *Boston Globe*, 2 November 1954, 9.
46 Abraham & Strauss ad, *NYT*, 26 November 1954, 12.
47 Marilyn Bender, "Coiffeur Here 'to Make a Revolution,'" *NYT*, 11 October 1962, 64.
48 Marie McNair, "Town Topics," *Washington Post*, 23 October 1962, B5.
49 Cawthon, "Glamour? They're Way Up There."
50 May Co. ad, *LA Times*, 17 September 1956, 30.
51 Bergdorf Goodman ad, *NYT*, 16 April 1961, 97; Bergdorf Goodman ad, *New York Herald Tribune*, 11 December 1960, 61; Marshall Field & Company ad, *Chicago Tribune*, 4 March 1963, 9; May Co. ad, *LA Times*, 2 April 1967, E7; Bergdorf Goodman ad, *NYT*, 16 April 1967, 103; Bergdorf Goodman ad, *NYT*, 21 April 1968, 121.
52 Christian Dior ad, *Vogue*, 15 October 1960, 25.
53 Frances Rowan, "Paris Is Here in Spring," *Washington Post*, 21 April 1958, B4.
54 "Confort Air France," *Échos de l'air/Bulletin mensuel Air France*, March 1947.

55 "Les Invalides, gare routière," *France-aviation* 8, no. 78 (May 1961): 3. See also "Que trouve-t-on aux Invalides?" *France-aviation* 8, no. 80 (July 1961): 9.
56 Simon, J-P, "Les chariots d'Orly et la campagne d'accueil," *Le Monde*, 18 April 1967, 13.
57 "La représentation régionale d'Air France aux Pays-Bas (Amsterdam-Hollande)," *France-aviation* 13, no. 140 (July 1966, (A13 N140): F.
58 J. LACREVETTE, "Jeunes filles en fleurs à Londres," *France-aviation* 8, no. 81 (August 1961): D.
59 Robert Cusin, "Un sourire … et ses racines profondes," *Air-France Revue*, no. 37 (April–June 1967): 3–5.
60 Cusin, "Un sourire … et ses racines profondes," 5.
61 Cusin, "Un sourire … et ses racines profondes," 3.
62 "L'hôtesse de l'air désire se marier … elle deviendra, hôtesse d'accueil!" *Aviation française*, 1 January 1947, 3.
63 "Vous Reconnaissez-Vous?" *France-aviation* 8, no. 77 (April 1961): E.
64 "Vous Reconnaissez-Vous?" *France-aviation* 13, no. 136 (March 1966): C.
65 "La femme et l'amour du travail," *Terre et ciel* 2, no. 8 (August 1948): 10.
66 Catry, *Sur les ailes*, 177–9.
67 "Air France Ups Age for Hostesses," *Washington Post*, 28 August 1969, A15.
68 "Intelligence Report," *Boston Globe*, 23 November 1969, B4.
69 Tania Bothezat, "But the More Paris Changes …," *Baltimore Sun*, 22 May 1960, 25.
70 Maurois, "Vocations nouvelles," 11.
71 Maurois, "Vocations nouvelles," 11.
72 *Journal officiel de la République française: Avis et rapports du Conseil économique*, 28 February 1959, 333.
73 *Journal officiel de la République française: Avis et rapports du Conseil économique*, 17 January 1960, 249–50.
74 François Xavier Aubry, "Conditions, moyens et limites d'une politique d'information au niveau départemental," *La Revue administrative* 25, no. 145 (January–February 1972): 67, 70–1, 73–6.
75 "A l'intention des touristes étrangers, ouverture d'une campagne d'amabilité et d'hospitalité," *Le Monde*, 7 April 1965, 24.
76 J.M., D.S., "L'équipement hotelier de la capitale: 'Une grande et belle ville, mais …,'" *Le Monde*, 6 November 1971, 17, 19.
77 Photograph, "'Hôtesse de Paris,' Model of Paris Exhibit, Sydney Trade Fair, 1961," State Library of New South Wales, Australia, exhibit 110055180.
78 "À l'Exposition française de Montréal," *Sud-Ouest*, 9 September 1954, 2.
79 "Women's World," *Baltimore Sun*, 14 May 1968, B4.
80 *Journal officiel de la République française: Avis et rapports du Conseil économique*, 28 September 1972.
81 Henry Wales, "Paris Girls Act as Guides for U.S. Tourists," *Chicago Daily Tribune*, 28 May 1950, G7.

82 "When in Paris …," *Christian Science Monitor*, 22 August 1956, 17.
83 "Hôtesses du rail," *Le Monde*, 30 June 1956, 8.
84 "Les plus aimables hôtesses du bon accueil," *Le Monde*, 18 June 1957, 9.
85 "Foire de Bordeaux 1966: Au carrefour de la tradition et du renouveau," *Sud-Ouest*, 18 June 1966, 14.
86 "Duyndam gagne l'étape et Stevens devient leader," *Sud-Ouest*, 9 March 1968, 8.
87 "Les souverains danois à Paris," *Le Monde*, 23 April 1955, 1.
88 "À partir du 4 juin, les parisiens assisteront aux représentations de la plus ancienne troupe du monde," *Sud-Ouest*, 1 June 1955, 12.
89 "Un centre des échanges pour les visiteurs étrangers," *Le Monde*, 18 May 1955, 6. Hostesses performed similar functions at various expositions and fairs throughout this period. See, for example, "Le XXXe salon de la machine agricole," *Le Monde*, 10 March 1959, 8–9. See also "Les fêtes de la saison de Paris," *Le Monde*, 21 March 1959, 13.
90 "Dans les coulisses du Congrès international de la chimie …," *Sud-Ouest*, 5 October 1961, 5.
91 Delestrée was one of several influential theorists of postwar tourism, a field that saw great development in France due to the economic needs of the nation. See Vukonic, "An Outline of the History of Tourism Theory," 12.
92 Delestrée, "Les nouvelles professions dans l'industrie de tourisme," 124.
93 Delestrée, "Les nouvelles professions dans l'industrie de tourisme," 127.
94 Delestrée, "Les nouvelles professions dans l'industrie de tourisme," 125.
95 Delestrée, "Les nouvelles professions dans l'industrie de tourisme," 125.
96 Delestrée, "Les nouvelles professions dans l'industrie de tourisme," 125.
97 Sénat de France, Notes from Séance, 9 December 1969, M. Marcel Anthionoz, secrétaire d'état au tourisme, 1545.
98 Laporte and Salin, *Hôtesse d'accueil*, 5–6.
99 Delestrée, "Les nouvelles professions dans l'industrie de tourisme," 125.
100 Laporte and Salin, *Hôtesse d'accueil*, 10.
101 Laporte and Salin, *Hôtesse d'accueil*, 11–12.
102 Laporte and Salin, *Hôtesse d'accueil*, 14–15.
103 The labour organizing that air hostesses and welcome hostesses participated in belies some of the passivity associated with the role of perfect hostess and its attendant emotions, but this project is more concerned with the creation and perpetuation of the role itself.
104 Delestrée, "Les nouvelles professions dans l'industrie de tourisme," 126.
105 Laporte and Salin, *Hôtesse d'accueil*, 18.
106 Laporte and Salin, *Hôtesse d'accueil*, 34–5.
107 Delestrée, "Les nouvelles professions dans l'industrie de tourisme," 126.
108 Laporte and Salin, *Hôtesse d'accueil*, 40–1.
109 Delestrée, "Les nouvelles professions dans l'industrie de tourisme," 126.
110 Laporte and Salin, *Hôtesse d'accueil*, 108–9.

111 Noyes Development Corporation, *Cosmetics Industry of Europe 1968*, 31.
112 Noyes Development Corporation, *Cosmetics Industry of Europe 1968*, 40.
113 Only the Americans and Japanese had larger beauty production industries in the postwar years. See Jones, *Beauty Imagined*, 366. Noyes Development Corporation, *Cosmetics Industry of Europe 1968*, 35.
114 Duchen, *Women's Rights and Women's Lives*, 159.
115 Delestrée, "Les nouvelles professions dans l'industrie de tourisme," 126–7.
116 "Front Matter," *La Revue Administrative* 22, no. 128 (1969).
117 Delestrée, "Les nouvelles professions dans l'industrie de tourisme," 126–7.
118 Roe, *La Vie d'une hôtesse d'Air France*, 38, inside back cover.
119 J-G M, "Vingt ans déjà …," *France-aviation*, no. 141 (August 1966): D–E.
120 Endy, *Cold War Holidays*, 169–71.

3 Hostessing Global Events

1 The Cannes Film Festival, while unquestionably important to France's burgeoning film industry and contemporary to this project, is recurring and far too vast of a subject to treat in this book. In my view, it merits its own separate exploration.
2 Henri De Linge, "Expo 58: Les hôtesses de France sont les plus gracieuses … affirment les hôtesses belges," *Le Figaro*, 4 April 1958, 5.
3 Despite the fact that the World Exposition was in Belgium, the French felt like they could draw tourists to France either before or after the events.
4 Henry Giniger, "France's Big Year," *NYT*, 2 March 1958, XX17.
5 Sénat de France, Notes from Séance, 11 February 1958, M. Edouard Bonnefous, ministre des travaux publics, des transports et du tourisme, 250.
6 Daniel M. Madden, "France Forging New Links in 'Friendship Chain,'" *NYT*, 3 May 1964, XX57.
7 "4 305 000 étrangers ont visité notre pays en 1956," *Le Monde*, 9 August 1957, 12.
8 Jean Prasteau, "Dans huit jours Bruxelles … ou cent ans d'expositions internationales," *Le Figaro*, 9 April 1958, 12.
9 "M. Pierre de Gaulle commissaire général de la section française de l'Exposition universelle de Bruxelles," *Le Monde*, 27 January 1955, 10; see also "'Nous serons en 1958 à Bruxelles les grands étalagistes de la France,' nous déclare M. Pierre de Gaulle, commissaire général de la section française," *Le Monde*, 22–23 January 1956, 8.
10 "'Nous serons en 1958 à Bruxelles les grands étalagistes de la France.'"
11 "À l'Exposition de Bruxelles en 1958 la France disposera de 3 hectares sur 50," *Le Monde*, 8–9 January 1956, 3.
12 "L'exposition internationale de Bruxelles," *Le Monde*, 9 June 1955, 16; "Les députés ont adopté plusieurs projets ainsi que les sénateurs," *Le Monde*, 31 December 1956, 5.
13 "Paris aura son pavillon à l'Exposition universelle de Bruxelles de 1958," *Le Monde*, 5 July 1957, 11.

14 "Sept merveilles, plus une, attendront les visiteurs de l'Exposition universelle de Bruxelles," *Sud-Ouest*, 27 January 1958, 3.
15 De Gaulle, Pierre, "Avant-propos," 9–10.
16 "'Nous serons en 1958 à Bruxelles les grands étalagistes de la France'"; see also "À l'Exposition de Bruxelles en 1958 la France disposera de 3 hectares sur 50."
17 Pierre De Vos, "M. René Coty est accueilli par M. Pierre de Gaulle Le président de la République reçoit le roi Baudouin à l'ambassade," *Le Monde*, 9 July 1958, 16.
18 "Quarante-trois nations," *Le Monde*, 15 April 1958, 10.
19 M. Guermantes, "Instants et visages," *Le Figaro*, 1 April 1958, 1.
20 Pierre De Vos, "Le roi baudouin a ouvert ce matin l'exposition de Bruxelles," *Le Monde*, 18 April 1958, 1.
21 "Bruxelles avant l'exposition," *Le Monde*, 29 January 1958, 9.
22 "La participation française," *Le Monde*, 15 April 1958, 10.
23 Raymond Cogniat, "Le protocole de la visite inauguration royale," *Le Figaro*, 17 April 1958, 15.
24 Henri de Linge, "Bonne présentation de tout ce qu'il montre, mais il en montre trop," *Le Figaro*, 28 April 1958, 12.
25 Balmain, "L'élégance française est sans frontières," 48. The government also promoted its upcoming Brussels display at Paris fashion week, in an effort to combine the many arenas where France excelled. See Jessica Daves, "Paris Collections," *Vogue*, 1 March 1958, 104.
26 Sénat de France, Notes from Séance, 11 February 1958, M. Edouard Bonnefous, ministre des travaux publics, des transports et du tourisme, 250.
27 One report noted that in all, 1,600 companies sent some form of support to the Exposition "to show off the achievements of our country to the world." See J. Castellane, "Pierre de Gaulle: Le pavillon français synthèse exceptionnelle de l'esthétique et de la technique," *Le Figaro*, 15 April 1958, 11.
28 "Les plus aimables 'hôtesses du bon accueil," *Le Monde*, 18 June 1957, 9.
29 "Une jolie hôtesse du Sud-Ouest au stand de la Presse à Bruxelles," *Sud-Ouest*, 22 February 1958, 3.
30 Pierre De Vos, "Des nationalistes flamands manifestent devant le pavillon français," *Le Monde*, 8 July 1958, 16.
31 "Le livre français à l'exposition de Bruxelles," *Le Figaro*, 15 October 1958, 16.
32 "Présence d'Air France à Bruxelles," *France-aviation* 5, no. 43 (June 1958, D–E).
33 Jean-Gérard Barraud, "M. Pierre de Gaulle: La France a tenu l'un des grands premiers rôles," *Le Figaro*, 17 October 1958, 14; "Palmarès de l'exposition de Bruxelles: France: étoile d'or, étoile d'argent, 169 grands prix," *Le Figaro*, 16 October 1958, 15; "Communiqué: Un grand succès français à Bruxelles," *Le Figaro*, October 1958, 9.
34 Hélène De Turckheim, "Pour le bal de Paris à Bruxelles luxe, charme, et beauté dans les bagages de l'élégance française," *Le Figaro*, 20 October 1958, 15.

35 M-A Dabadie, "Adieu de grâce et d'élégance de la haute-couture et de la mode parisiennes," *Figaro*, 4–5 October 1958, 7.
36 De Turckheim, "Pour le bal de Paris à Bruxelles," *Le Figaro*, 20 October 1958, 15; "Le 'Bal de Paris' rendez-vous de la jeunesse et manifestation de l'amitié Franco-Belge," *Le Figaro*, 27 October 1958, 14.
37 "1968: Le tournant," *L'Équipe*, 2 January 1968, 1.
38 Dauncey, "The Failed Bid for Lyon '68," 98.
39 "Winter Olympics to Open Tuesday," *Baltimore Sun*, 4 February 1968, A1.
40 "M. Herzog souligne devant le conseil des ministres les succès remportés par l'équipe de France," *Le Monde*, 7 February 1964, 15.
41 Quote from Jack Olsen, "A Shook-Up Town's Great Shape-Up," *Sports Illustrated*, 13 November 1967, 80.
42 Jack Olsen, quoted in "A Shook-Up Town's Great Shape-Up.".
43 "Lyon aurait de meilleures chances d'être choisie pour les jeux olympiques de 1968," *Le Monde*, 3 April 1963, 14.
44 Official Report/Rapport Officiel, Grenoble 1968, Comité d'organisation des Xèmes jeux olympiques d'hiver, 28.
45 Official Report/Rapport Officiel, Grenoble 1968, 29–30.
46 Jack Olsen, quoted in "A Shook-Up Town's Great Shape-Up," *Sports Illustrated*, 13 November 1967, 80; Gillian Thomas, "Grenoble – The Stage Is Set," *Boston Globe*, 7 January 1968, A23.
47 Shirley Povich, "This Morning ...," *Washington Post, Times Herald*, 9 February 1968, D1.
48 Jack Olsen, quoted in "A Shook-Up Town's Great Shape-Up,"; see also Daniel M. Madden, "Grenoble Girds for Olympics," *NYT*, 15 October 1967, 461; see also "Bobsled Test Is Canceled," *Baltimore Sun*, 10 February 1967, C8.
49 Official Report/Rapport Officiel, Grenoble 1968, Comité d'organisation des Xèmes jeux olympiques d'hiver, 30.
50 Povich, "This Morning ...."; Jack Olsen, quoted in "A Shook-Up Town's Great Shape-Up"; "France Assures Countries on Winter Olympic Set-Up," *NYT*, 3 May 1967, 56.
51 Official Report/Rapport Officiel, Grenoble 1968, Comité d'organisation des Xèmes jeux olympiques d'hiver, 34.
52 Official Report/Rapport Officiel, Grenoble 1968, 118.
53 Dauncey, "The Failed Bid for Lyon '68," 99.
54 Jacques Belin, "Grenoble, Aujourd'hui, Demain, et Après-Demain," *Sud-Ouest*, 19 February 1967, 9.
55 Thomas, "Grenoble – The Stage Is Set." Official Report/Rapport Officiel, Grenoble 1968, Comité d'organisation des Xèmes jeux olympiques d'hiver, 38.
56 Sénat de France, Notes from Séance, 20 November 1967, M. André Bord, secrétaire d'état de l'intérieur, 1513.
57 Jack Olsen, quoted in "A Shook-Up Town's Great Shape-Up"; Lloyd Garrison, "Grenoble Pays a High Price for Glory," *NYT*, 7 February 1968, 53. The *grenoblois*

had good reason to worry: the city only finished paying off its debt in 1995. Dauncey, "The Failed Bid for Lyon '68," 99.
58 Michel Clare, "Un avenir preoccupant," *L'Équipe*, 3 January 1968, 3
59 Gwen Morgan, "De Gaulle Officially Opens 10th Winter Olympics: 65,000 See Ceremonies in Grenoble's Stadium," *Chicago Tribune*, 7 February 1968, C1.
60 Official Report/Rapport Officiel, Grenoble 1968, Comité d'organisation des Xèmes jeux olympiques d'hiver, 187.
61 Official Report/Rapport Officiel, Grenoble 1968, 66.
62 Thomas, "Grenoble – The Stage Is Set."
63 Official Report/Rapport Officiel, Grenoble 1968, Comité d'organisation des Xèmes jeux olympiques d'hiver, 143–4.
64 Official Report/Rapport Officiel, Grenoble 1968, Comit. d'organisation des X.mes jeux olympiques d'hiver, 115–16.
65 Official Report/Rapport Officiel, Grenoble 1968, Comit. d'organisation des X.mes jeux olympiques d'hiver, 320.
66 Official Report/Rapport Officiel, Grenoble 1968, Comit. d'organisation des X.mes jeux olympiques d'hiver, 311–12.
67 Garrison, "Grenoble Pays a High Price for Glory."
68 Michel Clare, "Aux Jeux de Grenoble, même la glace sera en couleur pour l'ORTF," *L'Équipe*, 9 January 1968, 3.
69 "A.B.C. Gets Sponsors for 1968 Olympics," *NYT*, 15 June 1967, 95; Clay Gowran, "TV Today: Coverage of Winter Olympics Starts Tomorrow: ABC Posts 40 Cameras in France," *Chicago Tribune*, 5 February 1968, A9.
70 Official Report/Rapport Officiel, Grenoble 1968, Comité d'organisation des Xèmes jeux olympiques d'hiver, 149.
71 "Les plus grandioses des jeux d'hiver inaugurés par le général de Gaulle," *L'Équipe*, 6 February 1968, 1.
72 Official Report/Rapport Officiel, Grenoble 1968, Comité d'organisation des Xèmes jeux olympiques d'hiver, 250.
73 John Samuel, "Opening Ceremony above Politics," *The Guardian*, 7 February 1968, 17.
74 Shirley Povich, "De Gaulle to Make Sure Games Begin Late," *Washington Post, Times Herald*, 6 February 1968, D1.
75 Jim Murray, "De Gaulle at the Games: Unobtrusive as a Burglar," *LA Times*, 7 February 1968, B1; "Santa Monica Skier Fractures Leg in Drill for Olympics: Two Olympic Skiers Hurt," *LA Times*, 6 February 1968, B1.
76 Arthur Daley, "Sports of the Times: The Refrigerated Whammy, *NYT*, 4 February 1968, S2.
77 Povich, "De Gaulle to Make Sure Games Begin Late."
78 Morgan, "De Gaulle Officially Opens 10th Winter Olympics"; "Olympics Open Amid Ski Feud," *Atlanta Constitution*, 7 February 1968, 33.
79 Madden, "Grenoble Girds for Olympics"; "No School during Olympics," *Chicago Tribune*, 5 November 1967, J7.
80 "De Gaulle Opens Winter Olympics," *L A Times*, 7 February 1968, B1.

81 Fred Tupper, "60,000 See De Gaulle Declare Winter Games Open in Grandiose Setting," *NYT*, 7 February 1968, 53. The event (and entertainment for the Games more generally) was run by the Groupe de Paris, a company known for staging national events and grand expositions. Official Report/Rapport Officiel, Grenoble 1968, Comité d'organisation des Xèmes jeux olympiques d'hiver, 249–51.
82 Morgan, "De Gaulle Officially Opens 10th Winter Olympics."
83 Garrison, "Grenoble Pays a High Price for Glory."
84 Jean Bastaire, "'Show' et froid," *Esprit* 3, no. 169 (March 1968): 519–21. *Esprit* was a leftist journal, and despite these early laudatory remarks, Bastaire had no love for de Gaulle, whom he refers to in the piece as "a hideous fossil that no one believes anymore," and he did go on to lament the underrepresentation of developing countries.
85 Tupper, "60,000 See De Gaulle Declare Winter Games Open in Grandiose Setting."
86 "350 Hostesses Figure in Games," *Baltimore Sun*, 7 February 1968, C1.
87 Some were tasked with government officials and athletes, others with journalists, and others with tourists, but all appear to have served people in all categories.
88 Fernand Albaret, "Avec le sourire," *L'Équipe*, 19 January 1968, 3.
89 Anne Wyman, "A Dream Comes True," *Boston Globe*, 8 January 1967, B19.
90 Official Report/Rapport Officiel, Grenoble 1968, Comité d'organisation des Xèmes jeux olympiques d'hiver, 123.
91 "Grenoble: $224-Million Project Ready for Games," *NYT*, 4 February 1968, 262.
92 Michel Clare, "Plus du cinquième de l'effectif des CRS au service des jeux," *L'Équipe*, 18 January 1968, 2.
93 "Grenoble: $224-Million Project Ready for Games," *NYT*, 4 February 1968, 262.
94 Will Grimsley, "French Hostesses Dress Up Games," *Washington Post*, 31 January 1968, D2. Official Report/Rapport Officiel, Grenoble 1968, Comité d'organisation des Xèmes jeux olympiques d'hiver, 124. The official report lists the actual number as 372.
95 Official Report/Rapport Officiel, Grenoble 1968, Comité d'organisation des Xèmes jeux olympiques d'hiver, 125.
96 "Hôtesses de Grenoble," Interview with Christine Delacroix, 10 October 1967, INA, Collection RTF/ORTF, #CAF95011625.
97 Official Report/Rapport Officiel, Grenoble 1968, Comité d'organisation des Xèmes jeux olympiques d'hiver, 126.
98 Madden, "Grenoble Girds for Olympics."
99 Official Report/Rapport Officiel, Grenoble 1968, Comité d'organisation des Xèmes jeux olympiques d'hiver, 314.
100 Robert Colombini, "Indiscrétions de Grenoble: Comment M. Missoffe a été destitué en trois mots," *L'Équipe*, 26 January 1968, 3.
101 It is interesting that talk about sexuality became franker over the course of the period studied here – as seen in this quote in the open acknowledgment of France's commodification of female sensuality. Nevertheless, sexual mores had

196   Notes to pages 98–101

shifted far less than the term "sexual revolution," so associated with this age, would have people believe. For more, see Fishman, *From Vichy to the Sexual Revolution*.

102 Official Report/Rapport Officiel, Grenoble 1968, Comité d'organisation des Xèmes jeux olympiques d'hiver, 124.
103 Gwen Morgan, "Ancient Roman Town Today a City of Young Hope at 10th Winter Olympics," *Chicago Tribune*, 4 February 1968, B1.
104 Colombini, "Indiscrétions de Grenoble."
105 Fernand Albaret, "Galanterie et protocole," *L'Équipe*, 20–21 January 1968, 1.
106 Grimsley, "French Hostesses Dress Up Games."
107 Raymond Darolle, "Grenoble attend les jeux," *Sud-Ouest*, 17 December 1967, 13.
108 "Olympic Furs," *Chicago Tribune*, 14 August 1967, B2. Official Report/Rapport Officiel, Grenoble 1968, Comité d'organisation des Xèmes jeux olympiques d'hiver, 125.
109 Ginette Sainderichin, "Slalom," *Sud-Ouest*, 22 November 1967, 12.
110 Marian Christy, "Skiwear Combines Fashion 'N Function," *Boston Globe*, 27 November 1968, SKI7. Christy also cited the influence of the British and Polish Olympic uniforms, both of which incorporated fur as well.
111 Darolle, "Grenoble attend les jeux."
112 Will Grimsley, "Winter Olympics Open This Week," *Washington Post*, 4 February 1968, C1.
113 Morgan, "Ancient Roman Town."
114 I also wonder if the term bunny references the Playboy bunny, whose presence in American life was widely known, not least because of Gloria Steinem's undercover article about the Playboy Club. See Gloria Steinem, "A Bunny's Tale," *Show Magazine*, 1 May 1963, 90, 92, 94, 114.
115 Jacques Belin, "Harassante journée d'un journaliste," *Sud-Ouest*, 15 February 1968, 14.
116 Lloyd Garrison, "Criticism Runs Down as French Handle Games Like Clockwork," *NYT*, 13 February 1968, 2.
117 Grimsley, "French Hostesses Dress Up Games."
118 Colombini, "Indiscrétions de Grenoble."
119 Grimsley, "French Hostesses Dress Up Games."
120 Colombini, "Indiscrétions de Grenoble."
121 Colombini, "Indiscrétions de Grenoble."
122 "La révolte des bobeurs," *Sud-Ouest*, 15 February 1968, 14.
123 "La révolte des bobeurs."
124 Jim Murray, "Journalists Dish Out Olympic Pewter Medals," *LA Times*, 20 February 1968, B1; Joan Spindler, "Remembrance of Loves Past," *NYT*, 21 November 1965, 565, 570.
125 Fernand Albaret, "Boules de neige: Inquiétude pour les hôtesses," *L'Équipe*, 8 February 1968, 5.
126 "Solange Catry: Sa vie en l'air," *Versailles Magazine*, September 2009, 10.

127 Official Report/Rapport Officiel, Grenoble 1968, Comité d'organisation des Xèmes jeux olympiques d'hiver, 368.

4 Selling Postwar French Femininity

1. Bartky, "Foucault, Femininity and the Modernization of Patriarchal Power," 143.
2. French citizens were increasingly taking advantage of more leisure time (at least those among the middle and upper classes) and a strong French franc to travel internationally. See Rioux, *Fourth Republic*, 444, and Levenstein, *We'll Always Have Paris*, 208.
3. A.G., "Propos de la quinzaine," *Revue Des Deux Mondes* (1964): 311–12.
4. Sullivan, "France and the Vietnam Peace Settlement," 314–16. See also Sainteny, *Face à Ho Chi Minh*.
5. Jean Sainteny, Untitled article, *Air-France Revue*, no. 27 (June–August 1960): 9.
6. Endy, *Cold War Holidays*, 154–5. Sainteny also hired an American firm to promote France in the United States, but the ads I examine here were French productions.
7. https://www.siv.archives-nationales.culture.gouv.fr/siv/media/FRAN_IR_055375/d_667/FRCAC_20050260_169
8. https://www.siv.archives-nationales.culture.gouv.fr/siv/media/FRAN_IR_055375/c-8bo7sdd6j-18nfzv18r3w1b/FRCAC_20050260_303
9. https://www.siv.archives-nationales.culture.gouv.fr/siv/media/FRAN_IR_055375/d_168/FRCAC_20050345_168
10. https://www.siv.archives-nationales.culture.gouv.fr/siv/media/FRAN_IR_055375/d_162/FRCAC_20050345_162
11. They are reminiscent of art that centres on women as unknowing recipients of the male gaze, reinforcing women's unnaturalness in public. I do not think that the posters are portraying women as somehow unnatural in public, but rather as objects to be consumed by a viewer. For more on the male gaze, see Walker, *Material Girls*. See especially her chapter "Visual Pleasures," 50–65.
12. Air France Datebook, 1964, Éditions Sun Paris, Air France Museum.
13. "Couple on the Champ de Mars," Puzzle, 1970, Photograph by Alastair Miller, Imprimerie Thorbel, Air France Museum.
14. Unattributed tourist pamphlet, 1956, Air France Museum.
15. Tourist pamphlet, 1963, "Air France: The Largest Network in the World." Printer: Atelier Percival; Illustrator: Guy Georget; Photographer: Jacques Bulte; Photographer: U&O; Air France Museum.
16. Air France ad, 1963, OMDI Imprimerie, Air France Museum.
17. Air France ad, "Have You Done It the French Way?" *New Yorker*, 14 April 1975, 48.
18. See, for example, Delta ad, "Delta Is an Airline Run by Professionals," *The New Yorker*, 8 April 1974, 102.
19. See also Barry, *Femininity in Flight*, 178.

20 Air France ad, "Your vacation ... so much prettier!," 1963, Air France Museum.
21 Air France ad, 1970, "Summer Vacation 70 with Jet Tours Airtour," Air France Museum.
22 Air France ad, "The Rake's Guide to Paris," *Foreign Affairs* 47, no. 3 (1969).
23 Air France ad, "A Beautiful French Hostess," *Foreign Affairs* 46, no. 2 (1968).
24 Air France ad, "Ben Franklin's Guide to Paris," *Foreign Affairs* 47, no. 2 (1969).
25 Schwartz, *It's So French*, 103. See Weiner, *Enfants Terribles*.
26 See, for example, the scholarship of Ginette Vincendeau, Vanessa Schwartz, and Felicity Chaplin, whose excellent works deal with these three subjects in varying degrees.
27 Cécile Hanania. ""Poupée, anale nationale" ou La Marianne malade d'Alina Reyes," *French Review* 77, no. 5 (2004): 967.
28 JJSS was tapping into/creating a popular sentiment for this shift. A marketing firm polled the populace at 55 per cent in favour of modelling Marianne on a living woman in 1970. See Nesta Roberts, "Letter from Paris," *The Guardian*, 3 April 1971, 3.
29 Richard Vinen, "Bikinis and Breastplates," *History Today* 56, no. 4 (April 2006): 50–2.
30 "Why Brigitte? ... For 2 Very Good Reasons," *LA Times*, 11 March 1971, 2. See also Next Roberts, "Republican Hagiography ... Or Bust," *The Guardian*, 19 February 1972, 11.
31 "Names in the News," *Atlanta Constitution*, 11 March 1971, 3A.
32 "Why Brigitte? ... For 2 Very Good Reasons," *LA Times*, 11 March 1971, 2. Roberts, "Republican Hagiography ... Or Bust."
33 "Considers Bardot a Perfect 38,000," *Chicago Tribune*, 11 March 1971, 10.
34 "Why Brigitte? ... For 2 Very Good Reasons."
35 Trixie Belmont, "Bardot's Medal," *Baltimore Sun*, 17 May 1966, B6.
36 Agulhon, "Marianne, réflexions sur une histoire," 320.
37 "French Symbol to Show Bardot Influence," *Baltimore Sun*, 25 April 1971, K25.
38 "Marianne de l'an 2000," *Le nouvel observateur*, 14 October 1999, n.p.
39 "French Symbol to Show Bardot Influence."
40 "Friday Newsmakers," *Detroit News*, 6 December 1996, A2.
41 "Bardot Busts Removed," *Edmonton Observer*, 6 December 1996, C8; "And Brigitte Created Quite a Controversy," *Spokesman Review*, 10 December 1996, D2; "Friday Newsmakers."
42 "Bardot-Based Sculptures Now a Bust," *Seattle Post-Intelligencer*, 28 November 1996, A4.
43 Anthony Noel, "Sexy Roles out for Brigitte, Says Producer," *Atlanta Journal and Atlanta Constitution*, 21 September 1958, 9E. According to Vanessa Schwartz, Bardot "seemed to explode" into the US, despite being a relative unknown in France. Schwartz, *It's So French*, 122.
44 Patricia Pullan, "Still Fun in Future for Bardot after 40," *Baltimore Sun*, 24 September 1974, B1.

45 Vincendeau, *Companion to French Cinema*, 26.
46 Ad for Congress and Portage Movie Theaters, *Chicago Tribune*, 19 April 1958, B7.
47 "Les Américains ont découvert la bardolâtrie," *Paris-Presse L'Intransigeant*, 2 May 1958, 1.
48 Nat Hentoff, "Bob Dylan, The Wanderer," *The New Yorker*, 24 October 1964, 72.
49 Holmes, "'A Girl of Today,'" 51. While I think that French culture was in the process of creating a specific brand of femininity, rather than it being eternal, Holmes's point about Bardot's marketability is well taken. Vanessa Schwartz also points out to the fact that the French government and film industry mined its reputation in film productively on the international scene, and especially in the United States, thereby paving the way for Bardot's arrival and ascendance in the public eye. See Schwartz, "Who Killed Brigitte Bardot?," 149.
50 John McCarten, "Talk of the Town," *The New Yorker*, 2 May 1959, 36.
51 Gene Moskowitz, "Noted along the Seine: Trailing Busy, Peripatetic Brigitte Bardot – Capturing the Classics," *NYT*, 15 June 1968, X7.
52 Fishman, *From Vichy to the Sexual Revolution*, 117.
53 William K. Zinsser, "On: 'And God Created Woman,'" *New York Herald Tribune*, 22 October 1957, 22.
54 Crowther, Bosley, "Screen: French Import Brigitte Bardot Stars in 'And God Created Woman,'" *NYT*, 22 October 1957, 41.
55 Marjory Adams, "'And God Created Woman': Brigitte Bardot, Sinful Siren," *Boston Globe*, 31 October 1957, 30.
56 Joe Hyams, "Brigitte Bardot: Magic Mirror," *New York Herald Tribune*, 12 July 1956, A1.
57 Dodge, *Rich Man's Guide to the Riviera*, 35–6.
58 Hyams, "Brigitte Bardot: Magic Mirror."
59 Bosley Crowther, "Screen: French Import Brigitte Bardot Stars in 'And God Created Woman,'" *NYT*, 22 October 1957, 41.
60 Crowther, "Screen: French Import Brigitte Bardot Stars."
61 Adams, "'And God Created Woman.'"
62 Melvin Maddocks, "Brigitte Bardot at the Gary," *Christian Science Monitor*, 30 October 1957, 5.
63 Adams, "'And God Created Woman.'"
64 R.H. Gardner, "Sex Sold the Movie by Bardot," *Baltimore Sun*, 13 April 1958, F8.
65 Hyams, "Brigitte Bardot: Magic Mirror."
66 A.H. Weiler, "By Way of Report," *NYT*, 2 February 1958, X7.
67 Dick Schaap, "She Looked Sexy, Which Is Like Saying the Louvre Is a Museum: Not Like in Pottstown," *Boston Globe*, 17 December 1965, 52.
68 Herb Lyon, "Tower Ticker," *Chicago Tribune*, 27 December 1957, 18.
69 Maddocks, "Brigitte Bardot at the Gary."
70 Adams, "'And God Created Woman.'"
71 GMW, "Brigitte Bardot Real Dazzler in New Film," *LA Times*, 27 December 1957, B9.

72 Gardner, "Sex Sold the Movie by Bardot."
73 GMW, "Brigitte Bardot Real Dazzler in New Film."
74 Crowther, "Screen: French Import Brigitte Bardot Stars."
75 Paul V. Beckley, "The Formidable Brigitte Bardot," *New York Herald Tribune*, 18 May 1958, D1. Some Americans failed to appreciate the charms of Bardot, and the film was banned in several major cities and given a C rating by the Catholic Church's Legion of Decency. (See Schwartz, *It's So French!*, 136.) Perhaps most dramatically, in Philadelphia, the district attorney stormed a theatre where the film was five minutes underway and requisitioned all copies of the movie. He arrested movie theatre owners on charges of promoting obscenity. Likely, as with most banned objects, the publicity surrounding the raids only served to whet more people's appetites to see what, exactly, the film was about. See "Film Seizure Attacked: Mayor of Philadelphia Says Action May Be Illegal," *NYT*, 13 February 1958, 23; "Ban Brigitte Bardot Movie in Philadelphia, Seize Film," *New York Herald Tribune*, 12 February 1958, 14. Similar actions occurred in places as far flung as Fort Worth, where the city's censor board ban was upheld in court, as well as in Lake Placid, New York, where the local Catholic diocese banned congregants from patronizing the theatre where the picture was being shown. See "Movie Ban Upheld," *Washington Post*, 11 February 1959, A2; see also "Bardot Film Brings Catholic Ban on Lake Placid's Only Theatre," *NYT*, 2 August 1958, 19.
76 Sénat de France, Notes from Séance, 5 February 1963, M. Edouard Bonnefous, rapporteur spécial de la commission des finances, du contrôle budgétaire et des comptes économiques de la nation (Cinéma), 441.
77 "La production des films," *Informations sociales: Bulletin mensuel à l'usage des services sociaux/Union nationale des caisses d'allocations familiales*, June 1960, 27. Interestingly, at her peak Bardot was earning about $350,000 a film, a far cry from her male counterparts like Alain Delon and Jean-Paul Belmondo, who commanded $500,000 per picture. See Paul Sarlat, "The Industry: Actors' Salaries: Let's Make a Deal," *Film Comment* 11, no. 4 (1975): 30–1, 31.
78 Rioux, *The Fourth Republic*, 441.
79 Schwartz, *It's So French!*, 138.
80 Untitled, *Air-France Revue*, no. 24 (December 1958): 22.
81 "Quand voyage Brigitte Bardot," *France-aviation*, Supplément interrégional gratuit au no 135, 15 February 1966, H.
82 Wolters, Larry, "Mais Oui! Genevieve Talks of Life and Love," *Chicago Tribune*, September 13, 159, J31.
83 Joe Hyams, "This Is Hollywood," *New York Herald Tribune*, 20 September 1955, B6.
84 Hyams, "This Is Hollywood."
85 Dick Gray, "'I Don't Want to Be Sexy,' Corinne Calvet Declares," *Atlanta Journal and Atlanta Constitution*, 31 May 1964, 13D.
86 Hyams, "This Is Hollywood."

87 Don Alpert, "Auger – Sex Bomb Who Ignites 'Thunderball,'" *LA Times*, 28 November 1965, B4.
88 Alpert, "Auger – Sex Bomb Who Ignites 'Thunderball.'"
89 Charles Witbeck, "Ze '77' Accent Stays Wiz Her," *Chicago Daily Tribune*, 11 June 1960, C3.
90 Joe Hyams, "Sleepiest Girl in France," *Baltimore Sun*, 9 February 1958, W17.
91 "French Have Bare Interest in Nude Films, Actress Says," *Baltimore Sun*, 2 March 1964, 3.
92 "La revanche des vraies femmes," *Sud-Ouest*, 28 March 1967, 1. The question was part of an advertisement, enticing readers of major newspapers to buy the current issue of *Elle*, in which philosopher Raymond Abellio expounded on French femininity.
93 Larry Collins and Dominique LaPierre, "The Name Is Moreau (Not Bardot)," *NYT*, 21 March 1965, SM46.
94 Hyams, "To Love, Honor – Frighten," *New York Herald Tribune*, 19 February 1961, D11.
95 Hyams, "To Love, Honor – Frighten," *New York Herald Tribune*, 19 February 1961, D11.
96 Collins and LaPierre, "The Name Is Moreau (Not Bardot)."
97 Collins and LaPierre, "The Name Is Moreau (Not Bardot)."
98 Collins and LaPierre, "The Name Is Moreau (Not Bardot)."
99 Joe Hyams, "Brigitte Bardot: Magic Mirror," *New York Herald Tribune*, 12 July 1956, A1.
100 Hyams, "Brigitte Bardot: Magic Mirror."
101 Schaap, "She Looked Sexy."
102 Larry Wolters, "Mais Oui! Genevieve Talks of Life and Love," *Chicago Tribune*, 13 September 159, J31.
103 Hazel A. Washington, "This Is Hollywood," *Daily Defender*, 14 July 1958, 17.
104 Washington.
105 "Book Shows France's Youths at Work, Play," *Atlanta Constitution*, 10 July 1965, 15.
106 "Bien qu'enthousiasmée par la Californie, BB n'abandonnera pas Paris ... pour Hollywood," *Sud-Ouest*, 25 December 1965, 2.
107 Joe Hyams, "A Different Kind of French Girl," *New York Herald Tribune*, 13 March 1960, SM11.
108 Quoted in Schwartz, *It's So French!*, 149.
109 Fielding, *Fielding's Travel Guide to Europe* (1966), 829.
110 Lisa Tiersten's work has already demonstrated how French women's taste became a question of national and international anxiety in the late nineteenth century. That question, it appears, was settled in French women's favour by the time period covered in this book, when writers ascribed naturalness to French women's beauty. See Tiersten, *Marianne in the Market*.
111 Dorothy McCardle, "They Can Decide an Election: Women Out-Vote Males in France," *Washington Post and Times Herald*, 15 September 1956, F12.

112 There is a long history of the French beauty industry, but what is crucial here is its marketing on a global stage in a time of mass media, as well as during a time when the French were relying on aesthetics heavily as part of their national identity. The recognition of French aesthetic superiority by Americans would have been a coup both financially and in terms of prestige. For earlier context on the French beauty industry, see Holly Grout's *Force of Beauty*.
113 Peggy Massin, "The Oyster Is Her World," *LA Times*, 16 May 1971, D20.
114 Lydia Lane, "Egg Yolk Aids Skin and Hair," *LA Times*, 30 January 1961, A5.
115 "Beauty: Vogue's Ready Beauty," *Vogue*, 1 February 1968, 36, 86, 210.
116 Ad for Chic Parisienne Cosmetics, *WWD*, 17 April 1970, 42.
117 Ad for Parisienne Panel (Jantzen Foundations and Brassieres), *Vogue*, 1 April 1960, 61.
118 Jo Holley, "Hub Caps," *Bay State Banner*, 29 March 1973, 6.
119 "The Dresses: Summer Collections: J. Silverman," *WWD*, 27 February 1962, 29.
120 "Merci! Southland Tops East in Dress, Says Parisienne," *LA Times*, 13 March 1963, C1.
121 BB had, to some extent, bridged the versions of French women by starring in the film *La parisienne*, a romp in which the two protagonists attempt to outdo each other's sexual antics and make each other jealous.
122 Dodge, *Poor Man's Guide to Europe*, 7.
123 Olson, *Olson's Complete Motoring Guide to France, Switzerland, and Italy*, 409.
124 Olson, 409. Round-heeled was popular slang at the time for sexually easy women, based as it was on their heels on the ground, toes in the air, as though lying down on a bed. The distinction between gazing upon swimmers and cavorting with promiscuous women is condoned in this book; both are portrayed as sanctioned activities in the Riviera region.
125 Schmidt, *The Swimsuit: Fashion from Poolside to Catwalk*, 14–15.
126 Peggy Massin, "Fashions on the French Riviera," *Baltimore Sun*, 1 August 1966, B1.
127 John Handley, "Cannes: People-Watching Capital of Riviera," *Chicago Tribune*, 16 May 1971, H6.
128 Horace Sutton, "Bikini-Watching Cote d'Azur's Chief Industry at Ancient Spots Such as Miami and Waikiki," *LA Times*, 5 May 1957, E9.
129 Herb Daniels, "One Man's Week End: Riviera," *Chicago Tribune*, 12 April 1964, H52.
130 Eugenia Sheppard, "Riviera Still Bikiniland," *New York Herald Tribune*, 20 July 1962, 9.
131 "Bikini with the Holes Tolerates No Flab," *Baltimore Sun*, 10 August 1970, B4.
132 Elizabeth Bernkopf, "Bikini Suits Are Back in the Summer Swim," *Boston Globe*, 12 May 1959, 9.
133 Engel, *France: A Simon and Schuster Travel Guide*, 183.
134 Endy, *Cold War Holidays*, 7. See also Levenstein, *Seductive Journeys*, 247–8.
135 It is perhaps no accident that the Comité Colbert, the organization founded by Jean-Jacques Guerlain (of the famous perfume dynasty) to protect the sanctity

of French luxury brands and promote French creative genius to the world, had its origins in this time period (it was founded in 1954). I also want to point out that France has a long history of being associated with luxury goods and quality merchandise. See Lisa Tiersten's *Marianne in the Market* for more.
136 Endy, *Cold War Holidays*, 54. The promotion of shopping was not a one-way street; Endy also discusses how the US valued consumerism as a way for Americans to help shore up Western European finances amid the Cold War.
137 Notes from the French Senate, Séance, 20 June 1950, 1782–3.
138 Crane, *Fashion and Its Social Agendas*, 142. Crane also details how couture houses came to rely on brand diversification to remain profitable, branching out into now-familiar products like perfume and handbags, all goods marketed heavily toward American women.
139 Not every ad was from a French company, but a huge percentage of them were. See Crane, *Fashion and Its Social Agendas,* 211.
140 Quoted in Endy, *Cold War Holidays*, 19–20.
141 Martin, "Shopping: How to Spend," 105–25, 106.
142 Dodge, *The Poor Man's Guide to Europe*, 226.
143 Bertin, *Paris à la Mode*, 17.
144 Bertin, *Paris à la Mode*, 253.
145 Bertin, *Paris à la Mode*, 255.
146 Vitray, *Fashion for Cinderella*, 85.
147 Fielding, *Fielding's Travel Guide to Europe* (1966), 1024.
148 Martin, "Shopping: How to Spend," 105–25, 111.
149 Alak, *The Bikini: A Cultural History*, 101.
150 Eugenia Sheppard, "At Monte Carlo Beach: The Bikini Still Supreme along the French Riviera," *New York Herald Tribune*, 12 August 1960, 8.
151 Estella Atwell, "Dress 'Spiffy' for the French Riviera Set," *Chicago Tribune*, 4 April 1971, F8.
152 Engel, *France: A Simon and Schuster Travel Guide*, 19.
153 Engel, *France: A Simon and Schuster Travel Guide*, 2.
154 Fodor and Fisher, *Fodor's Paris*. This 1974 edition contains a lot of the same text as the 1952 version, but the part about the *Parisienne* has been expanded and given its own section.

5 The Gendering and Selling of France

1 Proulx and Keown, *Guide to France for Loving Couples*, 9.
2 See Levenstein, *We'll Always Have Paris*; Ring, *Riviera*; and Blume, *Côte d'Azur*, for more context on the Riviera's long history with tourism.
3 Endy, *Cold War Holidays*, 128.
4 Levenstein, *We'll Always Have Paris*, 207.
5 Endy, *Cold War Holidays*, 135.

6 See Levenstein, *We'll Always Have Paris*, 129–30.
7 See Levenstein, *We'll Always Have Paris*, 181–3.
8 Endy, *Cold War Holiday*, 104.
9 See Fishman, *From Vichy to the Sexual Revolution*.
10 See Hunt, *Politics, Culture, and Class in the French Revolution*; Agulhon's Marianne trilogy (*Marianne au combat, Marianne au pouvoir*, and *Les métamorphoses de Marianne*); and Gildea's *Marianne in Chains*.
11 Sutton, *Footloose in France*, 88.
12 Sutton, *Footloose in France*, 40.
13 I have been unable to find many references to it in the French press, but I think that, especially by the time of its second printing, French tourism officials were well aware of the many benefits of such sensualized marketing.
14 "Guidebook to Paris Lilts Like Gershwin," *Washington Post*, 26 December 1948, B7.
15 Beach Conger, "Travel Topics: Recent Travel Guides," *New York Herald Tribune*, 2 January 1949, C11; "Guidebook to Paris Lilts Like Gershwin," *Washington Post*, 26 December 1948, B7.
16 Joseph Henry Jackson, "Bookman's Notebook: Going to France?," *LA Times*, 14 December 1948, A5.
17 Samuel Putnam, "Guide to France," *NYT*, 5 December 1948, BR36.
18 "New Travel Book by Globe Writer Horace Sutton," *Boston Globe*, 4 April 1954, B6.
19 Segal, *Off the Beaten Track in Paris*, 6.
20 Thomas, "The Spirit of Paris: 'All Things to All Men,'" 59–60.
21 Thomas, "The Spirit of Paris: 'All Things to All Men,'" 60.
22 Sutton, *Footloose in France*, 54.
23 Dodge, *Poor Man's Guide*, 221, 223.
24 Martin and Martin, *Paris! And Its Environs*, 99.
25 Olivia De Havilland, "One of America's Most Beloved Stars Tells about the Whirlwind Romance That Turned Her into a Gay Parisienne," *Baltimore Sun*, 20 May 1956, WM10.
26 Wallenstein, *Red Canvas*, 90.
27 Air France ad, 1965, Éditions U&O, Air France Museum.
28 Air France ad, 1962, Fabricant: la Photolith, Air France Museum.
29 Air France ad, 1963, Photographer Jacques Bulte, Air France Museum.
30 Air Inter ad, 1970, "Weekend with Free Hotel," PARFRANCE Agence, SMEET Imprimerie, Air France Museum.
31 Fishman, *From Vichy to the Sexual Revolution*, chs. 7, 8.
32 Air Inter ad, 1970, "A Getaway, a Weekend, Your First Flight with Air Inter," PARFRANCE Agence, Air France Museum.
33 Air France ad, *Vogue*, 1 September 1968, 249.
34 Vitray, *Fashion for Cinderella*, 231.
35 Horace Sutton, "Eating, A Fine Art, in Burgundy," *Boston Globe*, 10 November 1957, B7.

36 Ruth Wagner, "It Concerns Romance and Beauty," *Washington Post and Times Herald*, 15 August 1967, C19.
37 Theodore H. White, Theodore H., "Crime Non-Passionel," *Palestine Post*, 3 March 1950, 5.
38 Proulx and Keown, *Guide to France for Loving Couples*, 17.
39 Proulx and Keown, *Guide to France for Loving Couples*, 28–9.
40 Proulx and Keown, *Guide to France for Loving Couples*, 149.
41 Proulx and Keown, *Guide to France for Loving Couples*, 149.
42 Proulx and Keown, *Guide to France for Loving Couples*, 37.
43 Proulx and Keown, *Guide to France for Loving Couples*, 78. Proulx and Keown invoke Bardot often, using her connection to a location as a selling point.
44 Proulx and Keown, *Guide to France for Loving Couples*, 91.
45 Proulx and Keown, *Guide to France for Loving Couples*, 107.
46 Fleer, "Paris at Night," 91–105, 102.
47 Fielding, *Fielding's Travel Guide to Europe*, 905.
48 Fielding, *Fielding's Travel Guide to Europe*, 909–11.
49 Fleer, "Paris at Night," 91–105, 95.
50 Fielding, *Fielding's Travel Guide to Europe*, 919.
51 Creed and Milo, *Paris and Its Environs*, 26.
52 Olson, *Olson's Complete Motoring Guide*, 231.
53 Olson, *Olson's Complete Motoring Guide*, 227–9.
54 Murray, *A Traveler's Guide to France*, 160.
55 Fielding, *Fielding's Travel Guide to Europe*, 989.
56 Sutton, *Footloose in France*, 220–1.
57 Sutton, *Footloose in France*, 223.
58 Jackson, *Living in Arcadia*, 200.
59 As Andrew Ross has argued, too often historians have treated the archives as the place to find "real" people and histories, and when those histories do not appear, or do not appear in ways familiar to contemporary eyes, or "the search for the sexual past always begin[ning] with the sexual present," we lose a wide swath of stories from underrepresented groups. Ross, "Sex in the Archives," 267–9.
60 Proulx and Keown, *Guide to France for Loving Couples*, 153.
61 Proulx and Keown, *Guide to France for Loving Couples*, 154.
62 Proulx and Keown, *Guide to France for Loving Couples*, 155.
63 Wallenstein, *Red Canvas*, 211.
64 Wallenstein, *Red Canvas*, 212.
65 *A Pocket Guide to France* (1951), 24, 35.
66 *A Pocket Guide to France* (1951), 35.
67 Mikes, "Some Popular Fallacies," 127–8.
68 Fielding, *Fielding's Travel Guide to Europe*, 819.
69 Fielding, *Fielding's Travel Guide to Europe*, 921.
70 Olson, *Olson's Complete Motoring Guide*, 234.

71 Olson, *Olson's Complete Motoring Guide*, 231.
72 Levenstein, *Seductive Journeys*, 202.
73 Levenstein, *We'll Always Have Paris*, 35-7.
74 Roberts, *What Soldiers Do*, 149.
75 Sutton, *Footloose in France*, 80.
76 Olson, *Olson's Complete Motoring Guide*, 428.
77 Gwen Morgan, "Paris in the Spring Like Paris of Old," *Chicago Tribune*, 23 April 1950, H6.
78 Segal, *Off the Beaten Track in Paris*, 96.
79 Willam Buchanan, "Paris in the Fall, Tra La … It'll Leave You Broke, Tra La," *Boston Globe*, 25 November 1965, 58.
80 Georges Menant, "The Paris Jungle," *Baltimore Sun*, 2 October 1966, S6.
81 H.P. Koenig, "To Really See Paris the Traveler Must Go on Foot: Way to Get Intimate View," *Chicago Tribune*, 9 May 1965, I16.
82 Betty Carrollton, "ESA's Rendezvous at Paris Pigalle," *Atlanta Journal and Constitution*, 24 May 1959, 7F.
83 Joseph Wechsberg, "'April in Paris' for New York," *NYT*, 24 April 1960, SM42.
84 "Old Favorites Back for Encores," *Atlanta Journal and Atlanta Constitution*, 8 September 1957, 9E.
85 Barry Bearak, "Art Deco Revival Miami Beach Comes Back into Vogue," *LA Times*, 14 February 1988, 1.
86 Adenike Adenitire, "This Week I Am Lovin'…" *New Nation*, 6 October 2008, 15.
87 "Earl Grant, 39, Composer, Organist," *Washington Post*, 11 June 1970, C4.
88 Fielding, *Fielding's Travel Guide to Europe*, 12.
89 François, "Paris: The Luxury Industry Capital," 34.
90 Newman, *Newman's European Travel Guide*, 109.
91 Newman, *Newman's European Travel Guide*, 84, 269.
92 Olson, *Olson's Complete Motoring Guide*, 223.
93 Olson, *Olson's Complete Motoring Guide*, 415.
94 Fielding, *Fielding's Travel Guide to Europe* (1966), 811.
95 Fielding, *Fielding's Travel Guide to Europe* (1966), 254.
96 Fielding, *Fielding's Travel Guide to Europe* (1966), 1298.
97 *France* (1973), 7.
98 *France* (1973), 8.
99 *France* (1973), 8.
100 *France* (1973), 11.
101 *France* (1973), 12.
102 Fielding, *Fielding's Travel Guide to Europe* (1966), 1026.
103 Dos Santos, "Discovering Paris: A Tour of the City," 29.
104 Thomas, "The Spirit of Paris," 58.
105 Thomas, "The Spirit of Paris," 61.
106 Arnoux, "Lettre à l'inconnu qui débarque à Paris," 2-5.

107 Segal, *Off the Beaten Track in Paris*, 24.
108 Olson, *Olson's Complete Motoring Guide*, 420.
109 Thomas, "The Spirit of Paris," 58.
110 Dos Santos, "Discovering Paris," 35.
111 *Paris* (New York: Random House, 1973), 45. (Prepared with the cooperation of the editors of *Holiday*.)
112 Bosley Crowther, "The Screen in Review: 'Under the Paris Sky,' French Import by Duvivier, Has Its Premiere Here," *NYT*, 6 May 1952, 35.
113 William Millinship, "The Romantic Revolting Seine," *Jerusalem Post*, 16 December 1963, 5.
114 Air France: Vacationing in Five Continents. 17, 19.
115 Martin and Martin, *Paris! And its Environs*, 219.
116 *Air France: Vacationing in Five Continents*, 19.
117 Horace Sutton, "Sunday in the Park Where All Paris Goes," *Boston Globe*, 18 May 1958, C1.
118 Creed and Milo, *All about Paris and Its Environs*, 196, 200.
119 Dos Santos, "Discovering Paris," 43.
120 Henry Miele, "He Who Misses Paris Cannot Say He Has Truly Seen France," *LA Times*, 27 February 1955, D9.
121 Henry Miele, "Touraine Romantic Heart of France," *LA Times*, 20 March 1960, E8.
122 Leonard J. Panaggio, "Romance of the Sorgue River," *LA Times*, 21 May 1972, I9.
123 H.P. Koenig, "Romantic Experience: Winding along Alsace's Wine Route," *Chicago Tribune*, 14 May 1972, F27.
124 Arthur Meeker, "He Relives Romantic Past of Ancient Beaucaire," *Chicago Tribune*, 17 March 1963, SW10. This depiction of Beaucaire as asleep, like Sleeping Beauty, is interesting because it suggests that Beaucaire is a passive place, where history happened, rather than an active place where current events matter in the world. The French government, while it certainly wanted to promote tourism, sought to attract people to France to take their money, yes, but it also wanted to reinforce that France mattered. As such, I doubt it would have found favour with Meeker's depiction.
125 Fielding, *Fielding's Travel Guide to Europe* (1966 edition), 822–3.
126 Blume, *Côte d'Azur*, 142.
127 Murray, *A Traveler's Guide to France*, 152.
128 Newman, *Newman's European Travel Guide*, 150, 154.
129 Thomas, "The Riviera and Monaco," 263.
130 Sutton, *Footloose in France*, 213.
131 Fielding, *Fielding's Travel Guide to Europe* (1966 edition), 957.
132 Arthur Meeker, "Romance Switzerland Is Much Like France," *Chicago Daily Tribune*, 17 September 1950, E1.
133 David Laird Watt, "Louisiana's Cajun Country," *Chicago Tribune*, 11 March 1973, C11.

134 H.P. Koenig, "Romantic Noumea: A Piece of France in the South Pacific," *Chicago Tribune*, 12 May 1968, G20.
135 *Air France: Vacationing in Five Continents*, 210.
136 "Little Bit of France in Caribbean," *Baltimore Sun*, 20 September 1964, GP15.
137 "Martinique a Paradox–France in Caribbean: Colorful-Isle Offers Fine Food, Buys," *Chicago Tribune*, 8 November 1964, I17.
138 H.P. Koenig, "Martinique Is More French Than France," *Chicago Tribune*, 19 October 1969, H1.
139 "Rhine River of Romance Now in Sewer Nearing Death," *Boston Globe*, 8 November, 52.
140 Carlyle Morgan, "Housing Needs Challenge France," *Christian Science Monitor*, 19 January 1965, 1.
141 Edmund K. Faltermayer, "Rhine Romance: Behind New Franco-German Accord Lie Self-Interest and Dreams of Past Glory," *Wall Street Journal*, 22 December 1958, 18.
142 Marcelle Fouquet, "Charles de Gaulle's Chinese Romance," *New York Amsterdam News*, 2 November 1963, 10.
143 Robert T. Hartmann, "Romance with a Nation: President Sets Out to Woo People of France," *LA Times*, 1 June 1961, 1.
144 David R. Francis, "French Finance Officials Keep World Guessing," *Christian Science Monitor*, 9 March 1968, 10.
145 Wayne Thomis, "Air France: On World's Skyways It Speeds Touch of Paris to 113 Cities," *Chicago Tribune*, 13 October 1965, B1.
146 Blake Ehrlich, "Europe: In England, The Roadside Signs Are Pun-happy, In France They're Sexy. And In Italy, Anything Goes!" *Baltimore Sun*, 9 September 1956, WM10.
147 Martin, "Shopping: How to Spend," 120.
148 Raymonde Alexander, "Romantic Spell of France Is Woven into US Work," *Atlanta Constitution*, 13 August 1962, 19.
149 Jean Baird, "New Evening Fashions in France Show a Wide Variety of Styles," *Christian Science Monitor*, 15 July 1946, 12.
150 Kathleen Geraghty, "The New Fashions from France," *Baltimore Sun*, 4 March 1962, E6.
151 Arnoux, "Lettre à l'inconnu qui débarque à Paris," 2.
152 Mikes, "Some Popular Fallacies," 129.

Conclusion

1 https://www.youtube.com/watch?v=f27zE-PdZZI. Retrieved 13 July 2020.
2 "France is the world's leading destination with 89.4 million foreign visitors in 2018. Tourism ... accounts for nearly 8% of GDP, €56.2 billion in tourism receipts and generates two million jobs directly or indirectly." Statistics from the French

Minister of Foreign Affairs: https://www.diplomatie.gouv.fr/en/french-foreign-policy/tourism/.

3 There is not necessarily consensus on women and work in the postwar period. Robert Gildea writes that "women had taken themselves out of the labour market after the war. Only 35 per cent of the working population were women in 1954, and the figure remained the same in 1968." Gildea, *France since 1945*, 148. Claire Duchen, however, pushes back on the static nature of those sorts of numbers, arguing for a focus on trends rather than the hard numbers offered by official analyses, which she finds masked the reality of women's own perceptions of their work lives, as well as the fluidity women experienced as workers. (For example, married women with children might come in and out of the labour force depending on their children's ages, a fact not accounted for in official statistics.) See Duchen, *Women's Rights and Women's Lives*, 129–30.

4 This was actually a global phenomenon; as Kathleen Barry points out, American airlines also pushed their hostesses to work harder and resisted any changes in their contracts, valuing what she refers to as overall "efficiency in the mass production of passenger care." Barry, *Femininity in Flight*, 105. Still, hostesses did win some victories. Barry demonstrates how the onset of jumbo jets actually put more hostesses on large planes, increasing solidarity among the members of the profession, who then could band together and demand more from companies, something she refers to as "occupational community." Barry, 197. See also Tiemeyer, *Plane Queer*.

5 Davey and Davidson, "The Right of Passage?," 196. American Airlines was the pioneer, hiring its first female commercial pilot in 1973; AA had three women pilots one year later. Air France was, however, the first major airline to hire a female CEO: Anne Rigail became CEO of AF in 2018, one of only nine women CEOs out of 120 major companies in France. (See the Gender Equality Index for France, 2019.)

6 Guiliano, *French Women Don't Get Fat*. Guiliano also has a similarly titled cookbook and a book of "secrets" of French women, as well as the *French Women Don't Get Facelifts*, a guide to aging like a French woman.

7 De la Fressange, *Parisian Chic*. See also Anne Berest's *How to Be Parisian Wherever You Are*; Jett, *Forever Chic*; Scott, *Lessons from Madame Chic*; Thomas, *Paris Street Style*.

8 Thomas, *The French Beauty Solution*; Callahan, *The Paris Bath and Beauty Book*.

9 Callan, *French Women Don't Sleep Alone*; Ollivier, *What French Women Know*; Postel-Vinay, *Home Sweet Maison*.

10 Von Mueffling, *Ageless Beauty the French Way*.

11 Druckerman, *Bringing Up Bébé*; Le Billon, *French Kids Eat Everything*; Druckerman, *French Children Don't Throw Food*.

12 Callan, *Parisian Charm School*; Malandrino, *Une Femme Française*; Frith-Powell, *All You Need to Be Impossibly French*; Ollivier, *Entre Nous*.

13 Pulled from one basic internet search for "French girl Instagram": "9 French Girls to Follow on Instagram for Endless Style Inspiration," https://www.huffpost.com/entry/french-girls-instagram_l_5cae25d0e4b03ab9f24f8314; "In Honor of Bastille Day, Here is Our Guide to Instagram's Chicest French Girls," https://www.lofficielusa.com/fashion/french-girls-instagram-fashion-follow; "25 Effortlessly Chic French Style Influencers to Follow on Instagram," https://frenchstyle.co/french-style-influencers/.

14 Research does show that women of colour tend to be more satisfied with their bodies than white women, suggesting a kind of Eurocentrism to this image of femininity, but not uniformly. Black college students, for example, especially at majority-white institutions, represent a divergence. See Kelch-Oliver and Ancis, "Black Women's Body Image"; Winter et al., "Toward an Understanding of Racial and Ethnic Diversity in Body Image among Women,"and Capodilupo and Kim, "Gender *and* Race Matter."

15 American women spend the most on beauty care products of any nation in the world, with the total market value at an astounding 93.35 billion dollars in 2019. The French company L'Oréal dominates the American beauty marketplace, capturing almost 30 billion dollars in 2018, around a third of that year's total spending. L'Oréal Finance Annual Report: https://www.loreal-finance.com/en/annual-report-2018/cosmetics-market-2-1/.

16 See Williams and Connell, "Looking Good and Sounding Right," and Peter Waring, "Keeping Up Appearances," both of which actually advocate for lookism, or discrimination based on adherence to beauty norms, and its sanction in employment law. For discrimination outside of the workplace as well as inside, see Deborah Rhode's *Beauty Bias*, which delves into how being perceived as unattractive can deeply impact a person's entire life.

Bibliography

Primary Sources

ARCHIVES AND OFFICIAL DOCUMENTS

Archives Nationales
Bibliothèque Forney
Bibliothèque nationale de France
French Judiciary Archives
French National Assembly Archives
French Senate Archives
Institute national de l'audivisuel (INA)
Musée Air France
Musée Carnavalet
Official Report/Rapport Officiel, Grenoble 1968, Comité d'organisation des Xèmes jeux olympiques d'hiver

NEWSPAPERS

Atlanta Constitution
Atlanta Journal and Atlanta Constitution
Bay State Banner
Boston Globe
Chicago Tribune
Christian Science Monitor
Daily Defender
Detroit News
Edmonton Observer
Florence Morning News
Guardian
L'Équipe

Le Figaro
Le Monde
Le Nouvel observateur
Los Angeles Times (LA Times)
New York Amsterdam News
New York Herald Tribune
New York Times (NYT)
The Observer
Palestine Post
Paris-Presse L'Intransigeant
San Francisco Chronicle
Seattle Post-Intelligencer
Show Magazine
Spokesman Review
Sud-Ouest
The Sun
Wall Street Journal
Washington Post

TRADE PUBLICATIONS AND MAGAZINES

Air-France Revue
Air France
Asian and Indian Skyways
Aviation française
Bulletin municipal officiel de la ville de Paris
Les Cahiers du GRIF
Échos de l'air
Échos de l'air / Bulletin mensuel Air France
Esprit
France-aviation
The French Review
Film Comment
Holiday
Informations sociales: Bulletin mensuel à l'usage des services sociaux /
    Union nationale des caisses d'allocations familiales.
Journal officiel de la République française. Avis et rapports du Conseil économique
L'Aérophile
L'Air
New Nation
The New Yorker
La Renaissance

La Revue Administrative
Revue des Deux Mondes
Sports Illustrated
Terre et ciel
La Tribune de Marseille et La Provence hôtelière, touristique et sportive
Versailles Magazine
Vogue (New York)
Women's Wear Daily (WWD)

BOOKS AND ARTICLES

Air France: Vacationing in Five Continents. Paris: Éditions U&O, 1968.
Arnoux, Alexandre, "Lettre à l'inconnu qui débarque à Paris," in Le Crapouillot, *Paris-guide*, 2–5. Paris: Le Crapouillot, 1951.
Balmain, Pierre, "L'élégance française est sans frontières," in *Entretiens et conférences donnés à l'auditorium du Pavillon de la France d'avril à octobre 1958*, 43–51. Paris: Commissariat Général de la Section française à l'Exposition Internationale de Bruxelles, 1959.
Beauvoir, Simone de. *The Second Sex*. Trans. Constance Borde and Sheila Malovany-Chevallier. London: Vintage, 2010.
Berest, Anne. *How to Be Parisian Wherever You Are*. New York: Doubleday, 2014.
Bernbach, Bill. *Bill Bernbach Said …* New York: DDB Needham, 1989.
Bertin, Celia. *Paris à la Mode*. Trans. Marjorie Deans. New York: Harper & Brothers, 1957.
Callahan, Chrissie. *The Paris Bath and Beauty Book: Embrace Your Natural Beauty with Timeless Secrets and Recipes from the French*. Kennebunkport, ME: Cider Hill Press, 2016.
Callan, Jamie Cat. *French Women Don't Sleep Alone: Pleasurable Secrets to Finding Love*. New York: Citadel, 2009.
– *Parisian Charm School: French Secrets for Cultivating Love, Joy, and That Certain* je ne sais quoi. New York: TarcherPerigee, 2018
Catry, Solange. *Sur les ailes de l'hippocampe*. Paris: Buchet Chastel, 1983.
Creed, Virginia, and Henry Milo, *Paris and Its Environs*. New York: Duell, Sloan and Pierce, 1955.
Daley, Richard. *A Priest and a Girl*. New York: World Publishing Company, 1969.
Decaux, Alain, *Les heures brillantes de la Côte d'Azur*. Paris: Librairie académique Perrin, 1969.
De Gaulle, Pierre, "Avant-propos," in *Entretiens et conférences donnés à l'auditorium du Pavillon de la France d'avril à octobre 1958*, 9–10. Paris: Commissariat Général de la Section française à l'Exposition Internationale de Bruxelles, 1959.
de la Fressange, Inès. *Parisian Chic: A Style Guide*. Paris: Flammarion, 2011.
Delahaye, Marcel. *Martine en avion*. Brussels: Casterman, 1966.

Delestrée, Hubert, "Les nouvelles professions dans l'industrie de tourisme." *Tourist Review* 19, no. 3 (March 1964): 123–33.
Desbruères, Henri, "Réalisations aéronautiques françaises: L'industrie de construction," 30 September 1958. Reprinted in *Entretiens et conférences donnés à l'Auditorium du Pavillon de la France d'avril à octobre 1958*, 341–9. Paris: Commissariat Général de la Section française à l'Exposition Internationale de Bruxelles, 1959.
Dodge, David. *Poor Man's Guide to Europe*. New York: Random House, 1953.
– *Rich Man's Guide to the Riviera*. Boston: Little, Brown, 1962.
Dos Santos, José A., "Discovering Paris: A Tour of the City," in Fodor, ed., *France in 1952*, 29–57.
Druckerman, Pamela. *Bringing Up Bébé: One American Mother Discovers the Wisdom of French Parenting*. New York: Penguin, 2014.
– *French Children Don't Throw Food*. London: Black Swan, 2012.
Dubreuil, Richard, and Hélène Dubreuil. *La journée de l'hôtesse et du stewart*. Paris: Éditions vivantes, 1979.
d'Unienville, Alix. *En vol: Journal d'une hôtesse de l'air*. Paris: Éditions Albin Michel, 1949.
Engel, Lyle Kenyon. *France. A Simon and Schuster Travel Guide*. New York: Simon & Schuster, 1973.
Fielding, Temple. *Fielding's Travel Guide to Europe* (1966 edition). New York: William Morrow & Company, 1966.
Fleer, Martin, "Paris at Night," in Fodor, ed., *France in 1952*, 91–105.
Fodor, Eugene. *France in 1952: With Maps*. New York: David McKay Company, 1952.
Fodor, Eugene, and Robert Fisher, eds. *Fodor's Paris*. London: Hodder and Stoughton, 1974.
François, Lucien, "Paris: The Luxury Industry Capital," in *France: The Nagel Travel Guide Series*, 32–5. New York: McGraw-Hill Book Company, 1964.
Frith-Powell, Helena. *All You Need to Be Impossibly French: A Witty Investigation into the Lives, Lusts, and Little Secrets of French Women*. New York: Plume, 2006.
Guiliano, Mireille, *French Women Don't Get Facelifts*. New York: Balance, 2014.
– *French Women Don't Get Fat*. New York: Vintage, 2007.
Hymans, Max. "L'Hôtesse de l'air." *Revue Des Deux Mondes (1829–1971)*, 1954, 261–5.
Jett, Tish. *Forever Chic: Frenchwomen's Secrets for Timeless Beauty, Style, and Substance*. New York: Rizzoli Ex Libris, 2013.
Laporte, Jeanne-Marie, and Marie-José Salin. *Hôtesse d'accueil: Guide de la parfaite jeune femme*. Paris: Éditions André Casteilla, Les nouveautés de l'enseignement, 1971.
Le Billon, Karen. *French Kids Eat Everything: How Our Family Moved to France, Cured Picky Eating, Banned Snacking, and Discovered 10 Simple Rules for Raising Happy, Healthy Eaters*. New York: William Morrow Paperbacks, 2014.
Malandrino, Catherine. *Une Femme Française: The Seductive Style of French Women*. New York: St. Martin's Press, 2017.

Mann, S.A. *Cosmetics Industry of Europe 1968*. Park Ridge, NJ: Noyes Development Corporation, 1968.
Martin, Alice, "Shopping: How to Spend – How to Save," in Fodor, ed., *France in 1952*, 105–25.
Martin, Sylvia, and Lawrence Martin, *Paris! And Its Environs*. New York: McGraw-Hill, 1963.
Maurois, Andre, "Vocations nouvelles," *Revue Des Deux Mondes (1829–1971)*, 1954, 3–12.
Mikes, George, "Some Popular Fallacies: The French … Without Tears," in Fodor, ed., *France in 1952*, 122–30.
Murray, Stuart. *A Traveler's Guide to France*. New York: Sheridan House, 1948.
Nadine, B. *Les 32 escales d'amour*. Paris: Éditions du Trèfle d'or, 1966.
Newman, Harold. *Newman's European Travel Guide*. New York: Henry Holt and Company, 1951.
Ollivier, Debra. *Entre Nous: A Woman's Guide to Finding Her Inner French Girl*. New York: St Martin's Griffin, 2004
– *What French Women Know: About Love, Sex, and Other Matters of the Heart and Mind*. New York: Berkley Books, 2010.
Olson, Harvey S. *Olson's Complete Motoring Guide to France, Switzerland, and Italy*. Philadelphia and New York: J.B. Lippincott Company, 1967.
Philippe, René, *Sylvie, hôtesse de l'air*. Paris: Éditions Gerard, 1955.
A Pocket Guide to France. Washington, DC: Armed Forces Information and Education Division, Department of Defense, 1951.
Postel-Vinay, Danielle. *Home Sweet Maison: The French Art of Making a Home*. New York: Dey Street Books, 2018.
Probst, Pierre. *Caroline en avion*. Paris: Hachette, 1977.
Proulx, Cynthia, and Ian Keown. *Guide to France for Loving Couples (The 31 Most Romantic Hotels and Inns in France)*. New York: Auerbach, 1971.
Puget, René. *The Long Haul*. New York: Simon & Schuster, 1964.
Roe, Claire Andrée. *La Vie d'une hôtesse d'Air France*. London: Longman, 1972.
Sainteny, Jean. *Face à Ho Chi Minh*. Paris: Éditions Seghers, 1970.
Scott, Jennifer L. *Lessons from Madame Chic: 20 Stylish Secrets I Learned while Living in Paris*. New York: Simon & Schuster, 2012.
Segal, Claire. *Off the Beaten Track in Paris: A Nash Travel Guide*. Los Angeles: Nash Publishing, 1973.
Servan-Schreiber, Jean-Jacques. *The American Challenge*. New York: Scribner, 1968.
Sutton, Horace. *Footloose in France*. New York: Rinehart, 1948.
Thomas, Isabelle. *Paris Street Style: A Guide to Effortless Chic*. New York: Abrams Image, 2013.
Thomas, James E. "The Riviera and Monaco: Roulette, Glamour, or Just a Suntan," in Fodor, ed., *France in 1952*, 263.
– "The Spirit of Paris: 'All Things to All Men,'" in Fodor, ed., *France in 1952*, 57–90.

Thomas, Mathilde. *The French Beauty Solution*. New York: Avery, 2015.
Vitray, Laura. *Fashion for Cinderella*. New York: Dodd, Mead, 1950.
Von Mueffling, Clémence. *Ageless Beauty the French Way: Secrets from Three Generations of French Beauty Editors*. New York: St. Martin's Press, 2018.
Wallenstein, Marcel. *Red Canvas*. New York: Avon, 1955.

Secondary Sources

Agulhon, Maurice, *Marianne au combat: L'imagerie et la symbolique républicaines de 1789 à 1880*. Paris: Flammarion, 1979.
- *Marianne au pouvoir. L'imagerie et la symbolique républicaines de 1880 à 1914*. Paris: Flammarion, 1989.
- "Marianne, réflexions sur une histoire." *Annales Historiques De La Révolution Française*, no. 289 (1992): 313–22.
- *Les Métamorphoses de Marianne: L'imagerie et la symbolique républicaines de 1914 à nos jours*. Paris: Flammarion, 2001.
Alak, Patrik. *The Bikini: A Cultural History*. New York: Parkstone Press, 2002.
Autier, Fabienne, Georges Trépo, and Gregory Corcos. *Air France, des années héroïques à la refondation*. Paris: Vuibert, 2017.
Barry, Kathleen M. *Femininity in Flight. A History of Flight Attendants*. Durham, NC: Duke University Press, 2007.
Bartky, Sandra Lee. "Foucault, Femininity and the Modernization of Patriarchal Power," in Katie Conboy, Nadia Medina, and Sarah Stanbury (eds.), *Writing on The Body: Female Embodiment and Feminist Theory*, 129–54. New York: Columbia University Press, 1997.
Barton, Nimisha. *Reproductive Citizens: Gender, Immigration, and the State in Modern France, 1880–1945*. Ithaca, NY: Cornell University Press, 2020.
Baum, Tom, "Working the Skies: Changing Representations of Gendered Work in the Airline Industry, 1930–2011." *Tourism Management* 33, no. 5: 1185–94.
Berenson, Edward. *Heroes of Empire: Five Charismatic Men and the Conquest of Africa*. Berkeley: University of California Press, 2011.
Black, Prudence. "Lines of Flight: The Female Flight Attendant Uniform." *Fashion Theory* 17, no. 3 (2013.)
- *Smile, Particularly in Bad Weather: The Era of the Australian Airline Hostess*. Perth: UWA Press, 2017.
Blume, Mary. *Côte d'Azur: Inventing the French Riviera*. New York: Thames and Hudson, 1992.
Bordo, Susan. *Unbearable Weight: Feminism, Western Culture and the Body*. Berkeley: University of California Press, 1993.
Bozo, Frédéric. *Two Strategies for Europe: De Gaulle, the United States, and the Atlantic Alliance*. Trans. Susan Emanuel. New York: Rowman & Littlefield, 2001.

Brogi, Alessandro. *A Question of Self-Esteem: The United States and the Cold War Choices in France and Italy, 1944–1958*. New York: Praeger, 2001.

Capdevila, Luc. "The Quest for Masculinity in a Defeated France, 1940–1945." *Contemporary European History* 10, no. 3 (2001): 423–45.

Capodilupo, C.M., and S. Kim. "Gender *and* Race Matter: The Importance of Considering Intersections in Black Women's Body Image," *Journal of Counseling Psychology* 61, no. 1: 37–49.

Chaplin, Felicity. *La Parisienne in Cinema: Between Art and Life*. Manchester: Manchester University Press, 2017.

Chaubet, François, ed. *La culture française dans le monde, 1980–2000 les défis de la mondialisation*. Paris: L'Harmattan, 2010.

– *La politique culturelle Francaise et la diplomatie de la langue: L'Alliance Francaise (1883–1940)*. Paris: L'Harmattan, 2006.

Cohen, Lizabeth. *A Consumers' Republic: The Politics of Mass Consumption in Postwar America*. New York: Alfred A. Knopf, 2003.

Cooper, Dana. *Informal Ambassadors: American Women, Transatlantic Marriages, and Anglo-American Relations, 1865–1945*. Kent, OH: Kent State University Press, 2014.

Crane, Diana. *Fashion and Its Social Agendas: Class, Gender, and Identity in Clothing*. Chicago: University of Chicago Press, 2000.

Curtis, Sarah. *Civilizing Habits: Women Missionaries and the Revival of French Empire*. New York: Oxford University Press, 2010.

Dauncey, Hugh, "The Failed Bid for Lyon '68, and France's Winter Olympics from Grenoble '68 to Annecy 2018: French Politics, Civil Society and Olympic Mega-Events," in *Olympic Games, Mega-Events and Civil Societies*, ed. Graeme Hayes & John Karamichas, 87–105. New York: Palgrave Macmillan, 2012.

Davey, Caroline L., and Marilyn J. Davidson. "The Right of Passage? The Experiences of Female Pilots in Commercial Aviation," *Feminism & Psychology* 10, no. 2: 195–225.

Dean, Carolyn J. *The Frail Social Body: Pornography, Homosexuality, and Other Fantasies in Interwar France*. Berkeley: University of California Press, 2000.

Dean, Deborah, "Recruiting A Self: Women Performers and Aesthetic Labour." *Work, Employment, Society* 19, no. 4: 761–74.

D'Hooghe, Vanessa. "How Stewardesses Obtained Equal Pay in the European Community (Belgium, 1968–1980)," in *Institutionalizing Gender Equality: Historical and Global Perspectives*, ed. Yulia Gradskova and Sara Sanders. New York: Lexington Books, 2015.

Duchen, Claire. *Women's Rights and Women's Lives in France, 1944–1968*. New York: Routledge, 1994.

Elmen-Gruys, Kjerstin. "Properly Attired, Hired, or Fired: Aesthetic Labor and Social Inequality." PhD dissertation, UCLA, 2014.

Endy, Christopher. *Cold War Holidays: American Tourism in France*. Chapel Hill, NC: University of North Carolina Press, 2004.

Enloe, Cynthia. *Bananas, Beaches and Bases: Making Feminist Sense of International Politics*. Berkeley: University of California Press, 2014.
Espérou, Robert. *Histoire du transport aérien français*. Saint-Malo: Pascal Galodé Editions, 2009.
Etcoff, Nancy. *Survival of the Prettiest: The Science of Beauty*. New York: Anchor, 2000.
Fernando, Mayanthi. *The Republic Unsettled: Muslim French and the Contradictions of Secularism*. Durham, NC: Duke University Press, 2014.
Fishman, Sarah. *From Vichy to the Sexual Revolution: Gender and Family Life in Postwar France*. New York: Oxford University Press, 2017.
Foucault, Michel. *Discipline and Punish*. New York: Vintage, 1979.
Garb, Tamar. *Bodies of Modernity: Figure and Flesh in Fin-de-siècle France*. London: Thames and Hudson, 1998.
Gibson, Emily Katherine. *The Flag: Gender and the Projection of National Progress through Global Air Travel, 1920–1960*. PhD dissertation, Georgia Institute of Technology, 2017.
Gildea, Robert. *France since 1945*. New York: Oxford University Press, 2002.
– *Marianne in Chains: Daily Life in the Heart of France during the German Occupation*. London: Picador, 2004.
Gordon, Mel. *Horizontal Collaboration: The Erotic World of Paris, 1920–1946*. Port Townsend, WA: Feral House, 2015.
Grout, Holly. *Force of Beauty: Transforming French Ideas of Femininity in the Third Republic*. Baton Rouge: Louisiana State University Press, 2015.
Ha, Marie-Paule. *French Women and the Empire: The Case of Indochina*. New York: Oxford University Press, 2014.
Halper, Donna L. *Invisible Stars: A Social History of Women in American Broadcasting*. New York: M.E. Sharpe, 2001.
Hamermesh, Daniel S. *Beauty Pays: Why Attractive People Are More Successful*. Princeton, NJ: Princeton University Press, 2013.
Harp, Stephen L. *Marketing Michelin: Advertising and Cultural Identity in Twentieth-Century France*. Baltimore: Johns Hopkins University Press, 2001.
Hochschild, Arlie. *The Managed Heart: Commercialization of Human Feeling*. Berkeley: University of California Press, 2012.
Holmes, Diana, "'A Girl of Today': Brigitte Bardot," *Stardom in Postwar France*, ed. John Gaffney and Diana Holmes. New York and Oxford: Berghahn Books, 2011.
Hunt, Lynn. *Politics, Culture and Class in the French Revolution*. Berkeley: University of California Press, 1984.
Jackson, Julian. *Living in Arcadia: Homosexuality, Politics, and Morality in France from the Liberation to AIDS*. Chicago: University of Chicago Press, 2009.
James, Carolyn, and Glenda Sluga, eds. *Women, Diplomacy and International Politics since 1500*. New York and London: Routledge, 2016.
Jones, Geoffrey. *Beauty Imagined: A History of the Global Beauty Industry*. New York: Oxford University Press, 2011.

Kamani, Aneel. "Doing Well by Doing Good: Case Study: Fair and Lovely Whitening Cream." *Strategic Management Journal* 28, no. 13 (Dec. 2007): 1351–7.
Kaplan, Laurence S. *NATO and the United States: The Enduring Alliance*. Boston: G.K. Hall, 1988.
Karia Kelch-Oliver, and Julie R. Ancis. "Black Women's Body Image: An Analysis of Culture-Specific Influences." *Women & Therapy* 34, no. 4 (2011): 345–58.
Kenny, Mary. "Forty Years On." *Studies: An Irish Quarterly Review* 92, no. 365 (Spring 2003): 7–12.
Krevsky, Margery. *Sirens of Chrome: The Enduring Allure of Auto Show Models*. Detroit: Momentum Books, 2008.
Kuisel, Richard. *Seducing the French: The Dilemma of Americanization*. Berkeley: University of California Press, 1993.
Lebow, Eileen. *Before Amelia: Women Pilots in the Early Days of Aviation*. Lincoln: University of Nebraska Press, 2002.
Levenstein, Harvey. *Seductive Journey: American Tourists in France from Jefferson to the Jazz Age*. Chicago: University of Chicago Press, 2000.
– *We'll Always Have Paris: American Tourists in France since 1930*. Chicago: University of Chicago Press, 2004.
Lorcin, Patricia M.E. *Historicizing Colonial Nostalgia: European Women's Narratives of Algeria and Kenya, 1900–Present*. New York: Palgrave Macmillan, 2012.
Mandel, Maud. *Muslims and Jews in France: History of a Conflict*. Princeton, NJ: Princeton University Press, 2014.
Marck, Bernard. *Les Aviatrices: Des pionnières aux cosmonautes*. Paris: L'Archipel, 1993.
– *Elles ont conquis le ciel: 100 femmes qui ont fait l'histoire de l'aviation et de l'espace*. Paris: Arthaud, 2009.
Martin, Morag. *Selling Beauty: Cosmetics, Commerce, and French Society, 1750–1830*. Baltimore: Johns Hopkins University Press, 2009.
May, Elaine Tyler. *Homeward Bound: American Families in the Cold War Era*. New York: Basic Books, 1988.
McKenzie, Brian A. "Creating a Tourist's Paradise: The Marshall Plan and France, 1948 to 1952." *French Politics, Culture & Society* 21, no. 1 (Spring 2003): 35–54.
Murphy, Ryan Patrick. *Deregulating Desire: Flight Attendant Activism, Family Politics, and Workplace Justice*. Philadelphia: Temple University Press, 2016.
Neiertz, Nicolas. "Air France: An Elephant in an Evening Suit?," in *Flying the Flag*, ed. Peter Lyth & Hans-Liudger Dienel. London: Palgrave Macmillan, 1998.
Nicolaou, Stéphane, and Élisabeth Misme-Thomas. *Aviatrices: Un siècle d'aviation féminine française*. Paris: Altipresse, 2004.
Nye, Joseph S., Jr. *Soft Power: The Means to Success in World Politics*. New York: PublicAffairs, 2004.
Pearson, Jessica Lynne. *The Colonial Politics of Global Health: France and the United Nations in Postwar Africa*. Cambridge, MA: Harvard University Press, 2018.

- "The French Empire Goes to San Francisco: The Founding of the United Nations and the Limits of Colonial Reform." *French Politics, Culture and Society* 38, no. 2 (June 2020): 35–55.
Peiss, Kathy Lee. *Hope in a Jar: The Making of America's Beauty Culture*. Philadelphia: University of Pennsylvania Press, 2011.
Pettinger, Lynne. "Brand Culture and Branded Workers: Service Work and Aesthetic Labour," in *Fashion Retail, Consumption Markets & Culture* 7, no. 2 (2004): 165–84.
Picton, Oliver. "The Complexities of Complexion: A Cultural Geography of Skin Colour and Beauty Products." *Geography* 98, no. 2 (Summer 2013): 85–92.
Read, Geoff. *The Republic of Men: Gender and the Political Parties in Interwar France*. Baton Rouge: Louisiana State University Press, 2014.
Reynolds, Sian. *France between the Wars: Gender and Politics*. London: Routledge, 1997.
Rhode, Deborah L. *The Beauty Bias: The Injustice of Appearance in Life and Law*. New York: Oxford University Press, 2010.
Ring, Jim. *Riviera: The Rise and Rise of the Côte d'Azur*. London: John Murray, 2005.
Rioux, Jean-Pierre. *The Fourth Republic*. Cambridge: Cambridge University Press, 1987.
Roberts, Mary Louise. *Civilization without Sexes: Reconstructing Gender in Postwar France*. Chicago: University of Chicago Press, 1994.
- *What Soldiers Do: Sex and the American GI in World War II France*. Chicago: University of Chicago Press, 2014.
Roche, Daniel. *Culture of Clothing*. Cambridge: Cambridge University Press, 1997.
Ross, Andrew Israel. "Sex in the Archives: Homosexuality, Prostitution, and the Archives de la Préfecture de Police de Paris." *French Historical Studies* 40, no. 2 (2017): 267–90.
Ross, Kristin. *Fast Cars, Clean Bodies: Decolonization and the Reordering of French Culture*. Cambridge, MA: MIT Press, 1995.
Rousso, Henry. *The Vichy Syndrome: History and Memory in France since 1944*. 3rd ed. Trans. Arthur Goldhammer. Cambridge, MA: Harvard University Press, 1994.
Sampson, Anthony. *Empires of the Sky: The Politics, Contests, and Cartels of World Airlines*. London: Coronet, 1984.
Scanlon, Jennifer. *Inarticulate Longings: The Ladies' Home Journal, Gender, and the Promises of Consumer Culture*. New York: Routledge, 1995.
Schmidt, Christine. *The Swimsuit: Fashion from Poolside to Catwalk*. London: Bloomsbury Academic, 2012.
Schwartz, Vanessa R. "Dimanche à Orly: The Jet-Age Airport and the Spectacle of Technology between Sky and Earth." *French Politics, Culture & Society* 32, no. 3; Special issue, Technology, the Visual, and Culture (Winter 2014): 24–44.
- *It's So French! Hollywood, Paris, and the Making of Cosmopolitan Film Culture*. Chicago: University of Chicago Press, 2007.
- "Who Killed Brigitte Bardot? Perspectives on the New Wave at Fifty." *Cinema Journal* 49, no. 4 (2010): 145–52.

Scott, Joan Wallach. *The Politics of the Veil*. Princeton, NJ: Princeton University Press, 2007.
Shepard, Todd. *The Invention of Decolonization: The Algerian War and the Remaking of France*. Ithaca, NY: Cornell University Press, 2006.
– *Sex, France, and Arab Men*. Chicago: University of Chicago Press, 2018.
Sontag, Susan, "A Woman's Beauty – A Put Down or Power Source," in *Essays of the 1960s & 70s*, ed. Susan Sontag and David Rieff, 803–5. New York: Library of America, 2013.
Stanley, Adam C. "Hearth, Home, and Steering Wheel: Gender and Modernity in France after the Great War." *The Historian* 66, no. 2 (2004): 233–53.
Stearns, Peter N. *Fat History: Bodies and Beauty in the Modern West*. New York: New York University Press, 1997.
Sullivan, Marianna P. "France and the Vietnam Peace Settlement." *Political Science Quarterly* 89, no. 2 (1974): 305–24.
Thibault, Philippe-Michel. *Mythologies à bord*. Paris: Gallimard-Loisirs, 2005.
Tiemeyer, Phil. *Plane Queer: Labor, Sexuality, and AIDS in the History of Male Flight Attendants*. Chapel Hill University of North Carolina Press, 2013.
Tiersten, Lisa. *Marianne in the Market: Envisioning Consumer Society in Fin-de-Siècle France*. Berkeley: University of California Press, 2001.
Tyler, Melissa, and Steve Taylor. "The Exchange of Aesthetics: Women's Work and the 'Gift.'" *Gender, Work and Organisation* 5, no. 3: 165–71.
Ugalde, Alain Pluckers. *Histoire des hôtesses de l'air: Les filles du ciel*. Paris: Broché, 2007.
Un siècle de chansons françaises: Vol. 1969–1979, 301 chansons françaises de 1969 à 1979. Paris: Chambre syndicale de l'édition musicale, 2006.
Vaïsse, Maurice. *La grandeur: Politique étrangère du général de Gaulle*. Paris: CNRS, 2015.
Vantoch, Victoria. *The Jet Sex: Airline Stewardesses and the Making of an American Icon*. Philadelphia: University of Pennsylvania Press, 2013.
Van Vleck, Jenifer. *Empire of the Air: Aviation and the American Ascendency*. Cambridge, MA: Harvard University Press, 2013.
Vielle, Bruno. *Air France, 1933–1944: Un turbulent décollage*. Paris: ETAI, 2011.
Vincendeau, Ginette. *Companion to French Cinema*. London: Cassell, 1996.
Vinen, Richard. "Bikinis and Breastplates." *History Today* 56, no. 4 (April 2006): 50–2.
Virgili, Fabrice. *Shorn Women*. London: Berg, 2002.
Vukonic, Boris. "An Outline of the History of Tourism Theory," in *The Routlege Handbook of Tourism Research*, ed. Cathy H.C. Hsu and William C. Gartner, 3–27. New York: Routledge, 2012.
Walker, Suzanna, *Material Girls*. Berkeley: University of California Press, 1995.
Walton, Whitney. *Internationalism, National Identities, and Study Abroad: France and the United States, 1890–1970*. Palo Alto, CA: Stanford University Press, 2010.

Warhurst, Chris, Diane van den Broeck, Richard Hall, and Dennis Nickson. "Great Expectations: Gender, Looks, and Lookism at Work." *International Journal of Work, Organisation, and Emotion* 5, no. 1: 72–90.

Waring, Peter. "Keeping Up Appearances: Aesthetic Labour and Discrimination Law." *Journal of Industrial Relations* 53, no. 2 (April 2011): 193–207.

Weiner, Susan. *Enfants Terribles: Youth and Femininity in the Mass Media in France, 1945–1968.* Baltimore: Johns Hopkins University Press, 2001.

Williams, Christine L., and Catherine Connell. "'Looking Good and Sounding Right': Aesthetic Labor and Social Inequality in the Retail Industry." *Work and Occupations* 37, no. 3 (August 2010): 349–77.

Winter, Virginia Ramseyer, Laura King Danforth, Antoinette Landor, and Danielle Pevehouse-Pfeiffer. "Toward an Understanding of Racial and Ethnic Diversity in Body Image among Women." *Social Work Research* 43, no. 2 (June 2019): 69–80.

Witz, Anne, Chris Warhurst, and Dennis Nickson. "The Labour of Aesthetics and the Aesthetics of Organization." *Organization* 10, no. 1: 33–54.

Woolf, Virginia. *Three Guineas.* London: Blackwell Books, 1963.

Zimmer-Tamakoshi, Laura. "What Is Holding Them Back?: Reflections on One Woman's Loss at the Polls: Usino-Bundi Open," in *Election 2007: The Shift to Limited Preferential Voting in Papua New Guinea*, 407–27. Canberra: ANU Press, 2013.

Index

32 Stops of Love (Nadine B.), 53
77 Sunset Strip (TV program), 123

Adams, Joey, 152–3
Adams, Marjory, 119, 121
advertising campaigns: Air France, 50, 51f, 110, 142f, 143–5, 144f, 146, 165; Air Inter, 113, 145
aesthetic standards, Air France hostesses, 67–8
Agence France Presse, 126
Agulhon, Maurice, 115, 139
Air France: advertising campaigns, 50, 51f, 110, 142f, 143–5, 144f, 146, 165; aesthetic hostess standards, 67–8; Brigitte Bardot, capitalization of, 122; depiction of Parisian parks, 159; French fashion, role in exporting, 65–6; French femininity promotion in US, 63; history of, 11, 21; hostesses' marital status, position on, 46–7, 49; married hostess litigation, 47–8; postwar modernization efforts, 16; relationship with French government, 10–11, 40; sexualization of hostesses, 52, 111–12
air hostesses. *See* hostesses, Air France
Air Inter, advertising campaigns, 113, 145
Air-France Revue, 29, 33, 38, 52, 70, 104

Alak, Patrik, 134
Albaret, Fernand, 98, 101
Alpert, Don, 123
ambassadrices: concept of, 4, 12, 17, 28; creation of, 33, 35, 126; role of, 57, 116, 165, 166. *See also* hostesses: Air France; hostessing, transition off the airplane
American soldiers: French women's attraction to, 150; notions of French femininity, 8; sexual aggression toward French women, 7, 137, 149, 151; views on France, 7, 152
Anthionoz, Marcel, 77
Arnoux, Alexandre, 157–8, 164
Ash, Agnes, 65
Aslan (French artist), 115
Atlanta Constitution, 64, 67, 125
Atwell, Estella, 134–5
Aubry, François-Xavier, 73
Auger, Claudine, 123

Baird, Jean, 163
Balmain, Pierre, 89, 98
Baltimore Sun, 120, 121, 161
Barbier, Anne-Marie, 47–8
Bardot, Brigitte: commodification of, 103, 118, 121–2; early life, 116; as face of Marianne, 113; fall from grace, 116;

Bardot, Brigitte (*cont.*)
  as French sex symbol, 113, 115, 125; *And God Created Woman* poster, 117f; objectification of, 121; photo of sculpture, 114; photos of, 120; retirement, 126; reviews of *And God Created Woman*, 118–22; Riviera identity, 128; role in *And God Created Woman*, 116–18, 134; as a translational figure, 20
Barnes, Leslie O., 63–4
Bartky, Sandra, 13–14, 103
Beaumont, Catherine, 37
Beauquier, Pierre, 35
Beauvoir, Simone de, 13
Beer, Jacqueline, 123
Belin, Jacques, 99
Bernheim, Nicole, 73
Bertin, Célia, 133
Bidault, Suzanne, 61
bikini, origin of, 129–31
Bohan, Marc, 32–3
Bonnefous, Édouard, 9–10, 86, 89, 121
Bonnet, Jacqueline, 74
Bord, André, 94
Boston Globe: on Air France hostesses, 64, 67; on Brigitte Bardot, 119, 121; on Grenoble hostesses, 93; on Grenoble Winter Olympics, 97, 99; on Pigalle, Paris, 153; on Rhine River, 162
Bourrel, Vincent, 75
Brussels World Exposition: Air France participation, 90–1; Belgian hostesses, 85; campaign to boost French tourism, 86–7; French femininity, display of, 89, 92; French government concerns, 85–6; French hostesses, 86, 88, 90; French hostesses' photo, 87f; French pavilion success, 87–8, 91; friendship chain, 86
Buchanan, William, 153

Calvet, Corinne, 123, 125
campaign for French resurgence, 12, 13, 15
campaign to attract Americans, 9–10, 131–2, 138
campaign to boost tourism, 57, 57–8, 73–5, 86–7
Capdevila, Luc, 13
Caroline en avion (Probst), 37, 43
Catry, Solange: about, 21–2, 41; on ageism and misogyny, 55; diplomatic mission in New York, 61; on ground hostesses, 71; on hostesses' smiles, 38; on hostesses' uniforms, 31; on mandatory retirement age, 48–9; marital status, 46; on marriage and hostesses, 49; photo of, 23f; on postwar civil aviation, 59; role as recruiter, 24–5, 26; role as trainer, 27, 28; role at Grenoble Winter Olympics, 97–8, 100, 101; on unwanted male advances, 53–4; on work relationships with males, 54, 55
Cawthorn, Frances, 67–8
"C'est ça la France!" (TV/radio program), 59
Chamereau (Air France hostess), 61
Charles de Gaulle airport, 17
Chicago Daily Tribune: on bikinis, 130; feminization of France, 160; on hostesses' uniform, 99; on Martinique French territory, 162; on nightclubs, 153; on Noumea French territory, 161; on tourism hostesses, 74
Chicago Tribune, 63
Christian Dior, 31, 65, 68, 132
Christian Science Monitor, 66, 75, 119, 162, 163
Clamat, Alain, 96
Coffee, Tea, or Me? 53
Cogniat, Raymond, 88
Colin, Paul, 90
Colombini, Robert, 100

commodification: of Brigitte Bardot, 103, 118, 121–2; of French femininity, 81–2, 105, 110–11, 126–8, 168
Confédération Général du Travail (CGT), 24
Connery, Sean, 123
Coty, René, 88
Couvreau, Jean, 60
Crane, Diane, 132
Creed, Virginia, 148, 159
Crowther, Bosley, 119, 121, 158
Cusin, Robert, 70–1

Daily Defender, 125
Daladier, Édouard, 11
Daley, Arthur, 95
Daley, Robert, 52, 54
Daniels, Heb, 130
Darde de Bénazé, Nicole, 25
Dardour, Gisèle, 71
de Gaulle, Charles, 92, 93, 94, 95, 97
de Gaulle, Pierre, 86, 90, 91
Delahaye, Gilbert, 37, 42–3
Delaplane, Stanton, 47
Delestrée, Dr. Hubert, 76–82
Demongeot, Mylene, 123–4
Deneuve, Catherine, 127
Desailly, Jean, 52
Desbruères, Henri, 11, 16, 61
Dior. *See* Christian Dior
disciplined femininity, categories of, 14
Doassans, Paul, 68
Dodge, David, 119, 128, 132–3, 141
Domergue, Anne-Marie, 47
Dorléac, Françoise, 52
Dos Santos, José A., 157, 158, 159
Dragon, Marie-Josée, 33, 44
Duchen, Claire, 50
Dumas, Pierre, 73
d'Unienville, Alix, 27, 35, 39–40, 43
Duphil (Air France hostess), 61
Dutronc, Jacques, 50, 52

Échos de l'air, 69
Échos de l'air (*Echoes of the Air*), 5
Endy, Christopher, 5, 9, 19, 82, 105, 138
Engel, Lyle, 131, 135
Enloe, Cynthia, 4

Faltermeyer, Edmund K., 162
Fargé, Annie, 127
Fashion for Cinderella (Vitray), 134, 146
feminization of France, 140, 155–64
Fielding, Temple: feminization of France, 156–7, 160; on France, 155–6; on French Riviera, 161; on French women, 126, 134, 149; on Paris nightclubs, 148; on prostitution ban, 151; on sex and romance in France, 154–5
Fishman, Sarah, 52, 118, 138–9
Fleer, Martin, 148
Fodor, Eugene, 156
Fodor's Guide, 132, 135, 148, 164
Footloose in France (Sutton), 139, 152
Foreign Affairs, 112
Foucault, Michel, 13
Fouquet, Marcelle, 162
France Economic Council, 58, 84
France-aviation, 28, 35, 47, 91
Francis, David R., 163
François, Lucien, 155
French Civil Code, 46
French Economic Council, 73
French fashion, 65–8, 126–7, 133–5
French femininity: American soldiers' notion of, 8; and campaign for French resurgence, 12, 13, 15; capitalization of, 3, 4; commodification of, 105, 110, 110–11, 126, 168; conflation with French actresses, 119, 123–4; contrast with masculinity in aviation, 17; disciplinary practices, 14; history of, 15; intersection with class and race, 17–18; intersection with fashion, 30–3;

French femininity (*cont.*)
for male pleasure, 135; Marianne, symbol of France, 115; pressure to conform to, 132, 134, 135, 166, 167; promotion in US, 63, 67, 103; Riviera women, 128–31; role of government in capitalization of, 14, 20, 166; shift to sensuality, 20, 52; as a soft power, 18, 167

French government: Brigitte Bardot, capitalization of, 126; Brussels World Exposition, capitalization of, 84, 86, 91–2; campaign to boost tourism, 58, 138, 147; capitalization of French femininity, 14, 19–20, 56, 75, 84, 91–2, 103–5, 164, 166, 168; investment in aviation, 21, 24; postwar modernization efforts, 16–18; relationship with Air France, 10–11, 40; role in creating ambassadrices, 126

French Olympic Committee, 93, 97, 102

French Riviera, 160–1

French tourism: campaign to attract Americans, 9–10, 57–8, 131–2, 138; Riviera, 129–31; sexualization of, 7, 8; as a source of soft power, 19, 52; travel guidebooks, rise of, 138

Friedlander, Paul, 130–1

friendship chain, 86

Gardner, R.H., 121

Garrison, Lloyd, 95, 99

Gibson, Emily Katherine, 16

Gilbert Marnier (character), 38, 45

Gildea, Robert, 139

And God Created Woman (film), 116–22, 134

Godbout, Jacques, 62

Goitschel, Anne-Marie, 4

Grenoble Winter Olympics: campaign to promote games, 94–5; Catry, Solange, role as chief hostess, 97–8, 100; grandeur of, 92, 95, 96; hostesses' discontent, 100; hostesses' performance, 96–7; hostesses' recruitment, 97; hostesses' role, 97, 98–9; hostesses' romantic encounters, 101; hostesses' uniform, 99; photo of hostesses, 102; pre-Olympic challenges/criticisms, 93–4; press coverage, 93, 94–5; success of, 101–2

Grimsley, Will, 98, 99

ground hostess duties, 70–1

The Guardian, 48, 95

A Guide to France for Loving Couples (Proulx and Keown), 137, 146–7

Hanania, Cécile, 114

Handley, John, 130

Hartmann, Robert, 162

Havilland, Olivia de, 143

Hecht, Gabrielle, 13, 16, 60

Heim, Jacques, 92, 129

Herzog, Maurice, 92

history of Air France, 11, 21

Hochschild, Arlie, 35, 40

Holiday, 156

Holmes, Diana, 118

hostess litigation, Air France, 47–8

hostesses, Air France, 65; as ambassadrices, 4, 15, 17; barriers to success, 50; emotional labour of role, 37, 39–40, 44; exchange program, 64; history of, 6, 9, 12, 21; mandatory retirement age, 48–9; maternal role, 41–5; mental health of, 40; motivation to join program, 26–7; photos of, 23f, 30f, 32f, 36f, 42f; physical appearance, emphasis on, 28–9; promotion of program, 27; qualities and qualifications, 5–6, 20, 22, 24–5; racial symbolism, 17–18; rationale for single status, 46–7; recruitment process, 22, 24–6; romances with passengers, 45;

romanticization of, 49–50; service attitude, 34; sexualization of, 52, 53, 62, 111–12; smiles as requirement of service, 35–41, 70–1; training process, 28; uniform mandate, 29–33; unionization efforts, 19, 49; work relationships with males, 54
hostesses, as translational figures, 103
hostesses' marital status, 46–7, 49
hostessing, transition off the airplane: campaign to boost tourism, 57, 73–5; capitalization of, 58f; commodification of, 81–2; complement to masculine French technology, 60–2; connection to femininity, 76–7; French femininity, promotion of in US, 63; ground hostess duties, 70–1; impact on cosmetics industry, 81; personalities, directives on, 80; photos of ground hostess, 69f; physical appearance, emphasis on, 78, 79–80, 82–3; presence at diplomatic events, 60, 62f, 68, 72, 75–6; private industries, 68; as representations of French culture, 63; in school curricula, 76; state-related positions, 74; training schools, 77
hostessing global events: Brussels World Exposition, 85–92; Grenoble Olympic Games, 86
Hulse, Jerry, 62
Hunt, Lynn, 6, 15, 139
Hure, René, 147
Hussein, King of Jordan, 61
Hutin, Maurice, 59
Hyams, Joe, 119, 123, 124, 126
Hymans, Max, 22, 25, 45, 46

Jacqueline de Valbon (character), 33, 38, 44, 45, 46
jeune fille, 8

Kennedy, John F., 162–3
Keown, Ian, 137, 146–7, 150
Kernel, Hélène, 32
Killy, Jean-Claude, 4
King Creole (film), 125
Koenig, H.P., 153, 160, 161, 162
Kuisel, Richard, 19

Lagarde, Françoise, 27, 60
Lamarque, Albert, 9
Lane, Lydia, 127
Laporte, Jean-Marie, 77–80
Lauwick, Hervé, 44
Le Crapouillot, 157
Le Figaro, 21, 25, 85, 86, 88
Le Monde: on ambassadrices, 12, 29, 60; on Brussels World Exposition event, 86, 88; on hostess competition, 75; on hostess selection process, 24; on hostess uniforms, 33; promotion of "*C'est ça la France!*" (TV/radio program), 59; on welcome hostesses, 73, 76
L'Équipe: on Grenoble Winter Olympics, 92, 93, 94, 97, 98, 100, 101; on Solange Catry, 97
Les 32 escales d'amour, 53
Levenstein, Roy, 152
Lévy, Raoul, 118
Liberté, 62
Lincoln Star, 47
Linge Henri de, 85, 88
litigation, married hostess vs Air France, 47–8
The Long Haul (Puget), 33, 38, 44–5, 46, 54
Los Angeles Times: on Air France hostesses, 61–2, 67; on Brigitte Bardot, 121; on Claudine Auger, 123; on *Footloose* travel guidebook, 140; on French fashion, 66, 128; on Grenoble Winter Olympics, 96; on Paris, 160
The Lovers (film), 124

228 Index

Maddocks, Melvin, 119, 120
Maggy, Marcel, 67
Malapert, Aude, 27
Malraux, André, 116
Manet, Edouard, 112
Marcus, Neiman, 65–6
Marianne, symbol of France, 15, 113, 115
Marillonet, Madeleine, 27
Marin, Christian, 74
Martin, Alice, 132, 134
Martin, Sylvia and Lawrence, 143, 159
Martine en avion (Delahaye), 42–3, 37
Massard, Armand, 93
Massin, Peggy, 127
Maurois, André, 73
McCarten, John, 118
Meeker, Arthur, 160
Menant, Georges, 153
Michèle Moreau (character), 54
Miele, Henry, 160
Mikes, George, 151, 164
Millet, Ingrid, 127
Millinship, William, 158
Milo, Henry, 148, 159
Mireille Daniele (character), 39, 45, 54
Montevecchi, Liliane, 125
Moreau, Jeanne, 124–5, 127
Morgan, Carlyle, 162
Morgan, Gwen, 99, 153
Moucot, Nicole, 37–8
Murray, Stuart, 149, 160

New York Herald Tribune, 119
New York Times: on Air France hostesses, 66; on Alexandre Raimondi, 67; on bikini body ideal, 130–1; on Brigitte Bardot, 119, 124; on *Footloose* travel guidebook, 140; on French fashion, 65; on Grenoble hostesses, 99; on Grenoble Winter Olympics, 95; on Jeanne Moreau, 124; romanticization of France, 158
New Yorker, 111, 118

Newman, Harold, 155, 160
nightclubs in France, 148, 153
Noel, Anthony, 116
Normandy campaign, 7
North American Newspaper Alliance, 116
Noumea French territory, 161
Nye, Joseph, 18

objectification of Brigitte Bardot, 121
Odette (character), 33, 39, 41, 43, 49
Olsen, Jack, 93
Olson, Harvey: on Antibes, 129; feminization of France, 155, 158; on nightclubs, 148; on Pigalle, Paris, 152–3; on prostitution ban, 151–2; on the Seine, 158
Orly Airport, 17, 61

Paar, Jack, 122
Panaggio, Leonard, 160
Paquet, Aimé, 10
Paris à la Mode (Bertin), 133
Paris! And Its Environs (Martin and Martin), 143, 159
Paris hostesses. *See* hostessing, transition off the airplane
Parisian parks, feminization of, 159
Parisiennes, 127–8, 135, 141, 153–4
Péricand, Michel, 59
Péron, René, 116
Philippe, René, 33, 39, 40, 43
Philippe Gambier (character), 45
Pierre Lachenay (character), 52
Pigalle, centre of sex tourism, 152–5
Pilon, Marie France, 72
Pinay, Antoine, 122
Pompidou, Georges, 127
Poor Man's Guide to Europe (Dodge), 132–3
postwar France: American GIs' view of France, 151; decolonization process, 16; female labour aesthetic requirements, 24; francophone

network, establishment of, 18;
modernization policy and efforts,
16–17; nationalization of aviation
industry, 11–12; promotion of
French femininity, 103; reputation
and military loss, 15–16, 18;
romanticization of France, 139–40;
state of economy, 8, 10
Pouget, Jules, 131
pressure to conform to French
femininity, 132, 134, 135, 166, 167
A Priest and A Girl (film), 52–3, 54
Probst, Pierre, 37, 41, 43
prostitution ban, 151–2
Proulx, Cynthia, 137, 146–7, 150
Puget, René, 33, 38, 44, 45, 54
Putnam, Samuel, 140

race and French femininity, 17–18
Raimondi, Alexandre, 67
Ravon, Georges, 52
Réard, Louis, 129
Red Canvas (Marcel), 143, 150–1
Renal, Georgette, 31
Riviera women, 128–31, 149
Roberts, Mary Louise, 7, 152
Roche, Daniel, 30
Rodgers, Shannon, 127
Roe, Claire Andrée, 39, 41, 49, 82
Roland, Philippe, 25
romanticization of France: American
GIs' view of France, 151, 152;
campaign to boost tourism, 110, 138,
143–5; comparison to Switzerland,
161; cuisine reputation, 147;
discretion of hotels, 147–8; fashion
and romance, conflation of, 163;
feminization of France, 140, 155–61;
gay tourism, approach to, 149–50;
nightclub experience, 148–9, 150,
152–3; Parisian parks, feminization
of, 159; Pigalle, centre of sex tourism,
152–4; portrayal in books, 146;
prostitution ban, 151–2; Riviera as
a romantic destination, 160; Seine
River, feminization of, 158; sexual
morality shift, 138–9; stereotypes
about French women, 151; ubiquity
of physical love, 143
Roos, Joseph, 37
Ross, Kristen, 13, 18
Roubert, Alexandre, 9
Roume, Ernest, 11

Sainteny, Jean, 147
Salin, Marie-Josée, 77–80
Salt Lake City Tribune, 48
Sampson, Anthony, 11, 17
San Francisco Chronicle, 47
Savreux, Robert, 35
Schwartz, Vanessa, 17, 113, 122
Scott, Joan, 14
Segal, Claire, 140–1, 153, 158
Seine River, feminization of, 158
Sentenac, Paul, 6
Servan-Schreiber, Jean-Jacques,
114–15, 116
sexualization of Air France hostesses, 52,
53, 62, 111–12
Shepard, Todd, 13
Sheppard, Eugenia, 67, 130, 134
Silverman, Jerry, 127
soft power, dynamics and use of, 18–19,
52, 89, 135, 167
Soft Skin (film), 52
Sontag, Susan, 15
The Spirit of Saint Louis (film), 60
Sports Illustrated, 93
Sud-Ouest: on Air France litigation loss,
48; celebration of successful hostess
candidates, 27; on French actresses,
124; on hostess age limit, 49; on
hostess selection process, 25; hostesses
and French Rugby team, 61; on
importance of hostesses, 37; special
edition on hostesses, 75

Sutton, Horace: on French Riviera, 161; on nightclubs, 149; on Parisian parks, 159; on Riviera women, 130; on sex and romance in France, 146; travel guidebook, 140; view of Paris, 139, 141, 152
Sylvie, hôtesse de l'air (Philippe), 33, 39, 40, 43

Terre et ciel, 61
Thiplouse, Madeleine, 54, 61
"*THIS* is France!" (TV/radio program), 59
Thomas, James E., 141, 157, 158, 161
Three Guineas (Woolf), 30
Thunderball (film), 123
Tillon, Charles, 11
"To an Air Hostess" (song), 53
tourism hostesses, 74. *See also* hostessing: transition off the airplane
tourism marketing, 57, 73–5, 104; campaign photos, 106–9, 142f; feminization of France, 139; romanticization of France, 110; sexualization of hostesses, 111–12
translational figures, 103, 136
travel guidebooks, rise of, 138, 140–1
Truffaut, François, 52
Truman, Bess, 61
Tupper, Fred, 95, 96
Turckheim, Hélène de, 92

uniforms, hostesses': criteria and guidelines, 78–9; glamourization of, 33, 65; Grenoble Winter Olympics, 99; history of designs, 31–3; importance of, 30. *See also* hostesses, Air France

Vadim, Roger, 116, 121
Vantoch, Victoria, 63

Van Vleck, Jenifer, 18
Vartan, Sylvie, 98
Versailles Magazine, 41
Vincendeau, Ginette, 116
Virgili, Fabrice, 13
Virieu, François-Henri de, 116
Vitray, Laura, 134, 146
Vogue, 65–6, 127, 132, 145
Vos, Pierre de, 90
Vulaines, Jacques, 37–8

Wagner, Ruth, 146
Wales, Henry, 74–5
Wall Street Journal, 162
Wallenstein, Marcel, 143, 150
Walton, Whitney, 8, 19
Ward, Clifford T., 53
Washington Post, 4, 64, 67, 93, 140
Watt, David Laird, 161
Wechsberg, Joseph, 152–4
Weiner, Susan, 113
Welcome Hostess: Guide to the Perfect Young Woman (Salin and Laporte), 77–8
welcome hostesses. *See* ground hostess duties; hostessing: transition off the airplane
Willoughby, Bob, 123
Winter Olympic Games, 1968, 4
Witbeck, Charles, 123
Women's Wear Daily, 66
Woolf, Virginia, 30
World News Service, 74

Young Girl (TV program), 27

Zinsser, William, 118–19

www.ingramcontent.com/pod-product-compliance
Lightning Source LLC
Chambersburg PA
CBHW022216090526
44584CB00012BB/570